DESERVING DESIRE

DESERVING DESIRE

Women's Stories of Sexual Evolution

BETH MONTEMURRO

RUTGERS UNIVERSITY PRESS
New Brunswick, New Jersey, and London

Library of Congress Cataloging-in-Publication Data
Montemurro, Beth, 1972–
Deserving desire : women's stories of sexual evolution / Beth Montemurro.
pages   cm
Includes bibliographical references and index.
ISBN 978–0–8135–7022–8 (hardcover : alk. paper) — ISBN 978–0–8135–6439–5
(pbk. : alk. paper) — ISBN 978–0–8135–7024–2 (e-book)
1. Women—Sexual behavior. 2. Women—Psychology. 3. Self-acceptance. I. Title.
HQ29.M653 2014
306.7082—dc23   2013046604

A British Cataloging-in-Publication record for this book is available from the British
Library.

Portions of Chapters 4 and 5 appeared in the article "Getting Married, Breaking
Up, and Making Up for Lost Time: Relationship Transitions as Turning Points in
Women's Sexuality," *Journal of Contemporary Ethnography*, 43(1) (February 2014):
63–93.

Visit our website: http://rutgerspress.rutgers.edu

Manufactured in the United States of America

For Madison, "I felt you in my legs before I ever met you."
(Tegan and Sara, "Nineteen")

CONTENTS

ACKNOWLEDGMENTS

First, I would like to offer my deep and sincere gratitude to the ninety-five amazing, dynamic, and diverse women whose stories made this book. I hoped that others would share my curiosity about changes in women's sexuality—beyond changes in sexual behavior—over the course of their lives. I was pleasantly surprised to find very many women who thoughtfully and generously volunteered their time and spoke with me about such a personal topic. I thank them all, truly, for sharing secrets, opinions, and pieces of their lives with me. And I am especially grateful to those who encouraged friends, mothers, daughters, or co-workers to participate as well. Several women spurred extensive chains of contacts, and I thank them for that.

I also recognize the many friends, colleagues, and family members who eagerly spread the word about my research and helped me recruit interviewees. My mother, Susan Montemurro, told everyone she knew over the age of thirty about the book and facilitated many contacts. Family members Madison Saurman, Christina Montemurro, Mary Montemurro, Lois Saurman, Kari Lupo, and Chris Riemer also helped to spread the word among potential interviewees. I thank my friends, who cheered me on and talked through research ideas with me. In particular, I thank Diane Saccone and Kim Maialetti, who each recruited several interviewees.

My colleagues at Penn State Abington really supported my work. Some volunteered for interviews; others offered encouragement. I am particularly indebted to Meghan M. Gillen, who eagerly and tirelessly read chapter drafts and offered both reassurance and helpful feedback. I thank Karen Halnon, my sociology compadre, for not only inspiration but also a pivotal conversation that led me to create concrete phases in the development of sexual subjectivity. And I recognize colleagues from my graduate school days, including Jim Dowd, whose work and thoughts helped me shape my chapter on aging and sexuality, and Joya Misra, who has a unique ability to reinvigorate my enthusiasm in my work and who, along with Diane Saccone, Ivy Ken, Don Riemer, and Kaya Van Beynen, helped me find the right title for this book. My work was very generously supported by several grants from Penn State University, all of which helped accelerate the pace of data collection and analysis by funding travel and transcription costs, among other things. For two years, I received the Career Development Professorship from Penn State Abington, which made a world of difference in my research progress. I also received a grant from the Rubin Fund, which supported travel to conduct interviews, and two faculty development grants, which supported wages for a research assistant in the summer, data analysis software, and professional transcription of interviews.

I was fortunate to have a number of excellent undergraduate research assistants who were supported by the Abington College Undergraduate Research Activities program. Allison Cooper helped organize demographic information and recruit interviewees. She also conducted and transcribed four interviews with women in their twenties. Beth Bleming assisted with data analysis and helped me figure out the nuances of Nvivo, and together we began microanalysis of the masses of interview data I had collected. She was also a huge help in maintaining momentum while I was on maternity leave. Jenna Marie Siefken not only helped immensely with coding but also crafted sexual development summaries. Additionally, she analyzed and wrote about interview data that would not fit into the narrative of the book. Even after graduation, Jenna maintained an interest in the project, which I sincerely appreciate. I would also like to recognize Susan Tomko for her fast, accurate, excellent transcription work.

Additionally, I would like to thank the staff at Rutgers University Press. It is nice to have the opportunity to work with this great group a second time. I thank Peter Micklaus for believing in this project in its early stages. I am also quite grateful for the amazing copyediting work of Dawn Potter, who made this book more accessible and helped find the right ways to clarify my ideas and my interviewee's stories.

Finally, thanks to my family for always supporting, encouraging, and understanding. Madison and Kate, your smiling faces at the end of a writing day meant the world. Thanks again to my mom for help with reference checking and indexing and to everyone else who made it possible for me to focus on this project and inspired me to keep at it.

DESERVING DESIRE

1 ◎ INTRODUCTION

> I don't think I've ever really sat there and thought ... what
> does sexuality mean to me? I think in society, unfortunately, our
> sexuality is defined negatively. ... When I just think of print ads and
> music videos and music, I don't think we're given enough opportunity
> to become comfortable and figure out what that actually means to
> us. I think society does play a big role in actually defining it for us. My
> mother never really sat down and had a talk about how my sexuality
> would play into me becoming a woman. Never had that conversation,
> so I had to kind of figure it out on my own. So I guess if I had to give
> you a definition, it would be hard for me to do because no one's ever
> really ... no one's asked me.
>
> —Monica, age thirty-five

Monica is an attractive, bright woman from a large northeast-ern city. She is a married, African American mother of two young children who works full time in the field of education. When we met to talk about the evolution of her sexuality, Monica confessed that, in college, she lied to friends about having had an orgasm. She did not know what it felt like to cli-max, so she just laughed along with friends when the subject came up. Her parents never talked to her about sex, nor was it something she discussed openly with friends. Recalling her sexual feelings as a young adult, she said, "It was so awkward because I didn't really know. I really wasn't comfort-able with my sexuality. I didn't really know about my desires at that point. It's like you're young and you really don't know about yourself and about your body."

As a teenager, Monica set limits on how far she would go sexually because she believed she was not supposed to be sexually active and feared what would happen if she were. In high school, she dated a boy who broke up with her because she would not have sex, yet "later we kind of took back up together, and then finally I was like 'I'm gonna do it.' I wish I—I wasn't in love with him. It was just kind of like—it was so disappointing. . . . Like, the kissing and the touching and all that, . . . I remember that felt good. But the actual act of sex the first time, that was just awful. It was painful and I remember thinking like 'What is that about? Like, is that it? Was that supposed to be it?' And really, I was like 'I don't really want to do that again.'"

In college, she dated a man who only wanted a secret hook-up relationship. Monica did not think much about her own desire or really understand her body until after she met and married her husband. For her, the comfort of her relationship with her husband—whom she could count on and who, unlike previous partners, respected her—helped her learn to enjoy sex and see herself as a sexual person. As she explored her sensuality and gained experience, she began to develop sexual agency: that is, the ability to appreciate physical pleasure and act as a subject who is entitled to such pleasure (Martin 1996). Furthermore, Monica was more comfortable having sex in marriage because such sex is sanctioned and she no longer had to worry about the stigma associated with premarital activities.

However, sexuality changed again for Monica when she had her first child. Now, as a working mother, she struggles against fatigue; and the time management necessary to maintain schedules and meet her children's needs has complicated and impeded her desire. Although she wants to maintain an active sex life with her husband and sees sex as important to their relationship, she often finds it impractical and unappealing after a long day.

Monica's story is unique in many ways; yet like the stories of the other ninety-four women with whom I spoke, it demonstrates how sexuality changes and how people, relationships, and experiences inhibit or bolster sexual agency. Parents who did not talk about sex, a painful first experience, and a partner who did not want to date in public stymied Monica's confidence in her body and her understanding of the pleasure she could derive from it. Sexual experimentation during college and a marriage to a supportive and encouraging partner, on the other hand, enabled her to discover *her* sexuality and start to develop subjectivity.

This book focuses on how and when heterosexual women experience changes in their sexuality—specifically on the development of sexual agency. I explore the ways in which momentous encounters, experiences, and life-course transitions affect the construction of women's sexuality and facilitate or inhibit the development of sexual subjectivity. I got the idea for this research when I was finishing my previous book, *Something Old, Something Bold: Bridal Showers and Bachelorette Parties* (Montemurro 2006), in which I examined how public sexual expression was approved at bachelorette parties and chastised at bridal showers. What struck me was the brevity of time in which expressions of sexuality were sanctioned and how quickly some women I interviewed for that study disconnected from the single-woman role they played at the bachelorette party. When I attempted to solicit photographs for my book, only two women agreed without hesitation. Others flatly refused, commenting that pictures of themselves with exotic dancers, random men, or penis-shaped water bottles were too embarrassing. Sexualized play was not something they wanted to have immortalized in print. Several women specifically said, "I'm married," or "I'm a mom now," as if this explained everything. But for me, it did not. I wanted to know why these women were uncomfortable about showing that side of themselves and what specific elements of being married or a mother made such displays inappropriate. Does the comfort of monogamy allow for increased understanding of sexuality and sexual satisfaction? Or does sexuality lessen in importance once one has a permanent partner? Are mothers so culturally desexualized that even playful mocking of sexuality can be interpreted as irresponsible? And, more critically, why are women uncomfortable about expressing their sexuality in general?

As the women I interviewed celebrated anniversaries, became or tried to become pregnant, had children, or divorced, I became curious about how other transitions were affecting their sexuality. So I set out to answer those questions empirically with women diverse in age, generation, and relationship status. I wondered if the women who had declined to share their pictures were unique. After all, a couple of women did say I could use any pictures, and one commented that a published picture of her biting the tag off a man's boxers would show her daughter that she was "cool one day."

In my own life, I was experiencing transitions that made the political personal in ways that I did not imagine when I first thought about undertaking this research. In my mid-thirties, I found myself suddenly single and faced with the prospect of dating, really for the first time. I pondered differences in my appearance and desirability from my twenties to thirties but also realized sensations of excitement and anticipation when faced with the adventure of having new relationships and sexual experiences. My single days were short-lived, however, and within a few years (all while working on this book) I was engaged, married, then pregnant, and (now) mother of a toddler. I also turned forty and began to think about aging. I found I knew much more and entered my second marriage with greater confidence, experience, and understanding of the importance of sexuality to me, not just in expression of a relationship. Going through the low days of feeling as if I would never be in another relationship but also faced with the opportunity to start over, I had time to truly consider what was important to me and to seek it out. These transitions inspired me and helped me connect with and learn from my research participants personally as well as professionally.

SEXUAL SUBJECTIVITY

Studying sexuality and women's sexual agency is important because sexuality has been linked to physical health and emotional well-being. Sexuality is a prime source of identification (Weeks 2006). Those who report higher levels of sexual satisfaction have been found to have higher levels of marital satisfaction, longer-lasting relationships, and better physical health (for example, Heath 1999; Hinchliff and Gott 2004; Renaud, Byers, and Pan 1997; Rutter and Schwartz 2012; Yeh, Lorenz, Wickrama, Conger, and Elder 2006). Women who have greater sexual agency are likely to feel more comfortable with their bodies and more entitled to sexual pleasure, and they tend to enjoy sex more (Schalet 2011; Waskul, Vannini, and Wiesen 2007). They also have higher levels of sexual satisfaction than do those who lack sexual self-confidence (Kiefer and Sanchez 2007).

At its core, this book is a study of the development of sexual subjectivity. Sexual subjectivity can be defined as possessing agency in sexual interactions—that is, having sexual desire and the ability to act on that desire (Martin 1996). It is about being a willing and eager participant in sexual encounters rather than a passive object and about having the ability to derive pleasure from one's body. Sexual subjectivity is also about feeling in control of sexual decision making and acting purposefully and confidently. The more comfortable and agentic women are in expressing their sexuality and communicating their desires, the greater their feelings of intimacy with partners and the greater their partners' ability to satisfy them (MacNeil and Byers 2005).

Though empirically based understanding of women's sexual subjectivity is still in its early stages, foundations are primarily located in studies of adolescent sexual development (Schalet 2009). Most research on the development of sexuality finds that girls are objectified in early sexual experiences; even though some may feel desire, they are often passive in sexual situations and judged when they are sexually assertive (Martin 1996; Thompson 1995; Tolman 2002). In her compelling analysis of interview data from pubescent girls and boys, Karin Martin (1996) found that girls had considerable anxiety about their bodies as well as about why and when to engage in sexual activity: "As girls reach puberty and enter the new realm of adult female sexuality, they feel ambivalent about growing up and anxious about their new bodies. Because female sexuality in our culture is associated with dirt, shame, taboo, and danger, girls are scared and unsure of their new bodies. They rarely take pleasure in and often feel that they are not in control of their bodies" (11). These feelings are carried into sexual relationships. Rather than feeling a sense of agency in sexual encounters, girls feel like sexual objects who have participated in an experience that was about securing a relationship or giving in to pressure from boys. This frequently results in a physically painful first experience because girls are not aroused. Essentially, most girls in Martin's study lacked sexual subjectivity.

Study of the issue of sexual subjectivity and girls' entitlement to and feelings of sexual longing has expanded in the new millennium. In *Dilemmas of Desire* (2002), Deborah Tolman noted that girls do have sexual feelings, are curious, and want to explore their urges. However, they are aware of the consequences associated with expressing their feelings. According to Tolman, girls' expression of sexual passivity in stories of sexual encounters may in fact be a cover story that masks their desire with gender-appropriate behavior. Moreover, yearning for sex cannot be conflated with confidence about acting on such feelings. In Tolman's (2002) study, as in others (Allen 2003; Hamilton and Armstrong 2009; Schalet 2010; Tanenbaum 2000; Thompson 1995; Wade and Heldman 2012), the awareness of judgment can be enough to quell desire or action. Girls learn that desire is something boys have and experience dilemmas as they figure out how to deal with physical longing in a culture that tells them not to act on it. Although Tolman's, Martin's, and Louisa Allen's (2003) studies identified girls who possessed sexual confidence and who were described as having agency, they were the minority.

Studies of young women in their late teens and early twenties also show a dearth of sexual confidence, pleasure-driven action, or freedom in sexual decision making. Nicola Gavey, Kathryn McPhillips, and Marion Dougherty (2001) described situations in which young women had unwanted sex or failed to insist on condom use with casual partners. And Laura Hamilton and Elizabeth Armstrong (2009) found that, though some upper-middle-class college women wanted to have casual sex and preferred hooking up to relationships, they were reluctant to pursue extra-relationship sex because they were well aware of how they would be judged.

One explanation for heterosexual women's other-focused sexual activity is gendered socialization and the consequent internalization of a "male sex-drive discourse," which suggests that "men are perpetually interested in sex and that once they are sexually stimulated, they need to be satisfied by orgasm" (Gavey et al. 2001, 922). In other words, this ideology reinforces the notions that men's sexual climax and satisfaction are primary in a sexual encounter and that men's ejaculation marks the epitome and completion of the sexual act. A similar ideology regarding women's sexual satisfaction does not exist, nor is it necessary for "sex" to have happened: sex is defined primarily by heterosexual intercourse and men's orgasm (Daniluk 1998).

Validation of women's sexual pleasure or satisfaction was absent from the narratives of girls and young women in the studies I've just mentioned, and the lack of language to communicate their yearning reinforced their status as primarily sexual objects. Such discourses inextricably bind women's sexuality to heterosexual relationships (Daniluk 1998; Hamilton and Armstrong 2009; Rutter and Schwartz 2012). We can understand girls' and women's lack of sexual subjectivity because feminine sexuality is constructed as something that is expressed to another person or done for another person. There is little evidence that girls or women possess a strong sense of personal sexuality or derive personal pleasure from their bodies independent of relationships.

Women's lack of sexual subjectivity is also a product of the fact that many women do not know how to talk about their bodies in ways that would allow them to experience sexual gratification beyond intercourse (Daniluk 1998). Dennis Waskul and his colleagues (2007) discussed the idea of "symbolic clitoridectomy," which is the "bracketing of the clitoris by means of linguistic and discursive erasure" (152). In other words, the primary center for sexual pleasure in women's bodies is an organ that is rarely named, let alone discussed. In sex education, when studying human anatomy, girls do not learn about the clitoris, nor are they taught to understand its function. Women in Waskul et al.'s study reported discovering its capacity for pleasure by surprise. Women's lack of knowledge and information about their own bodies, coupled with taboos about female masturbation and gendered norms regarding initiation of sex, reinforces girls' and women's sexual objectification.

Culture matters, however. Not all girls possess this same ignorance and fear. Several studies find that middle-class Dutch and Danish teenage girls have greater sexual self-confidence than do their American peers, due to the cultural acceptance of teenage sex (Schalet 2011; Sternheimer 2003). The normalization of sex in these contexts creates a climate in which young women are not shamed for sexual desire and sexuality is seen as a regular aspect of identity.

Clearly, much more work needs to be done to understand the development of sexual subjectivity. The vast majority of research on sexual subjectivity concerns either adolescents or the sexual experiences of college-aged women. So as I began thinking about the topic, I wondered, what happens after the teenage years? Did the girls that Martin (1996), Tolman (2002), and Thompson (1995) interviewed develop more confidence to act on sexual feelings as they grew older? And how did earlier experiences influence the construction of their older sexual selves? Were the women that Gavey and her colleagues (2001) interviewed still having unwanted sex, either casually or in committed relationships? Did they develop their own "sex-drive discourse" that boosted their self-assurance? Were they in relationships in which they were able to express their sexual desire? Did they seek sexual gratification or pleasure motivated by personal desire?

Sexual subjectivity is about having power—power to act confidently, power to make decisions about sex with which one feels comfortable, power to say no to sexual advances when uninterested, and power to claim the right to seek pleasure and enjoy one's body. In some ways, then, expressing or embracing sexual subjectivity is an act of gender deviance. Compliance with expectations of femininity involves passivity and receptive sexual desire, and women constantly see their sexuality defined this way in American popular culture (Daniluk 1998). So how do women become more comfortable with their bodies? When do most begin to enjoy sex, to feel confident and positive about engaging in it? When do they start to experience sexual pleasure? When and how do women become sexual subjects and feel in control of their bodies? As someone asked me, does it get better as women become older? If and when sex changes, what precipitates increased or decreased sexual agency? In the existing literature, discussions of *women's* sexual subjectivity are rare. The way in which sexual subjectivity is cultivated and developed throughout women's lives is conspicuously absent from the research on women's sexuality, and it is that process which I explore in this book.

SETTING THE CONTEXT: STUDYING WOMEN'S SEXUALITY THROUGH THE LIFE COURSE

Few empirical studies look at multiple generations of women or explore the way in which life-course transitions affect the construction of women's sexuality. Laura Carpenter and John DeLamater (2012) rightly point out the need for life-course evaluation of sexuality, given that an individual's sense of sexuality is developed over time and is the result of both positive and negative experiences as well as the acceptance or rejection of cultural scripts. And Lisa Wade and John DeLamater (2002) found that stage in life mattered more than race, social class, religion, education, or parental status in predicting the acquisition of new sexual partners.

Examinations of women's sexuality through the life course have focused primarily on changes in sexual frequency associated with specific stages such as marriage (Elliott and Umberson 2008) and pregnancy or childbirth (for example, Ahlborg, Dahlof, and Hallberg 2005; Apt and Hurlbert 1992; De Judicibus and McCabe 2002); specific transitions such as virginity loss (Carpenter 2005); or significant experiences such as contracting a sexually transmitted disease (Nack 2008). Studies that focus on aging often look at particular stages of sexual development such as menopause and later life (for example, Carpenter, Nathanson, and Kim 2005; Dillaway 2012; Hinchliff and Gott 2004, 2008; Levy 1994; Loe 2004b; Meadows 1997; Vares, Potts, Gavey, and Grace 2007). Alternatively, they are presented as self-help texts (Ellison 2000) or guides for counseling professionals who work with girls and women (Daniluk 1998), or they include little data analysis (Rose 2003).

Carpenter and DeLamater (2012) developed the Gendered Sexuality over the Life Course (GSLC) model, a framework based on the notion that sexuality is constructed from both positive and negative experiences during one's lifetime, which have a continuous and cumulative impact. Carpenter and DeLamater asserted that gendered sexual scripts and related power disparities create very different sexualities for men and women. Their model calls for a close examination of the trajectories, transitions, and turning points that define our sexual selves. Positive earlier experiences often yield greater agency later in life, while deleterious experiences can produce a negative sense of sexuality going forward. The model also posits that the timing of a transition during one's life and the sociohistorical context are pertinent in making sense of its impact on sexuality. I use the GSLC model, exploring how and when life-course transitions act as turning points in the cultivation of sexual subjectivity.

SEXUAL SCRIPTS AND DOUBLE STANDARDS

The way in which women define their sexuality and the degree to which they feel entitled to sexual desire are influenced by cultural characterizations that are transmitted through media images, family norms, religious doctrine, and messages from peers (Daniluk 1998). These images and ideologies shape sexual scripts that guide girls and women in sexual encounters. As William Simon and John H. Gagnon (1984, 1986, 2003) noted, individual and interpersonal sexual behavior is influenced by cultural scenarios or scripts. Sexual scripts can be seen as social guides that shape individual awareness and actions. These scripts operate on three levels. First, *cultural scenarios* are norms for sexual expression, such as the belief that women are sexually passive and men are sexually aggressive, and thus women who initiate sex or men who are less interested than their partners in sex are viewed as deviant. Second, *interpersonal scripts* dictate interaction between sexual partners but are informed by cultural scenarios so that even private interactions have public influences. A woman's hesitation to approach a man she finds desirable or to publicly express her sexuality are examples of how the internalization of cultural scenarios creates interpersonal scripts that constrain behavior. Finally, *intrapsychic scripts* are the cognitive understandings and processing of both interpersonal scripts and cultural scenarios. These are the conversations that individuals have with themselves as they negotiate sexual situations and consider others' reactions to their behavior. For example, the married woman who wishes her husband were more sexually adventurous or would engage in more foreplay evaluates their situation mentally based on her understanding of cultural constructions of men's and women's sexuality and gendered discourses of desire (Elliott and Umberson 2008; Gavey et al. 2001; Tolman 2002).

There is considerable evidence that sexual scripts reinforce gendered double standards and create double binds for women (Hamilton and Armstrong 2009). Research on American society consistently confirms that men and women have been held to different standards with respect to premarital sex, casual sex, and initiation of sexual encounters (Bogle 2008; Crawford and Popp 2003; Fasula, Miller, and Weiner 2007; Kiefer and Sanchez 2007; Rutter and Schwartz 2012). For example, women who initiate sexual encounters or are rumored to have participated in casual sex are viewed as "easy" and labeled as sluts or whores for such behavior (Fullilove, Fullilove, Haynes, and Gross 1990; Tanenbaum 2000). Women are made well aware of double standards via media and the reactions of others. The internalization of these double standards functions as a social control over women's sexuality and serves both to keep women in line and to punish those who express sexual desire in contexts deemed socially inappropriate (Bartky 2010), thus impeding the development of sexual subjectivity for women as a class.

While working on this book, I paid attention to the promotion and rejection of sexual double standards in media as well as general depictions of women's sexuality, which I viewed as a way to gauge the promotion of sexual subjectivity at large. I saw some evidence of increasing acceptance of women's desire and agency. Advertisements on television for K-Y lubricants and Herbal Essences shampoo show women initiating sex or in post-orgasm ecstasy, and the fact that commercials for "personal massagers" appear on network television indicates growing understanding of the importance of women's orgasm and sexual pleasure (Steinberg 2010). Women can buy vibrators at Duane Reade, Walgreens, CVS, and other drug stores (Howard 2011). Television programs such as *The Secret Life of the American Teenager* feature plotlines concerning girls' masturbation, and magazines such as *Cosmopolitan* publish articles about how to teach a partner to perform cunnilingus. The erotic novel *Fifty Shades of Grey* topped the *New York Times* bestseller list.

At the same time, however, Georgetown law student Sandra Fluke was chastised and called a slut for publicly advocating that insurance companies cover the cost of birth control pills (Lowder 2012); and in her song "I

Wanna Go (All the Way)," Britney Spears sings about feeling ashamed of her desire and having to control her sexual urges. The lyrics in this song epitomize the contradiction associated with contemporary images of women's sexuality and the way in which women are socialized to believed that they are not entitled to sexual pleasure. This is precisely the message that American girls and women receive from media and culture at large. Show your sexuality, make yourselves look appealing to men, but for their benefit, not your own. Shame on you if you seek sexual satisfaction or pleasure, particularly through self-gratification.

Given that Britney Spears, an icon of hypersexuality, links shame and sexual desire, I find it hard to imagine that most everyday girls and women are sexually self-confident or possess feelings of entitlement to sexual pleasure. As Shirley M. Ogletree and Harvey J. Ginsburg (2000) have asserted, girls and women in American culture are taught "to be sexy not sexual" (925). This is why research such as mine is so very important. Women receive mixed messages about the public and private expression of sexuality and are aware of the consequences of deviant displays. It is important to provide insight from women at different points in life to determine how they negotiate these confusing directives and how and when sexual agency increases or decreases.

THE DEVELOPMENT OF SEXUAL SUBJECTIVITY

In this book I explore how several generations of women feel about their sexuality and the ways in which life-course events, individually and cumulatively, affect the development of sexual subjectivity. I focus on different generations in order to explore the influence of historical context. Ken Plummer (2010) noted that sexuality should be interpreted on the basis of generation because language, habits, significant historical events, symbolic objects, and narratives vary depending on when an individual has come of age. So as I worked on my research, I wondered, for instance, if women in their twenties and thirties, who came of age in the late 1980s, the 1990s, and the early part of the twenty-first century, would be more sexually liberal than older women were, given changes in media images of sexuality and moderate transformations in the cultural climate regarding women's sexual behavior. By asking women about their sexual development, including early influences and experiences meaningful in shaping sexuality, I have been better able to understand the context of relationships and sexual self-image as women age. In addition, by analyzing women's sexuality as cumulative, I have been able to investigate significant episodes and transitional periods that helped to define women as sexual beings.

Using the foundation provided by previous studies of sexual development and sexual subjectivity, I look at how women see themselves and act as sexual subjects in relationships. More generally, I find that sexual subjectivity develops through a complex multistage process (see table 1.1). As children, girls learn about sex; and the ways in which parents, peers, religion, and media regard sex leads them to *develop a stance* on sexuality that shapes their experiences going forward. In other words, girls think about sex and form a perspective or attitude about it and their future involvement in it. At this point, girls think less about having sex and more about how they feel about it theoretically. Stances include "sex is taboo or bad," "sex is a mystery to investigate," "sex is confusing," "sex is natural," and "sex is for love or marriage." If a girl initially views sex negatively or with anxiety, then she is less likely to imagine herself as sexually active in the future and generally experiences more conflict and anxiety when she does actually have sex. In contrast, girls who have a positive or normalized view of sex are less conflicted about sexual activity when they move to the next stage because they do not have to justify their behavior or change their position about it.

After girls absorb information about sex from other sources, and as they begin to experiment themselves, they enter the second phase of the process: *learning through doing*. In this phase girls and women develop a concrete

TABLE 1.1. Phases in the Development of Women's Sexual Subjectivity through the Life Course

1. Developing a stance

2. Learning through doing

3. Validation, affirmation, and encouragement and first sexual relationships of consequence

4. Self-discovery through role and relationship changes

5. Self-discovery through embodied changes

6. Self-acceptance

understanding of sex that allows them to discover their bodies in new ways. Sex shifts from an abstract idea to a real experience and, by experimenting, girls and women start to learn how they are viewed by boys and men. Their initial stance on sex may change or be reinforced. Girls or young women with unfavorable early experiences may discover that a "sex is taboo or bad" stance is legitimate and be slow to engage in subsequent sexual activity. Alternatively, pleasurable encounters may inspire young women with a "sex is taboo or bad" stance to change their view.

In mainstream American culture, most people expect girls or women engaged in heterosexual sexual activity to have partners, and there is a tremendous emphasis on dating and romantic relationships (for example, Bogle 2008; Hamilton and Armstrong 2009; Holland and Eisenhart 1990). Thus, for most women, acquiring a committed sexual partner has great significance. During such relationships they often move on to the next stage of the process: *validation, affirmation, and encouragement.* Committed relationships such as marriage are founded on trust and respect in ways that are meaningful for women's sexuality. The vulnerability of sexual exposure and trusting a spouse with secret fantasies or private thoughts increases intimacy and can build confidence. When a partner validates a woman's sexual desirability and encourages her desire, she begins to feel more comfortable with her body and her sexual longings (Daniluk 1998).

The next stage in the process is *self-discovery through role and relationship changes,* which the women I interviewed most often experienced during motherhood or divorce. Motherhood is desexualized (Friedman, Weinberg, and Pines 1998; Montemurro and Siefken 2012), so women becoming more comfortable with their sexuality in relationships with committed partners must reassess the situation when they become pregnant or have children. Taking on the role of mother calls for a shift in perspective from self- to other-oriented, and women must grapple with their feelings about self-indulgence and their own sexuality. For mothers of young children, this is generally a phase in which sexual subjectivity is stifled.

Another significant role change occurs when relationships dissolve. Given the sexual nature of marital relationships, divorce and remarriage act as turning points in women's sexuality: now they are forced to think about new sexual partners. Often, divorce inspires self-discovery and ultimately greater sexual subjectivity as women have a chance to reflect on and seek out satisfying relationships and have sex on their terms. Many women born before 1960, for example, found dating after divorce liberating because they had greater agency than when they dated before marriage.

Self-discovery continues in the next phase of the development of sexual subjectivity: *self-discovery through embodied changes.* The physiological changes associated with becoming a mother—pregnancy and related hormone shifts, childbirth, and breastfeeding—all influence women's perception of their sexuality. In some cases, women are objectified as their body becomes a functional necessity for someone else. But a number of women noted the experience of giving birth as powerful and important in understanding the capacity of their bodies and their strength, which led them to feel prouder of and more comfortable with themselves.

Changes associated with the physical process of aging also influence the development of sexual subjectivity. As women reach the end of their fertility, some struggle with what this shift means for them as women. Others, particularly those who are dating or in newer relationships, see menopause as liberating because they no longer have to worry about pregnancy or plan dates around their menstrual cycles. More generally, women reflect on their desirability as they veer away from conventional norms of attractiveness. When they imagine themselves as others see them, they have a difficult time feeling alluring. Yet some women also noted that with age comes knowledge about their bodies and the ability to experience pleasure in ways they have never done before, which enhances their sexual self-confidence.

The final stage is *self-acceptance,* which is achieved through aging, maturity, and accomplishments in other areas of life. When women find increased comfort in their bodies and feel entitled to pleasure, when they accept their appearance, even if they believe others might see them as wrinkled, heavy, or old, they demonstrate self-acceptance. Such women have gained self-confidence from progressing through the earlier stages and from living in their bodies for many decades. Pleasing others is no longer their primary mission, and they make decisions about sex purposefully and judiciously.

Women move through these stages at different paces, and their experiences influence when, whether, or how they move to another stage. Older women I interviewed, those born before 1960, did not have information about sex and were disadvantaged by a lack of recognition of women's sexual desire and sexual scripts that deemed women's sexual satisfaction to be irrelevant in sexual encounters. Such women were likely to see sex as either unspeakable or debauched when they were young, and most had few premarital sexual experiences. The majority married in their early twenties, and most of their husbands were their first sexual partners. Marriage and the attention of men validated their sexual desirability, which frequently stimulated sexual desire. Yet many husbands of this generation were also inexperienced and left their wives dissatisfied. Older women who divorced in their thirties, forties, or fifties were often pleasantly surprised by new lovers and the increased power they felt in new relationships.

Younger women, those born in 1960 or later, knew more about sex and had more sexual experience going into their twenties than older women did. For most of the younger women I interviewed, this gave them an advantage in the development of sexual subjectivity. Premarital sexual activity was normative, at least in committed relationships. These women married later, dated more people, and learned more about their sexual desire before committing to a partner. Yet younger women dealt with mediated hypersexualization of women and mixed messages about sexual display and the communication of sexual desire. For younger women, marriage was consequential in the development of sexual subjectivity because it gave them confidence that their partner respected them and valued them for more than their bodies. This helped them feel more comfortable about being sexually vulnerable and expressing their desires. Marriage also allowed younger women who were conflicted about a premarital promiscuous sexual identity to redefine themselves in ways that preserved femininity and made them feel okay about sex.

Religion, ethnicity, family attitude toward sex, and sexual experience influenced the development of sexual agency. Overall, women I interviewed who were raised as Catholics or in other conservative Christian religions, immigrant women or first-generation American women, and those whose families forbade discussion of sex were slower to develop sexual agency than were women who were raised Jewish or whose families had normalized sexual development. The initial stance that girls developed about sex—whether they saw it as natural and positive or deviant and anxiety-producing—had lasting influence on the development of sexual subjectivity. Negative, fearful perspectives made it difficult for women to accept their own desire or feel entitled to sexual gratification and pleasure.

Episodes in women's lives mediate or suppress the development of sexual subjectivity. Sexual abuse or assault, waning desire, physiological changes that complicate spontaneity in sex, and the dissolution of relationships confound this process and thus explain why some women possess more or less agency as they age. It is important to bear in mind that these stages are not necessarily sequential or only experienced at one point in life. Women can and do progress back and forth through these stages during their lives, though most of the women I interviewed over the age of forty did experience them in a similar way. As Carpenter and Delamater (2012) suggested, previous sexual experiences shape future experiences and influence the significance of life-course transitions. At each stage in the process, sexual subjectivity can be enhanced or stifled by women's expectations of what they think should happen as well as what actually happens and with whom.

STUDYING SEX

This book is based on in-depth interviews with ninety-five women between the ages of twenty and sixty-eight, most of whom were heterosexual and lived in the northeastern United States (see table 1.2). The women were diverse in terms of demographics, experiences, and feelings about sexuality. (See appendixes A and B for more detail on sample and methodology.) Overall, they were more educated than the general population is, with one-third of the women holding bachelor's degrees and another third holding graduate degrees. I found few differences in their experiences that I could tie to social class, probably because more than three-quarters of my interviewees identified themselves as middle or upper middle class. Had more of my sample been working class or living below the poverty line, I might have been able to draw more conclusions about the relationship between socioeconomic status and sexual subjectivity. However, I did notice that working-class women and those without college degrees (and who were not currently pursuing a degree) appeared to have thought less about their sexual development and sexuality than did those with higher education. This was particularly true among women born before 1960.

I interviewed women who were very sexually conservative and did not believe or engage in premarital sex. A few women were considerably more liberal and confidently described copious sexual experimentation with different or multiple partners and a focus on physical pleasure. Most, however, were in between these two extremes and practiced serial monogamy. Several older women were involuntarily celibate due to their partner's physical problems or their own inability to find a partner. I found it surprising

TABLE 1.2. Summary Demographics of Interviewees (N = 95)

Age at Time of Interview	Percent of Total (N)
Twenties	21 (20)
Thirties	21 (20)
Forties	20 (19)
Fifties	19 (18)
Sixties	19 (18)
Race/Ethnicity	
White	72 (68)
Black	14 (13)
Asian	10 (9)
Hispanic	2 (2)
Middle Eastern	2 (2)
Biracial	1 (1)
Self-Reported Socioeconomic Status	
Working class	22 (20)
Middle class	52 (49)
Upper middle class	26 (25)
Upper class	1 (1)
Education	
High school education or less	6 (6)
Some college	24 (23)
Associate's degree	5 (5)
Bachelor's degree	34 (33)
Graduate degree	30 (28)
Marital Status	
Married	50 (48)
Never married	25 (24)
Divorced	17 (16)
Separated	5 (5)
Widowed	2 (2)
Parental Status	
Mothers	61 (58)
Not mothers	39 (37)
Residential Location	Percent of Total (N)

(continued)

TABLE 1.2. (continued)

Urban	30 (28)
Suburban	66 (63)
Rural	4 (4)
Current Religious Identification*	
Christian (other than Catholic)	33 (31)
Catholic	20 (19)
None/atheist	24 (23)
Jewish	8 (8)
Agnostic	6 (6)
Buddhist	1 (1)
Spiritual	7 (7)

* The religion in which women were raised was generally more important in the development of sexual subjectivity than was their current religion. Most of the women with no current religious identification were raised with formal religious influences.

that the majority of women were uncomfortable talking about sex in general and that they did not talk about sex with mothers, sisters, or friends and laughed at the idea of talking about sex with their fathers or men friends. For these women, sex was a very private topic, which made their openness and honesty in interviews compelling, moving, and fascinating. It seems that these women wanted to talk about sex but had reservations about doing so, especially when their thoughts were unsolicited. I am overwhelmed by the generosity of these women, and I deeply appreciate their candor, sincerity, and desire for understanding and validation. In earnest, several asked if other women had shared similar experiences and if the way they felt was "normal," and they expressed deep concerns about self-acceptance and controls over the expression of women's sexuality.

I related to their concerns, not only in my experience as a newly (re)married woman, a woman on the cusp of her forties, and a new mother, but also as a woman reared in American culture. I learned from them and especially appreciated the stories of women who came into their own after devastating breakups and then found confidence and self-assurance they might not have otherwise possessed. I am inspired by their quests for self-discovery and their willingness to include me in the process. Because this is not a random sample of women, I cannot generalize from the experiences of the women I interviewed to all or most women. Yet while there are numbers of women out there who are not like the women I interviewed, I suspect many heterosexual American women's own stories will resonate with what they read here, as did mine.

Each of the following chapters focuses on a stage in the development of sexual subjectivity. In chapter 2, I explore *developing a stance,* considering the primary influences on women's sexuality and how they have shaped women's early sexual development. In chapter 3, I focus on early sexual experiences and the acquisition of information about sex: *learning through doing.* In chapter 4, I consider sexual relationships of consequence, such as marriage, and the role that *validation, affirmation, and encouragement* play in the development of women's sexual agency. In chapters 5 and 6, I discuss *self-discovery through role and relationship changes such as divorce and motherhood.* In chapters 7 and 8, I explore *self-discovery through embodied changes,* focusing first on the physical experience of motherhood and then on aging and menopause. In chapter 9, I examine *self-acceptance,* evaluating women's experiences throughout these stages and summarizing how and when women's sexual agency and subjectivity are enhanced or stifled.

2 ☙ DEVELOPING A STANCE
Sowing the Seeds of Sexual Subjectivity

When I got my period [my mother] just said, "Now that you have
your period, don't let any boy ever touch you [*laughs*]. Don't let them
do anything, okay?" I said, "Okay." I didn't know what that meant. I
didn't know that at that time you became fertile. I didn't know that,
she didn't tell me that. She just said you just have to watch out now for
boys. That's how I learned. I was like so uninformed, and so were all my
girlfriends. We didn't know.

—Hannah, age sixty-six

I met Hannah, a petite Asian American woman, married for
forty-three years, at her home in a northeastern suburb on a cold winter day.
She was talkative, had a wonderful laugh, and eagerly shared stories of how
she had learned about sex and the lack of information available for girls who
came of age in her day. In young Hannah's household, sex was not a topic
for discussion. Her parents never mentioned it, nor did she witness any
intimacy between them. In fact, the conversation I quote in this chapter's
epigraph was the only remotely sexual one she ever remembers having with
her mother.

Hannah's early knowledge about sex and her mother's vague handling of
it were typical not just of women from her generation but of most of the
women I interviewed. Parents rarely addressed sex openly, and few women
said that, as girls, they understood how the changes in their body at puberty

related to their sexuality. Moreover, girls in Hannah's cohort received little information from sources such as school or media. When asked about television programs that shed light on sex or sexual relationships, most interviewees in their fifties and sixties laughed. Hannah commented, "I grew up with *Ozzie and Harriet* and *I Love Lucy*, you know? I mean, innocence beyond innocence." Several women in their sixties mentioned the Federal Communications Commission rules of the time, which prohibited even married couples, such as Lucy and Ricky of *I Love Lucy*, from sleeping in the same bed and thus suggesting any sort of sexual interaction (Douglas 1995).

In other words, women who came of age in the 1950s and early 1960s had few media models of sexualized women. Accessible television programs, magazines, films, and books rarely addressed sex directly or in an enlightening way (Douglas 1995). As girls, the women I interviewed seldom spoke openly with friends because most were equally clueless. When I asked Hannah about discussions of sex with peers, she again chuckled, smiled, and said, "First of all, we didn't even know how you got pregnant, you know? I didn't know about semen.... Like, disgustingly, I thought a guy peed inside of you, and that's how you got pregnant. And that's why we thought it was disgusting, just like an 'eww!' you know? But that's what we knew."

Girls such as Hannah were put off by inaccurate information and the fear of broaching a taboo topic. Although they knew that some girls did engage in sex, those girls were deemed "bad" or "fast." Gossip about such girls traveled quickly: "It was like 'oh, my God!' Back then it was 'she got into trouble,' you know?" "Trouble" served as coded language for unplanned teen pregnancy, a necessary euphemism because it was shameful to discuss the situation directly. Without any education about sex from parents, friends, media, or school, along with implicit messages about the degradation of sexually active girls, Hannah formed a stance about sex before she engaged in it herself. For her, as an adolescent, sex was taboo—something to avoid speaking of entirely.

Developing a stance, or position, on sex is the first stage in the development of sexual subjectivity. As girls learn about sex and take in information from sources such as friends, parents, media, and religion, they start to consider how they themselves see it. At this stage, few think about their own involvement in sex; rather, they become aware of it as an activity and figure out how they feel about it. As I discussed in chapter 1, *sexual subjectivity* is defined as possessing agency in sexual encounters—that is, having sexual desire and the ability to act on it (Martin 1996). Sexual subjectivity is about being a willing or eager participant in sexual encounters rather than a passive object. It is about deriving pleasure from one's body and about feeling in control in sexual decision making, whether that means turning down or initiating sexual encounters. Being a subject means that a woman has the ability to act on her feelings and to know what she does and does not want to do with her body.

To begin to develop sexual subjectivity, then, girls must first understand what sex is and take a stance on it. Girls have to weigh their parents' opinions, media direction, socialization from religion and peers, and the gendered societal messages they receive and discern their own feelings about sex. Rather than merely parroting their parents' or religion's perspective, girls who are taking a stance develop their own opinions about sex that shape their decisions going forward.

As I mentioned in chapter 1, five stances represent the childhood attitudes of the women whom I interviewed. They are, in order of frequency, "sex is taboo or bad (or taboo and bad)," "sex is confusing," "sex is a mystery to investigate," "sex is for love or marriage," and "sex is natural." Stances were influenced by religion, family, media, culture, and generation. Although I readily determined most women's early perspective on sex, I found that, for some, it was less clear cut. In these cases, I classified them as having a combination of two stances. I could not determine the stances of two women because I lacked information about their early socialization and sexual feelings.

DON'T ASK, DON'T TELL: "SEX IS TABOO OR BAD"

Good girls don't ask for sex. Good girls don't talk about sex. Good girls let boys take the lead in sexual encounters. The research on adolescent girls' sexual development and desire corroborates girls' internalization of these proscriptions (Martin 1996; Tolman 2002). Sexual double standards abound and limit women's sexual subjectivity by treating girls' sexual assertion or confidence as aggressive and deviant (Fasula, Miller, and Weiner 2007; Fullilove, Fulliloe, Haynes, and Gross 1990; Hamilton and Armstrong 2009; Holland, Ramazanoglu, Sharpe, and Thomson 2004; Tanenbaum 2000). I heard this sentiment over and over from interviewees—both explicitly when women described messages they received from family and religion and implicitly in women's attitudes about appropriate sexual expression (Montemurro and Gillen 2013a, 2013b; Montemurro and Siefken 2012). Women were hesitant to talk about sex, which indicated their general discomfort with the subject. I was truly surprised by how few women had discussed sex with friends or close family members.

Forty-one of the women I interviewed had a "sex is taboo," a "sex is bad," or a "sex is taboo and bad" stance. Adopting a stance involves negotiating and sorting through information from others and then deciding for oneself how sex should be viewed. Girls fell into one of three categories. Those in the "sex is taboo" category internalized implicit messages from parents, peers, and religious leaders about the consequences of sexual activity and then determined that they, too, were not going to talk about sex. In contrast, girls in the "sex is bad" category were told explicitly that sex is bad. They had some parental discussion of sex, usually in the form of communication that girls who had sex before marriage were corrupt, sinning, and worthy of condemnation. These women told me that the message from their family was "don't do it" or "good girls wait for marriage" However, most of the forty-one interviewees with this stance saw sex as both taboo and bad when they were girls. Women who were in their forties, fifties, or sixties at the time of the interview were more likely to have a "sex is taboo and bad" stance than were women in their twenties or thirties. I most often found this stance among women who grew up in homes in which sex was not discussed at all, who did not talk explicitly with friends, or who did not hear about sex through formal institutions such as school or religious organizations. Girls with a "sex is taboo" stance dealt alone with confusing messages and questionable images of what sex actually is. Recall, for instance, Hannah's description of how women get pregnant. Another interviewee, Charlotte, remembered overhearing a perplexing metaphor involving dipping a French fry into ketchup. They felt uncomfortable asking questions to acquire accurate information and were well aware of the moral judgment reserved for girls who expressed an interest in sex. Even though they experienced no explicit discussion of sex, most women with this stance told me they knew that others viewed sex as bad. They understood that if they were involved in sex or even communicated curiosity about it, there would be serious trouble.

"That Catholic Guilt": The Influence of Religion

Most of the women I interviewed with a "sex is taboo and bad" stance were raised as Catholics or in other conservative Christian denominations. Such women recalled being aware of the stigma reserved for "bad girls." Leigh, a sixty-five-year-old white divorced woman, said that her parents never talked to her about sex; but she felt pretty sure that her father would have disowned her if he had found out she was sexually active—particularly if she got pregnant. When Leigh's older sister accidentally became pregnant as a teenager, "I got the message [from him] loud and clear: 'If this happens to you,' and these are his words, 'I'll kill you and I'll kill him, and I don't care if I go to jail, just know it.' And I knew he meant it because he was nuts that way."

Leigh had been raised as a Catholic, and the church's position on sex shaped her early ideas about it. "I knew there were [church] rules . . . that you shouldn't do that, that everything was wrong. Masturbation was wrong, sex was wrong, dirty thoughts were wrong, porno movies were wrong, everything was wrong. It didn't stop me from doing any of those things [later] but, you know, I knew they were wrong. . . . The message was 'don't do it,' you know? Everything's wrong with it, everything's wrong with the things that feel good." Leigh understood that her family and her religion disapproved of sexual activity. As a girl, she did not want to disappoint her father and was fearful of being labeled as bad. She was not able to change her stance until early adulthood, and even then she grappled with guilt about doing something she had been raised to view as wrong.

Not only did her parents and her religion communicate that sex was immoral, but her peers also labeled sexually active girls as bad. This was true for many of the women I interviewed in their fifties and sixties. Leigh described the expectations for sexual behavior among girls in her high school: "The dominant message in high school was that [sex] was not the norm and only the bad girls did that. So if you did that you—probably everybody was gonna find out about it because the guys were gonna talk about it."

Like Hannah, Leigh did not learn about sex from her parents, the media, or her religion; and the general taboo against asking about sex left her confused and clueless into her early twenties—essentially until she had a chance to experiment for herself. Thus, when a cousin first explained the concept of fellatio to her as a young adult, Leigh said she was "flabbergasted. I didn't know what the hell to think. Nobody I knew ever talked about that or knew about that or—I thought it was, like, so bizarre, you know, forever. And I have to be honest, even in my first marriage, I can't say that [sex] was wild and crazy. It was a much more conservative, settled kind of a relationship." Although Leigh noted that she had participated in sexual activity before marriage (but only after she was engaged), she felt conflicted about it and still struggled with her youthful "sex is taboo and bad" stance.

The stance she cultivated as an adolescent affected her sexual behavior through her twenties. After her husband was tragically killed during the Vietnam War, Leigh became a young single mother. Several years later, when she finally was ready to date, she still felt uncomfortable about the idea of sex outside of marriage, given the strong "sex is bad" message she had received as a girl.

> I was widowed for five years and [then] remarried. . . . I think . . . if I had the freedom that today's women have, I would have had an affair with that man for as long as it was—or, if I decided to, marry later. But once I became sexually active with him, I had to get married. So it was different for me because I was still following the rules, there were rules. And if I broke the rules, I knew what the consequences of that was, and the consequences were—not my mother but my father, God rest his soul, could walk out of my life and never see me again. And he loved me more than anything, but that was the consequence. You break *my* rule, you don't see me anymore.

Leigh's sexual decision making was thus influenced by her parents and the religious doctrine instilled in her as a child, even after she became an adult and went through two marriages. She felt conflicted about nonprocreative sexual activity as a young woman in her first marriage, though she deeply loved her husband and felt it was okay for them to have intercourse. She married for the second time because she wanted to be intimate with her boyfriend and could not shake her father's view of her and the idea that she would be a bad girl if she were to have sex outside of marriage. Though her perspective shifted during her late teens and twenties, the "sex is taboo and bad" stance she had cultivated as a young girl still acted as an impediment to sexual subjectivity and confidence.

Even as adults, many women whose first stance defined sex as taboo or bad found it difficult to enjoy sex without feeling guilty. Those who felt this way had initially seen sex as scary, had parents who emphasized its immorality, and had few experiences later in life to counter that image. For example, Robin, a forty-eight-year-old white mother of three, married for twenty-eight years, was visibly nervous during our interview. She joked when she sneaked in and out of my office about people seeing her and thinking she was overly interested in sex. For her, sex was not a comfortable subject—not even with people she knew well, such as close friends or family or even her husband. Robin firmly believed sex should be reserved for marriage and primarily for procreation. "I don't know if it was from [my parents] or going to Catholic school, but I guess it was both, you know, that you don't just—no sex, you know? You just don't fool around. . . . Sex is a sacred thing for marriage. And that was drilled into my head." Her parents never talked directly about sex, nor did she ever ask her mother any questions. Yet the message was clear: sex is bad. Although her peers were sexually active, she was not. Robin confided that she was "just always afraid." She remembers being appalled by her friends' behavior. "I was like God, you know [*laughs*], 'I can't believe her, in bed with him again!'" Even though she came of age in the 1970s, when attitudes about casual sex were notably more liberal than they had been in earlier decades, for her, sex was immoral.

Robin's first "significant" relationship—the first that involved anything more than kissing—began when she was seventeen. When I asked how that relationship had influenced her sexuality or whether it allowed her to learn anything about her own desire, she wrinkled her brow and shook her head.

> I'm a tough one with this because the desire was always held back because of whatever was drilled into my head growing up, you know? So the desire was always—I was always afraid to—I think to let my feelings—I think I even have a problem with that today. I mean seriously to just let go, you know? . . . I guess family, my mom, although it wasn't said, I just knew. It was like one of those things where you go into the store, you wouldn't touch one thing, you know what I mean? . . . I just knew I could never have sex because if something happened I would be like—that would be awful back then. So my desires were always held back.

Robin received messages from multiple sources telling her that sex was debauchery and that if she engaged in it, she would be a sinner. As an introduction to sex, this strong message inhibited her from feeling connected to her own sexuality. She never got past the rhetoric and still struggles with the idea that sex can be pleasurable or that it is okay for her to enjoy it, feel entitled to it, or express desire. Robin was thus seriously influenced by the perspective of her parents and her interpretation of the position of the Catholic church. Unlike other women whose stances on sexuality have changed many times during their lives, she still embraces and maintains a "sex is taboo or bad" stance today. Though she did not tell me that she does not like sex (even though she does not really enjoy or pursue it), it is still fraught with guilt and conflict for her. In fact, she says her husband is frequently trying to get her to "loosen up" and enjoy intimate moments. Sometimes she feels more amorous when they have been out to dinner and she has had a few drinks. She confessed, "He wants me to be sexual and let go and, you know? . . . That's why I say with the alcohol it does kind of [*laughs*] help." However, the disinhibiting effect of drinking is ephemeral, and she says by the time they go home she usually just wants to go to sleep.

Robin was one of the few women I interviewed who did not consider herself a sexual person. She said she wished she could be more so because she knows it is important to her husband, but she is not and has never been comfortable with her sexuality. She is particularly uncomfortable about discussing it with her partner. Tentatively, she confided, "I'll tell you what I'm bad at, verbal communication. . . . Like sex, what you enjoy and stuff like that." She intimated that her husband wants her to tell him what she likes and does not like in the bedroom, but she cannot bring herself to do it. She wished she could turn her husband on and tell him what she wants because she believes, as a married woman, she should be able to say such things to him. In contrast to girls and women who feel as if they need to suppress desire to avoid judgment, Robin wanted to induce it as a means of pleasing her husband. Performing desire requires emotion work—calling up the sentiments one feels are important in a relationship to maintain intimacy (Elliott and Umberson 2008)—and Robin wanted to work on evoking those feelings, mostly for her partner's benefit. Yet the stance she had constructed as a child was limiting her.

To increase sexual subjectivity and gain confidence, women need motivation and means for self-exploration: that is, they need not only to want to do it but also to gain the courage to seek out information about how to do so or to engage in masturbation. Dennis Waskul, Phillip Vannini, and Desiree Wiesen (2007) noted that the body can be "made meaningful in action, transaction, and practice" (170). Once women in their study "discovered" their clitorises and explored their bodies, they experienced greater sexual subjectivity. Thus, if women such as Robin are motivated and comfortable enough to try new experiences, they may gain sexual confidence. However, given the weight and duration of Robin's negative perspective about sex, she is unlikely to change. Internally, she wrestles with the residue of the "sex is taboo and bad" stance and the rationale that sex is okay for married women. That she cannot speak about sex to her friends, other than vaguely joking about ways to deflect her husband's pursuits, indicates that she remains heavily influenced by her initial perspective on sex and has had few experiences that have inspired her to change her view. The other phases in the development of sexual subjectivity did not affect Robin as they did other women because she has never shed the sense that expressing desire or enjoying sex, even after marriage, will make her a "bad girl."

As girls, women from earlier generations were more likely than younger women to adopt a "sex is taboo or bad" stance. Yet I interviewed a couple of women in their twenties and thirties who did as well. I met Marisa, a petite, white, communications professional born in 1978, in a quiet small-town café located in the scenic, rural, northeastern artist's community where she had been raised. Marisa had been dating her boyfriend for more than two years and, at thirty, was eager to move to the next stage in their relationship. They had lived together briefly, but Marisa moved out because she felt he was taking her—and her cooking and cleaning—for granted, which was particularly troubling, given that she was not his wife.

Although she was struggling to implement what she felt was a fair balance of labor, Marisa knew she did not want a relationship like her parents', in which her mother waited on her father and cultivated her appearance to please him. When she was younger, however, she thought this was how relationships between married couples were supposed to be. "My mom was always the pretty—she always did herself up before she left the house. She wouldn't even come out to get the mail without makeup on, so hair is done, makeup is done. She was always a little size 1. So that's the way I viewed everybody. My dad on the other hand was this strict Italian who—everything needed to be done for him. He did not lift a finger until recently." Marisa felt she needed to make it clear to her boyfriend that she was not comfortable with a parallel situation, nor did she want to live together indefinitely with no commitment to marry.

Marisa had been raised by Catholic, Italian American parents with traditional values, not only about the gendered division of labor in the home but also about sex. For example, they censored what their children were allowed to watch on screen, fast-forwarding through the salacious parts as a way to preserve their innocence. Thus, religion and old-fashioned family values had a greater influence on Marisa than they did on most members of her generation. Though most of her peers with whom I spoke were curious about sex during adolescence, Marisa remained fearful of being disowned or disappointing her family. Her father did not talk about sex openly but made it clear, as Leigh's father did, that she would be kicked out of the house if she became pregnant. Her stance as an adolescent, greatly influenced by her parents and religion, was that "sex is taboo and bad." She did not fully reject it as a possible future activity, but she remained concerned about its consequences and clearly understood that she was expected to view it as wrong.

In her study of parents' approach to teenage sexuality, Amy Schalet (2011) noted the significance of national culture at large. Comparing the way in which Dutch and American parents treat their children's burgeoning sexuality, she noted that American parents dramatized and attempted to manage or control it, while Dutch parents normalized it and aimed to maintain a supportive and safe environment for sexuality to develop. In other words, Marisa's parents' efforts to censor their daughter's exposure to sex are consistent with the mores of contemporary American culture, even for girls born in the 1970s or later.

Despite her conservative upbringing, Marisa developed an interest in boys as she grew older, and she began to see things differently. In her midteens she fell in love and thought about having sex with her boyfriend. She struggled with changing her stance on sex, given her parents' disapproval, but ultimately decided to confide in her mother and ask for help obtaining birth control.

> When I turned sixteen, I started dating my first love and I talked with him about having sex. I was terrified because my dad was like "If you come home pregnant, you're disowned," and he was serious. Unlike other people [who] would say that and not mean it, my dad would. He would change the locks and that would be it, so I was terrified. I said to my first love. "Let me talk [to] my parents first and see if I can get on the pill." So I talked about it with my mom, and I was like "I want to have sex and I want to be on the pill and I don't want to get pregnant. If I do, dad will kill me," and she was like "All right."

When her mother eventually told her father that Marisa had birth control pills, he found the package and threw them at his daughter. Such a response underscored the drama of her sexual development.

According to Schalet (2011), American parents feel a responsibility to prevent or control teen sex because they believe teenagers are ruled by raging hormones and incapable of emotional depth in romantic relationships. Thus, even though Marisa was being responsible and her mother had reluctantly agreed to help her get birth control pills, Marisa still felt awkward about the subject and well aware of her parents' disapproval. Yet she exhibited sexual subjectivity in her behavior. Though fear of pregnancy motivated her decision to obtain birth control pills and she did not actually become sexually active until her early twenties, she started to make decisions for herself and develop a new stance that blended her parents' beliefs with hers. Like most of the women I interviewed, she began to change her stance after she became aware of her sexuality and became sexually active. But her initial "sex is taboo and bad" " stance influenced her behavior going forward because it caused her to seriously debate the "right" thing to do as regards birth control. At age thirty, she continued to ponder what her role as a wife should be with respect to her boyfriend's domestic and sexual expectations. How much should she be concerned with pleasing him, and how much could she expect him to please her?

For most of the women I interviewed, a "sex is taboo or bad (or taboo and bad)" stance complicated their development of sexual subjectivity. When girls see sex as immoral or something they should not even mention, they are less likely to feel okay about experimentation or imagine themselves in sexual situations. They worry they will be viewed as bad if they have sex and struggle with the idea of disappointing their parents. Like the girl whom Karin Martin (1996) interviewed who "couldn't picture herself having sex" (72), many women who internalize the message that girls who have sex are unscrupulous seem to advance slowly to the next stage of sexual subjectivity: *learning through doing*. They tend to move furtively so that their parents do not know what they're up to, or they engage in seriously committed relationships that meet parents' approval.

"Respect Yourself": The Influence of Culture

The women I interviewed who were reared in conservative cultures or by immigrant parents with traditional views saw sex as taboo when they were girls. Irina, age forty-seven, who grew up in what was still the Soviet Union, noted that sex was never discussed—not on television, not with family, not with friends. Adena, age thirty, raised as a Muslim in Turkey, also remarked that talking about sex was forbidden. She recalled a story of a young woman in her college dormitory who had committed suicide after people discovered she had lost her virginity. Likewise, all of the Asian women I interviewed, both those born outside the United States and first-generation Asian Americans, recognized the influence of their conservative cultures.

Jamie, the daughter of Chinese immigrants, now age forty and a married mother of two, described the pressure she felt to respect her parents' values and how their views led her to develop a "sex is taboo " stance. As we sat outside on a park bench on a warm spring day, she nervously told me how sexuality was approached in her home and in her culture. "It was not talked about. . . . When I got my period—and actually because it was, like in Chinese—it was called like 'that thing.' It wasn't even called like a period or anything. Like it was, like that thing you got, you know? It wasn't talked about, really, . . . but you kind of understood, like don't come home pregnant, you know what I mean?"

A shy, quiet woman, Jamie described herself as a "good girl" growing up, concerned about pleasing and honoring her parents and following their advice. She struggled to fit in and be like her peers, but she always felt different. Her family ate different food and talked and interacted in their own way, and she felt the expectations to help her family were greater than those she observed among her friends. "I just grew up different. It's not even—you didn't just look it, but I mean just—you were just different. You know what I mean? Like the rules in my house were different than the rules in your house, you know?"

The parents kept a watchful eye over Jamie and her older sister, and she spent most of her time after school and on weekends helping out in her family's business. "I remember my sister [in high school] wanted to date, and my mother said, 'What are you gonna be, a streetwalker?' . . . I think that [my sister] was more, she was more of an experimenter than me. . . . And she was older, so I think she was trying to strike out. But I saw, like she'd have all these troubles with my mom and stuff, so I was like forget that, you know what I mean? Like it's not worth it for me." Whereas her sister tried to express independence and be more like her westernized peers, Jamie shied away from doing anything that would displease her parents.

Sex was also taboo for Jamie because it felt personally irrelevant, given that she could not imagine herself involved in it. Media images of ideal beauty did not feature Asian women, so she did not feel attractive or desirable. "It was hard because it was all for white women, so it would be like, oh, blond hair, you know, lighten your hair—well, that would never happen, you know what I mean? Or, you know, like the makeup. As we have the double folds in our eyes, . . . some of that was not gonna happen." Because Jamie never felt appealing, she did not believe boys would be interested in her and had little curiosity about sex throughout her adolescent years. She stayed in the first phase of sexual subjectivity for longer than most of the other women of her generation whom I interviewed because she did not see sex as personally relevant until she went away to college and met her future husband.

Jamie's peers also reinforced the "sex is taboo " stance. Sex was something they did not discuss at all in junior high school; and later, when they did begin to consider it, they agreed that abstinence was the best practice. Jamie said, "I hung around with like a lot of good girls, so we all sort of felt the same way, you know, wait till marriage for sex. We weren't like the popular girls, which I think . . . probably would have [given us] . . . a different message, you know what I mean? Like we didn't even date." Jamie was born in 1969; and although it was common for girls of her generation to have sex before marriage (Laumann, Gagnon, Michael, and Michaels 1994), she resolved to wait and was the only married woman born after 1960 who told me she did not have sex until her wedding night.

Jamie's "sex is taboo " stance affected her sexuality going forward. She said it took a long time to feel comfortable with her body and sexuality and that she felt very tentative with her husband in the early stages of their intimate relationship. Although ultimately her husband's validation and the experience of pregnancy, childbirth, and motherhood influenced her significantly, she, like other women raised in conservative cultures or religions, had a hard time shedding her original perspective. Reflecting on the influences of her past, she said, "I think actually it took me a little bit of time. Probably if I had sex in my [early] twenties, I would have been more comfortable in my thirties, but I wasn't very comfortable with sex until later, you know? Like I think like now I'm probably at the height of my comfort—in sex."

A number of other women whose first perspective on sex was taboo or bad lamented this influence on their sexual development. Like Jamie, they felt fearful in early sexual experiences or betrayed by their physical feelings of arousal. They lacked the opportunity to discuss sex with anyone and found the communication of desire problematic. Michelle Fine (1988) has suggested that there is a "missing discourse" of girls' sexual desire in public schools. While reproduction is addressed, desire is ignored, and thus women complete sex education with little knowledge about their bodies beyond mechanics. Men's arousal is addressed by way of erection, ejaculation, and conception, yet women's is not because it is deemed irrelevant to reproduction. Girls are disadvantaged by the lack of formal information or any acknowledgment that sex is about more than producing children. This perpetuates the notion that men are more sexual than women are and that men have sexual needs that must be satisfied once they become aroused. Moreover, many women do not know how to talk about their sexual pleasure or their genitalia in ways that would allow them to experience sexual gratification beyond intercourse. Masturbation in general and women's masturbation in particular continue to be stigmatized, and efforts to include information about it as a way of helping teens delay sexual intercourse have met considerable resistance and protest (Rutter and Schwartz 2012). When sex is off limits for discussion or seen as shameful and anxiety-producing, women are stifled in their development of sexual subjectivity.

When women fail to learn about their bodies' capacity for sexual pleasure and believe they are not supposed to talk about sex—especially not about wanting sex—they feel distanced from desire. When they receive the message that girls who are interested in sex or have sexual feelings are bad, they learn that desire is not something women should have. Thus, desire is masculinized (Fine 1988; Tolman 2002). Women are clearly socialized to understand that it is their role to be desirable, which reinforces sexual objectification and makes sexual subjectivity more challenging. Many of the women I interviewed, particularly (but not only) older women with little sexual experience, let their partners take the lead in sexual encounters. Several reported that it was not until well into their sexual lives that they were able to achieve orgasm or were sure that they knew what it felt like to climax. So there are great consequences to initially viewing sex as taboo or bad. Girls who start out with this perspective approach the next phase, *learning through doing*, with a disadvantage in the development of sexual subjectivity. For women such as Robin, Leigh, and Jamie, the influence of this first phase is so significant that they struggle to change their views.

SEX IS A MYSTERY TO INVESTIGATE

Some girls' understandings of sex often began with poorly hidden *Playboy* magazines or life-science encyclopedias on the family bookshelf. Frequently they read these sources furtively; the girls sensed that they should not be looking at such pictures and descriptions but were intrigued and wanted to see more. Of the women I interviewed, seventeen set out as girls to investigate and accumulate clues that would help them figure out what sex was all about. Sometimes they had been told that sex was bad or should not be discussed; yet they were sincerely curious, so they rejected those messages.

Hope, a twenty-one-year-old Asian American premed student, contacted me after seeing a recruitment flier posted at her college. I met her on her campus during an extended break between classes. She described herself as single, though she explained that she had a complicated relationship with a guy she was "sort of" seeing and hooking up with. Like Jamie, Hope was raised by immigrant parents (in her case, born in the Philippines) who encouraged her to be conservative and save sex for marriage. Unlike Jamie's parents, however, they did not entirely avoid discussing sex and were demonstrative in their love and affection for one another. At an early age Hope was also exposed to sexual images on television and sexual content in books, which stimulated her curiosity. She remembered seeing an erotic scene in a movie at about the age of four; and as she got older, the more she watched the more she wanted to know. In her view, television and magazines were educational.

> There was actually a show I watched on MTV when I was younger, and it exposed me to a lot of like things that I had never seen before. It was called *Undressed*. . . . So I mean like basically the title of the show is like it just like opens your eyes on everything. I was really young, too—like preteen—so knowing those things made me more susceptible to that—because I did start becoming sexually active at a pretty young age. And media has a lot to do with how you know how to do it—how you know how to express yourself and you know how to send out the signals and everything. . . . [And] Howard Stern. He would have like girls on the show and they'd be almost naked and you become familiar with parts of the body and some people are more prudish when it comes to that. But it's like you have one, I have one, too. . . . And you

just learn, too, I guess, about what people do when they're being intimate and how to do it. 'Cause I guess the show *Undressed* was like "Oh, I've never done this before, how do you do it?" [*laughs*]. They give you a tutorial basically on the show. It's like "Okay, well, now I know how to do it." . . . *Seventeen* or *Cosmo* those kind of—some months they would have those special articles like, you know, "How to Be Crazy in Bed," or "Twenty Ways to Make Your Man Go Wild." And I was like "Oh, well, might as well read it because I'm interested." It just makes—it actually helps you if you're having trouble to be more sexual or express yourself better, you know how. . . . So that has had an impact because I know I was really interested in sex when I was younger and I think it has—I like to read—I think it had a lot to do with TV and books.

Hope's exposure to media was not censored as it was for women who saw sex as taboo, so she had freedom to explore her curiosity about sex. Nonetheless, her conservative upbringing did weigh on her. She confided that she cried after she lost her virginity because she felt as if she had done something wrong and could never go back to being the innocent girl her parents wanted her to be. Yet before she became sexually active, she was eager to learn about sex and voraciously consumed all information she encountered. Her curiosity and the availability of information for women of her generation inspired her "sex is a mystery to investigate" stance.

Born in 1987, Hope grew up in an environment saturated with images of hypersexuality in which the sexualization of teenage girls was normative. She knew where to find pornographic content on the Internet and commented that popup advertisements featuring lesbian eroticism made her curious about homosexuality and allowed her to develop an appreciation for the sensuality and beauty of women's bodies. Of the women I interviewed who had a "sex is a mystery to investigate" stance, 70 percent were in their twenties or thirties. Sexual content was far more available for women of these generations than it had been for older women. Women who came of age in the late 1970s, the 1980s, and the 1990s were more likely to talk about feeling influenced by the sexualized imagery they saw in advertisements and on television. Whereas older women had the television models of *Leave It to Beaver* and *I Love Lucy*, women in their twenties and thirties discussed suggestive images from *Sex and the City*, *Three's Company*, *The Love Boat*, *Dawson's Creek*, and *Beverly Hills 90210*, which they saw as influential or helpful as they constructed their sexuality.

Given the frank and graphic depiction of girls' and women's sex lives on these shows, younger women had more resources as they conducted their investigations. Unlike Hannah or Leigh, who grew up in the 1950s, or Robin, who grew up in the 1970s, girls who came of age in the 1980s and 1990s simply had greater access to information about sex through multiple sources, and the advent of the Internet made such inquiry private and relatively easy to accomplish.

Some women in their fifties and sixties told me they were quite curious about sex as adolescents but were often thwarted in their attempts to learn. Tamara, a forty-eight-year-old single, African American real estate professional, found sex to be mysterious and intriguing when she was younger. When I asked what her family told her about sex while she was growing up, she said, "Don't do it, from my mother. She never, we never had that discussion with her, nor did we want to. There were four girls in our family. She was strict, she was a strict mom, and we just didn't talk to her about anything. I had a boyfriend, my first boyfriend, and I was fourteen and we didn't do a thing but kiss. I was too afraid. And we dated all through high school." Although Tamara was fearful, she was also fascinated by the idea of sex and sought information about it. She was disappointed by her sex education classes (as were most of the women I interviewed, who said they learned, at most, the mechanics of menstruation and reproduction) but discovered a book at home that she read intently. "We had a health book, a medical book at home, I remember this big book and I would turn to it. It's like that was the dirty book. I would go into the room, close the door and look at the page of how the baby was born and how it actually came out, and that was like scary. And then [when someone else was around] I [would] put that back and leave the room because I wanted to take my time and read it and see it instead of just acting like 'Oh, yeah, I know what that is.' I had to read it for myself." For Tamara knowledge about sex was critical. She wanted to understand it on her own—to know what peers were talking about when the subject came up and not have to pretend that she understood. She remembered really scrutinizing that medical book until she felt clear about the process of reproduction.

Girls with a "sex is a mystery to investigate" stance still often got the message that sex was bad or a subject to be avoided; however, they did not accept or adopt this perspective. Instead, their curiosity was abetted by a changing tide in cultural attitudes about sex, first influenced by the sexual revolution of the late 1960s and 1970s and later by the media's hypersexualization of girls and women. Girls such as Hope and Tamara were able to satisfy their curiosity by seeking out books and other media that addressed sex or by talking to friends about it. Their "sex is a mystery to investigate" stance facilitated movement to the *learning through doing* phase because they had no inconsistencies to overcome. For girls with this stance, moral proscriptions had less repressive power. Because information was available, they gained knowledge and thus a cumulative advantage.

SEX IS CONFUSING

Most of the women with whom I spoke had cultivated a clear stance on sex during adolescence and before becoming sexually active. Fifteen women, however, dealt with conflicting perspectives from peers, parents, media, and religion, which left them puzzled about how they personally should feel about sex. As girls, they struggled to develop their own perspectives because their interest in sex was both encouraged and discouraged. Ultimately, they felt confused about sex as an abstract concept and had mixed emotions and turbulent experiences as a result. Girls with a "sex is confusing" stance often talked about sex with parents and/or peers, but they lacked a clear moral position. These girls did not think sex was bad, but neither did they see it as natural or tied primarily to love and marriage. Many heard a combination of these sentiments and had trouble forming their own opinions.

Younger women, those born after 1970, were more likely to have a "sex is confusing" stance because women born earlier were more likely to have received a straightforward "sex is taboo or bad" message. As I've discussed, these younger women were saturated with sexualized media content. This was an aid for girls with a "sex is a mystery to investigate" stance, but it was problematic for others. For instance, Marcia, an Asian American college student, who was twenty-two and single at the time of our interview, commented on the negative influence of contemporary media.

> *Cosmopolitan* definitely. The cover. Like it always has like these beautiful girls, you know, on the front, and they always look good. Even though I know it's like Photoshopped or computerized, it still influences the way I think sometimes, . . . like everything in that magazine is about like how a girl should please a guy. . . . Like for 101 sex tips, like I think about it, "Oh this is pretty good, we got to try it," . . . and [these magazines] definitely portray a certain girl's aspect

of sexuality because they make you think like "this is what you got to do to impress a guy you like, and to show off how sexy you are you have to dress this way, or you have to do these things in bed with a guy."

As a woman in her twenties Marcia reflected on the images she saw during her adolescence. American culture emphasized hypersexuality; and even as a young girl, she felt confused by what she saw and how she was supposed to act and dress. Like other daughters of immigrants whom I interviewed, she knew her parents disapproved of premarital sex and the consequences associated with getting caught having sex. "I was raised in a traditional environment where you're not supposed to do that. Like my parents still yell at me if I'm wearing shorts because I'm showing too much. They're really conservative, and they're really traditional, where in the Asian culture you can't show a lot of skin or it will be frowned upon by society." As for her parents' messages to her about sex and morality: "'Dress conservatively. Stay a virgin. Don't have boyfriends because career is first.' That's about it. Oh, 'Don't talk to guys. Like don't talk to nobody, no males. Come home after school. Your body's important. You're pretty, that's all that matters. You should care about what we would think about you.' . . . Like they say what they don't want you to do—like don't have sex." Among her friends and at school, she realized that girls who got more attention were those who expressed sexuality, usually by wearing tight clothes. Yet she also was well aware of the stigma and shaming directed toward girls who were sexually active outside of relationships. These mixed messages made it difficult for Marcia to cultivate a perspective on sex.

Jessica was a white thirty-eight-year-old married mother of two living in the outskirts of a large eastern city. She, too, was raised by parents who did not talk openly about sex. Through her Catholic upbringing, she got the message that sex was bad and that she should "not think about it. . . . It didn't exist." But her exposure to media and her visceral reaction to the music of Prince, Michael Jackson, and Madonna told her otherwise. At about the age of twelve, she saw Madonna perform the song "Like a Virgin." "I was in Catholic school, and just seeing how she would be with the cross and wearing a white gown and rolling around on the floor, I thought, 'That's awesome! I want to be like that! I want to be sexy and beautiful and who cares about all those things that my parents and everybody want me to be!'"

Despite her carefree declaration, she felt guilty about investigating sex yet preoccupied with it. Although she went on to have varied sexual experiences and relationships, she told me these mixed messages had long-term consequences. "I think that when I had any inklings of it as an adolescent—I was interested in any little tidbit I could grab out there, I latched on to it. And I think growing up that way made me be a little bit more promiscuous than I may have been if it had been a little more a part of our lives or discussed or brought up in any way, shape, or form instead of being this little secret thing, like 'Oh no, don't talk about that.'"

Jessica's mother barely addressed sex with her and seemed uncomfortable when her daughter first menstruated, passing the responsibility for full explanation to Jessica's sister, seven years her senior. Her mother's embarrassment over Jessica's pubertal development and questions about sex perplexed Jessica and made her question her budding curiosity. Eventually, she chose to become sexually active but still felt conflicted about whether or not it was the right thing to do.

When sex is initially viewed as confusing, the development of sexual subjectivity is complicated. This perspective often led women to second-guess their actions and regret their subsequent sexual experiences because they lacked confidence in sexual decision making and feared doing the wrong thing and being judged for it. Like those who viewed sex as taboo or bad, girls who adopted a "sex is confusing" stance generally began the experiential stage disadvantaged in the development of sexual subjectivity.

About half of the women who developed "sex is confusing" stances were sexually assaulted or molested as girls. Girls who grew up in a culture that told them they should not be sexual but who then were regarded sexually by others struggled to develop their own perspective on sex. In other words, when sexual experience came before the development of a stance, girls had difficulty figuring out how they viewed sex in their own right. For example, when I initially asked Jacqueline, a vivacious, recently separated, forty-four-year-old African American mother of six, about her first sexual experience, she told me she did not really remember, laughing nervously about how she had blocked it out because it was so bad. Later in the interview, she revealed that she had been sexually molested by a stranger when she was twelve and that the experience had hindered subsequent sexual relationships. Tearfully, she recalled the terrible encounter:

When I was about twelve . . . I was after school and the building was empty, virtually. There were a few teachers and I was in Miss A's room cleaning the board and I had a pail of water and I went to go empty the water in the water cabinet that was in the hallway, at the end of the hallway. And as I'm walking to the cabinet this man comes out of the stairwell, a very big burly man wearing a beige trench coat and a hat and a suit. I can still remember what he looks like today. I can still smell what he smelled like. And he asked me where was Mr. B's room. And now I know he read the name off the door, which was opposite, and I said his room is right there but he's not there . . . and I said he's down there somewhere, and I proceeded off to the water cabinet. And I'm in the water cabinet emptying out the pail and I noticed the room was getting dark. And then I noticed a hand around my mouth and I started screaming. Then this man proceeded to violate me [whispers]. And I'm screaming and screaming. And I grabbed a can of Lysol and I sprayed him with it. And it must have got in his eyes and he let me go and I don't know where this voice came out because, as I said, I was [small], and I screamed this gut-curdling scream and he let me go. And he took off out [of] the cabinet and he ran. And they said they heard me like four floors down. And everyone came running and I was just standing there. I can remember my dress was torn and I was screaming, screaming. . . . But that was my first introduction to sexuality. And I can remember saying, "Well, maybe if I didn't have breasts, maybe if I didn't look so much like a little woman, that this wouldn't have happened to me," not understanding that that was the sick mind of a pedophile.

Jacqueline's traumatic ordeal left her scared of sex, her developing body, and men. She wondered if because she looked older she had somehow encouraged the attack. The aftermath of this event—when she felt people knew and judged her and her parents forbade her from going out—made her even more confused about her sexuality and development. "And that was a really hard time for me, a really hard time, . . . to be away from school for a couple of days and then to come back and everyone is whispering, you know. . . . My mom became more sensitive to my goings and comings, and so I became a prisoner, like it was my fault. And my young mind couldn't understand she was trying to protect me. I took it, internalized it as 'they think it's my fault, I did something wrong.' So when I had my first sexual encounter, like I said, I really don't remember how I felt because, you know, I had had such a negative experience prior to that." Jacqueline was thus deprived of the opportunity to develop a perspective on sex. Her parents' decision to control her and not let her play outside as an adolescent sent the message that she was at fault in the molestation. Yet she had not really thought about sex or felt aware of her sexuality before being sexually assaulted. So sex was confusing because she was labeled with a sexual identity with which she did not identify. In subsequent relationships this complicated her expression of agency and her development of sexual subjectivity. Jacqueline spent most of her life feeling confused about sex, her sexuality, and desire. Like women with a "sex is taboo or bad" stance, she did not feel entitled to express sexuality or sexual desire until her late thirties, when she developed new channels for communicating it and her marriage began to unravel.

The experience of being sexually abused as a child can have lifelong consequences, including greater likelihood of sexual assault as an adult, difficulty maintaining intimate relationships and asserting desire, and emotional unavailability in adult relationships (Browning and Laumann 1997; Carbone-Lopez 2012). It is not just these experiences, however, that create obstacles in the development of sexual subjectivity. The perspective one develops as a result of the reactions of others in the aftermath of molestation and the messages that parents, peers, and significant others convey about sex influence sexual decision making and the expression of agency. Feeling confused about sex in general makes it difficult to have the confidence or desire to think about it personally in a way that is free from coercion, violence, or guilt.

SEX IS NATURAL

Ten of the women I interviewed had adopted a "sex is natural" stance as girls. Like other stances, this one was largely influenced by parents' views on sex. Girls with a "sex is natural" stance usually had parents who normalized sex and girls' physical development as a regular part of growing up, an attitude that aided the girls' development of sexual subjectivity. I learned that parents with a medical background were more likely to be matter of fact about sex and provided far more information than did most other parents. This commonality was particularly notable among women in their forties, fifties, and sixties. As Gail, a sixty-five-year-old retired white woman, explained, "in my family it was a good thing to be a woman, good thing to be female. And my father was—would sort of joke and play, and be playful about sex. My father's a doctor, so it was . . . my father who told me about sex. Because it was a very clinical discussion, . . . so he was—it was natural. Natural is what I would say. It's a natural part of life. Sex is a good thing. It's something to enjoy. Both parents indicated that it was something to be enjoyed." This idea that sex is a normal, healthy part of life gave Gail the freedom to ask questions and come to her own conclusions about it.

Religion also positively affected the initial stance of some of the women I interviewed. As girls, younger Jewish women—those in their twenties, thirties, and forties—had more progressive views and liberal stances on sex than did most other women. Eve, a forty-eight-year-old white married mother of two who works in education, described her family as "that classic Woody Allen Jewish family, like it's all out on the table—oh, my God, it's all out there, . . . there's no sexual hangups." While most women told me that they would not go to their mothers with questions about sex, Eve noted that she did question her mother, who "spoke to [my sister and me] very directly at a very early age about sex, but in an appropriate way, and in a good way. It was like one of the few things she actually did really well, I have to say. . . . [She] taught us to be very—like that your body is your own, is personal and private and don't let anybody touch you until you're older and you say it's okay, those kinds of things." Though her mother warned her about sex, she also underscored its normality and the importance of feeling in control of one's body. Having a mother who acknowledged her daughters' sexual development and created an open dialogue inspired Eve's view of sex as natural, even before that stance became personally relevant.

When Eve began to develop breasts earlier than most of her peers, she became self-conscious and tried to cover them with baggy clothes or long hair. She remembered feeling unattractive and undesirable, so sex was unimaginable for her. Yet she knew she could always question her mother, and she viewed sex as normal for adults in committed relationships, both of which gave her sexual subjectivity when she became sexually active. As she told me, her mother's influence and the lack of religious proscriptions about sex enhanced her sexual agency. "I was always very, I was protective of myself, and I felt like I was very strong and I made my own decisions, like when it was right for me to kiss someone, or even to have, you know, to lose my virginity or whatever. I totally made those decisions."

Kara, an engaged twenty-five-year-old woman who was raised Jewish, explained why she thinks Jewish women are generally more liberal about sex. "I know it's a mitzvah if you have sex on the Sabbath because you might procreate and you're relaxing on the Sabbath. So I think Judaism is a little bit different than some of the Christian religions in that sex isn't deemed a sin as frequently. . . . At least in my congregation I wasn't raised with guilt about sexuality or being a woman or my body." Kara recognized the sexual hangups and guilt frequently associated with Christianity and felt significantly influenced by her open-minded parents, who helped her learn to view sex as natural. "My mom's a [psychologist] so I learned where babies come from very young . . . and very correctly, the proper names for things. So I understood my body better than most children did. You know, there's a funny story where my half-sister . . . who's eight years older than me— who fell off a bike and the handlebar hit her in her vagina and I said, 'Oh, did you hurt your clitoris?' And I was six and she was fourteen and she was like 'What's a clitoris?'" In addition to talking about sex in a matter-of-fact way, Kara's parents modeled the naturalness of sex in their behavior: "[They] slept in the nude or when I was very young would shower with us, so I didn't feel like the opposite sex body was behind closed doors or dirty or bad or anything like that."

Like Eve, Kara maintained an open dialogue with her parents as she matured and began to experiment sexually. The fact that she did not feel she was keeping secrets eliminated feelings of guilt and bolstered her confidence in the choices she made.

> I was very open with my parents about choices I was making: you know, talking to my parents about going to the gynecologist and getting on birth control before I had sex for the first time. . . . I felt very responsible in terms of having talked to my parents and having gone on the pill and was with a boyfriend and, you know, felt very adult and mature in those senses. Yes, so I think it set a tone for my sexuality, whereas had that been awkward fumbling in the backseat of a car, it may have had a different impact. . . . I think it actually set a nice tone for me in terms of making decisions jointly with partners about when was the right time and where and how and what people liked or didn't like.

Kara's ease in talking about sex as a pre-adolescent and her comfort with her body were encouraged by her upbringing. This attitude helped to minimize the anxiety she felt when talking about sex with future partners. Seeing sex as natural before she thought about engaging in it, recognizing it as a topic that was always open for discussion, clearly benefited her as she developed sexually. When teens are able to talk to their parents about sex and when the culture supports and encourages sexual responsibility and agency, as is the case in the Netherlands, teens tend to feel more confident about sex and sexual decision making (Schalet 2011). In the case of my interviewees, those who grew up with a "sex is natural" stance generally did not have to hide their sexual relationships and had parents who were receptive to the topic of sex, which encouraged the development of sexual subjectivity.

SEX IS FOR LOVE OR MARRIAGE

Sex is socially constructed as an expression of love or a means of securing love. Girls' and women's first sexual experiences are often influenced by a belief that having sex is a way to prove their love (Martin 1996; Thompson 1995) or the idea that their virginity is a special gift for their partner (Carpenter 2005). This ideology comes from a culture that romanticizes sex and idealizes love and romantic relationships (Holland and Eisenhart 1990; Martin 1996). Yet only ten of the women I interviewed had adopted a "sex is for love or marriage" stance as girls. This was probably due to generational influences that made even talking about sex as children deviant for most of them. Only two women over the age of forty described this as their first stance on sex. On the whole, women were far more likely to adopt this stance later, when they transitioned to the *learning through doing* phase.

Girls who developed a "sex is for love or marriage" stance rarely had open discussions about sex. Instead, they constructed their stance based on observations of other relationships, conversations with peers, and encouragement from parents to "wait for the right person." For example, Amber, a thirty-four-year-old single white woman, was raised with the awareness that she was supposed to be "good." She was told "to not sleep around, to be careful with who I'm with and what I'm doing, but to be comfortable with who I am as a sexual person. . . . Basically it was 'save yourself for the right person, be careful—be careful with who you are with and what you're doing with them.'" Amber interpreted "the right person" as someone for whom she had deep feelings, a message supported by media images that told her that love is critical in a relationship and that self-respecting girls don't just "give it away." Sex was not taboo or bad, nor was it mysterious or natural. Her first perspective on sex was that it was reserved for serious relationships. Although she still felt hesitant and unsure, her initial stance on sex made her feel "confident in limiting what was going to happen" when she began experimenting with boys in junior high school. When boys pressured her to go further than she wanted to, she acknowledged feeling turned on and enjoying such early sexual experiences. Nonetheless, she held back because she retained her belief that she should wait for "the right person."

Two older women, one in her fifties and one in her sixties, also shared this perspective. They were more invested in the "sex is for marriage" aspect of this stance because, from what they understood, premarital sex was wrong. Unlike girls who learned to see sex as taboo or bad, girls with a "sex is for love or marriage" stance saw sex as perfectly acceptable, as long as it took place in the right relationships. Often, parents modeled loving relationships, and this greatly influenced girls' views. Paige, a retired sixty-four-year-old white woman, described how her parents' behavior shaped her stance, even though they did not do well in talking about sex directly. "Actually my mother and father were very physically in love, so they displayed that kind of loving, touching, kissing. They were very romantic. Um, so I always—we always had a good feeling about marriage, relationships. As far as giving me a book to read about what to do about this and that, they failed miserably. . . . I don't think there was a lot of information out there that they could look to. But I still had a good feeling of life as what it would be like to have sex and stuff like that." Paige's comments about her parents' affectionate relationship shed light on one of the major influences on her ideas about love, marriage, and sexuality. Because she had few other sources of information, their demonstrative marriage served as a critical inspiration. For some women, the "sex is for love or marriage" stance provided an advantage going forward because it gave girls a justification for waiting to have sex when they did not feel ready. It gave them confidence, as Amber noted, about setting limits and feeling in control of their sexual decision making. For others, however, it produced guilt or anxiety when they engaged in premarital sexual activity with the "wrong" person.

CUMULATIVE ADVANTAGES AND DISADVANTAGES ASSOCIATED WITH TAKING A STANCE

Positive stances that encouraged sexual exploration or normalized sex ("sex is a mystery to investigate," "sex is natural") or sanctioned it in relationships ("sex is for love or marriage") bolstered girls' development of sexual subjectivity. Those who cultivated these stances were usually raised in liberal families, had open parents, and were born after 1960. Negative stances ("sex is taboo and bad") and weak stances ("sex is confusing") inhibited girls' sexual self-assurance because eventually they had to come to terms with doing something they had believed or were told was wrong. Girls reared in families that did not talk about sex, who had conservative religious or ethnic backgrounds, and who were born before 1960 were more likely to possess such negative stances.

Stances change throughout most women's lives. After the women I interviewed became sexually active, some changed their attitudes completely—going from "sex is taboo and bad" to "sex is amazing and how could I have ever thought this was something I should not do?" For others, this first phase in the development of sexual subjectivity was more influential than the other phases were. In other words, stances are dynamic and thus indicate sexual subjectivity. A subject takes a stance; a subject has an opinion about sexuality. Once girls develop a stance, they move to the next phase in the development of sexual subjectivity, *learning through doing*, when they become aware of their own sexuality and start to imagine themselves becoming involved in sexual activity.

3 ๑ LEARNING THROUGH DOING

Early Exploration and Experience

Until I actually experienced it, it's all Greek, it's all mechanics. It's all wonderful on paper. But until you actually put it into play—it didn't mean anything, really.

—Gretchen, age forty-two

Few women I interviewed approached initial sexual encounters feeling confident or prepared. Most said they only really understood sex after they had experienced it. Although some had read books or heard sketchy and confusing accounts from friends, the majority—particularly those born in the 1940s and 1950s—said they did not truly "get it" until they began to do it. Their first real understanding of sexuality was accomplished in the *learning through doing* phase. Sexuality is shrouded in mystery and taboo; so when girls experiment, they begin to make sense of it through their bodies. They start to understand sex in a direct and sensual manner that gives them a new viewpoint, one in which sex is no longer abstract. Women piece together information from what they have heard, been told, or seen; process it with their own experience; and develop an understanding of sex on a new level. They then begin to see themselves not just as kids or girls who know what sex is but as young women who might someday (or soon) have sex.

This phase in the development of sexual subjectivity involves the growth of a sexual self, a new element of girls' and women's identity. As George Herbert Mead (1934) wrote, we are not born with a sense of self; we develop it in the process of social interaction. The same is true with a sexual self. As girls mature, they recognize this new aspect of their identity and construct a sexual self based on understanding and internalizations of sexual scripts (Simon and Gagnon 1984). Developing a sexual self is a critical step in the cultivation of sexual subjectivity. To feel confident, make decisions about sexual activity, and act on sexual desire, girls must first see themselves as sexual and recognize sex as an activity in which they can, might, or will engage. Girls can want to do it or not want to do it, but being able to imagine the possibility or make a choice about their level of participation is important in fostering sexual subjectivity (Martin 1996). Of course, American sexual scripts complicate girls' sense of ownership or confidence in their sexuality. As Amy Schalet (2011), among others, has found, American adolescent girls are expected to be good, but being good and being sexual are mutually exclusive. Girls must negotiate cultural barriers that discourage their desire as well as feelings and experiences that cultivate it (Tolman 2002).

A SEXUALITY OF HER OWN: THE AWAKENING OF SEXUAL FEELINGS

Early Awareness

First sexual feelings inspire girls to think about themselves as sexual beings. And early sexual experiences, when consensual, allow them to develop their sexual selves further as they began to discover new physiological sensations and see themselves as independent and mature. About 60 percent of the women I interviewed noted that they became aware of their sexuality when they started to feel attracted to boys or when boys (or men) started noticing them. Most often this happened during adolescence, when they were between the ages of ten and thirteen (with women in their fifties and sixties noting awareness at later ages than did women under fifty). For some women, however, it was earlier. These early bloomers remarked that they detected this shift during play: all of a sudden, they were not just part of big groups of kids playing together but *boys* and *girls*.

Several interviewees also recalled prepubescent sexual encounters and feelings. Bridget, age twenty-five, recollected this feeling at eight years old. "There was one boy I had a crush on ... and I remember we would play tag around the garden and I would catch him and kiss him and kiss him all over his face, like little pecks or whatever. So that was the first time I was like 'Oh, I'm in love, it's a boy,' things like that." Others told of sexual touching or experimenting with other children and commented that, even as young girls, this made them aware of new bodily sensations that they later interpreted as sexual. Such play taught girls something new about their bodies or their relationships with boys. Only in retrospect did some acknowledge these experiences as the beginning of their sexual development. Thus, for some of the early bloomers, the *learning through doing* and *developing a stance* phases happened simultaneously.

Feeling "Tingly" and Exploring One's Body

Most girls became aware of sexuality around the time of puberty. Hearing people talk about sex led them to realize that they could have it. Many women recalled experiencing a new physical sensation, in response to either a sexual image, a person, or an encounter, as a turning point in their sexual development. As one woman in her sixties remembered with a smile, "When you start getting those feelings when you had makeout sessions, which you know, I didn't get to do that too often because my father was so strict. . . . You're thinking, 'God, what was that? Why is that?' You know? And you didn't connect the two, not when I was young because I didn't know any better. . . . I think the first time you ever become aware of it is when you're kissing and something goes on in parts of your body that you didn't know you had [*laughs*]."

Delia, age sixty and African American, noted that physical feelings moved her sense of sexuality from abstract to personal:

> Oh, [I was] probably about fourteen, and there was a boy that I really, really, really, really, really liked, and I was having feelings in my body that were different from what I had ever felt before. And I just thought that this boy was so cute and I just thought that I loved him. And he probably didn't even know that I existed, but I definitely was feeling the flips in your stomach and the kind of contractions that your body goes through when you are feeling that sexual attraction. . . . Well, what started to become clear was some of the stuff that my mother had talked to me about, what men and women do when they're in love and they have sex and how your body responds. And it's like okay, well, I kind of get that now, it's beyond theoretical. It's beyond the little stuff in the book and all of that. This is "Oh! This can really happen."

Delia and other women remembered the initial physical feelings of being aroused and recalled trying to make sense of them. They were both intrigued and anxious about this change because it made them see boys differently, caused their hearts to race, and fostered awareness that they were entering new chapters in their lives. Although initially they did not realize that the feeling was arousal or know how it related to their sexuality and maturation, these early experiences and feelings were the germination of their sexual selves. This was how they began to discover what their sexuality meant and how they felt about direct involvement in it. As Delia said, sex was no longer merely "theoretical." The things that her mother had told her and that she read about were really happening *to her.*

Physical feelings of arousal triggered several women's desire to explore their own bodies. Eight women, half of whom were in their twenties at the time of the interview, said they became aware of their sexuality when they first masturbated. This often began as play as a young child and became connected to sexuality when they felt desire and realized they enjoyed the feeling of sexual release. Holly, a twenty-one-year-old white college student, for example, noted that she did not remember having strong sexual urges as a girl but that she began to touch herself and found it pleasurable. "When I was ten, I think that was the first time I masturbated and I was like 'Oh, I don't even know how I figured it out!' [*laughs*]. But, uh, yeah, I didn't feel sexy or anything like that, but it was the first time I realized that this is something fun to do."

For Holly, masturbation was a physical release and a way of exploring and learning about her body. Although it took a while for her to link this behavior to her sexuality, she was learning about her body by masturbating, which enabled her to be more aware of what was pleasing to her when she later engaged in partnered sexual activity. In this case, masturbation, whether as a child's play or as an older girl's conscious exploration, is a prime example of *learning through doing,* the second phase of developing sexual subjectivity. When girls explore their bodies independently, they better understand their sexual functioning and can become more confident about sex throughout their lives. Masturbating as a child, particularly when done without guilt or shame, can be beneficial for girls later in life. They enter into sexual situations with partners already aware of what it feels like to have their genitals touched and comfortable with the sensation of being turned on.

Getting Noticed and Having Crushes

Forty-five of the women I interviewed marked sexual awakening as having a crush or feeling attracted to boys, and another twelve marked it as the moment when boys started paying attention to them as more than friends. Charlotte, a thirty-six-year-old white married mother with a toddler, said that although she had crushes on boys, she didn't really feel an awareness of her sexuality until boys started noticing her. "I guess I started feeling more attractive to other people, like when I was my second year in high school. 'Cause up into—starting in like sixth grade I was always interested in boys but they weren't interested in me. . . . I don't think it was boys that necessarily gave me the confidence but they made me aware of the fact that maybe I was becoming more attractive, because I had no idea."

Charlotte felt insecure about her appearance, saying she was "homely" until she "blossomed" as a teenager, and could not imagine boys' being attracted to her even though she was infatuated with them. In fact, the first time a boy telephoned her, she was convinced it was a joke because she was so used to rejection. But once boys started showing interest, she began to realize her desirability and thus felt more self-assured. It was not, she said, that boys simply made her feel more confident. Rather, their attention allowed her to see herself in a different way and recognize that she was moving into a new stage of her sexuality. Sex was no longer abstract; and though she was timid and naïve about sexual experiences, she was curious and confident enough to want to experiment with kissing and touching, once her desirability was validated by boys' attention. Like several other girls who noted that boys' interest inspired a new perspective on sex, Charlotte learned through these interactions to see herself in a different light.

Exposure to *Playboy* and Other Erotic Media

Some women remembered first feeling aroused when they came upon suggestive publications such as pornographic magazines or Judy Blume's novel *Forever*. Though they often felt confused by their bodies' physical responses to these images, such feelings made them curious, and they liked the way they felt. Several had very precise memories. Kara, age twenty-five, felt that her heterosexuality was confirmed as soon as she saw actor Patrick Swayze's back in the movie *Dirty Dancing*. A couple of women specifically mentioned coming across soft-core pornography and being intrigued and aroused by it. Jessica, age thirty-eight, married, and white, began to ponder the complexity of her sexual feelings when "my parents and I were staying at a hotel, and there was this cable channel that came in that of course we didn't have at home that was showing like this Texas kind of burlesque show, and there was this woman stripper. And looking back it's so obvious. I was like 'Oh my God, this is really turning me on, I don't know why.' I didn't see that as being a normal thing or anything I'd mention to my friends because I hadn't heard anyone else say anything like that, so I kept that very secret for a very long time." In all of these cases, these early feelings of arousal were a surprise and, for girls such as Jessica, a secret. Many of these girls had a "sex is a mystery to investigate" stance and thus were actively seeking out information about sex, though some came across it by accident. Yet whether their discoveries were intentional or not, most knew that this feeling was not something they could discuss with others, either because they were not sure if it was normal or right or because they feared judgment from others.

A number of women, mostly those born after 1960, said they discovered their fathers' pornography collections and were transfixed by the images. Amanda, age thirty-nine, white, divorced, and a mother of two, said, "I think it was my father's *Playboy* in the bathroom, probably."

BETH: Do you remember feeling it changed anything or that anything was different once you felt this awareness?

AMANDA: Well, I definitely wasn't disgusted by it. So I think the feeling of not being disgusted by it and being more intrigued probably set my whole life on that sexual path . . . as far as like a curiosity.

Seeing pictures of naked women made these girls think about their own bodies in a new way, yet most felt guilty or uncomfortable at the same time. Thus, although Amanda and other women found *Playboy* arousing, they knew that this should be kept secret. None of the women who mentioned being titillated by sexualized media spoke of sharing that information with others or asking mothers or friends about what they had seen or felt.

Puberty As Exception

I found it striking that very few women connected awareness of sexuality to puberty. When girls first menstruated, only a handful related the development to their sexual maturity. Given their understanding that this topic, which they somehow connected to sex, was taboo, most were too embarrassed to question their mothers or anyone else. Women recalled feeling unprepared, and several told me they thought they were dying when they first saw menstrual blood. Only then did their mothers, with little or no discussion, quickly show them how to use pads or tampons. Older women remembered fumbling with sanitary belts and metal clips, and many born before 1960 said that their introduction to puberty came in the form of a mail-order kit with an informational booklet, which their mothers wordlessly handed to them. Though a few women born in the 1970s or later received more detailed explanations and, in a couple of cases, celebrations, most did not know what was happening before they got their periods.

Menstruation marks puberty and sexual maturity in a very clear way. Thus, the fact that many girls have little knowledge of the changes in their bodies helps to explain their lack of sexual subjectivity. As Karin Martin (1996) noted, puberty evokes ambivalence and fear as girls learn that "female sexuality is associated with dirt, shame, taboo, and danger" (15). When girls are ignorant about physical changes and lack control over their own bodies and how they are changing, the process of alienation from the body begins (Martin 1996; Thompson 1995; Tolman 2002). So although menstruation may be the first *physical* step in the transition to developing a sexual self, it was rarely a turning point in the development of a sexual self or sexual subjectivity among the women I interviewed. Only seven described experiencing puberty as the beginning of their awareness of their sexuality, and only a couple specifically mentioned menstruation as a significant episode in their social-sexual development.

Feelings about Feeling Sexual

Many of the women with whom I spoke noted that feeling aware of their sexuality generated a great deal of angst during their adolescence. Although some enjoyed the physical sensations, more felt confused and scared about changes in their body, which is not surprising given the lack of information they possessed and the cultural taboos surrounding adolescent desire (Fine 1988; Martin 1996; Tolman 2002). Kelly, age thirty-five, married, and white, said, "It made me very awkward around boys, whereas before I wasn't. It made me feel constantly embarrassed, constantly ugly, constantly insecure [*laughs*]. It made things much more complicated." Feeling sexually aroused made many girls uneasy. Those who initially saw sex as taboo, bad, or confusing were conflicted about feeling something they believed they were not supposed to feel, desiring what they should not desire. Furthermore, with the exception of those who initially viewed sex as natural, girls generally lacked both reliable information and confidants and had nowhere to turn to discern whether or not their feelings were normal. Like girls whom Deborah Tolman (2002) and Louisa Allen (2003) interviewed, they recognized the feeling of desire, they enjoyed or were intrigued by their arousal and interactions with boys, but they felt guilty due to their initial stances.

Feelings of confusion were especially acute among older women who lacked validation of their burgeoning sexual feelings. Unlike women born in the 1970s or later, who were often open with peers, had consistent exposure to media images that normalized hypersexuality, and had access to books or television shows that dealt frankly with teen sex, women from older generations had few places to look for support. Rose, age sixty-five, remembered the apprehension she felt in the early days of her sexuality. "Some boy likes me, he came over to my house and I just felt this little, zzzzz, you know? . . . Fear, it was fear. Because I knew we weren't supposed to do anything—a lot of fear in my life. . . . There was curiosity. But then when he finally did kiss me, I jumped up and I took a book and I threw it at him." Rose's ambivalence was very clear. She liked this boy, wanted to spend time with him, and so invited him into her house. She was curious but afraid, and her reaction indicates that most of her unease related to how she would be judged if she "let" something happen. Before this experience, she had believed that sex was bad and had learned that "nice girls wait" until marriage. She did not want anyone to think she was not a nice girl.

Women from older generations also feared, as girls, that people would judge them if they found out that they had been turned on or were sexually curious. Iris, age fifty-eight, recalled feeling exposed when a boy commented on her reaction to their "makeout session": "He made a remark that I was getting wet, and I remember being embarrassed by that and thinking like 'Oh, just, I don't want to hear it!' You know, like bleh! So I was not—I was I think maybe a little scared or something like that, but not so much that I was being sexual but that my cover was gonna be blown. . . . I mean, I could get wet before and like I was the only one who knew it, so my privacy was like broached or interfered with. I didn't like that." On her own, Iris could control her arousal; it was her secret. She did not like the idea that this boy knew something about her because it made her sexuality public.

When women move from having a stance on sex without imagining direct involvement in it, to feeling aroused and/or to masturbating, and then to sexual experimentation with a partner, they make important shifts in the development of a sexual self. The sexual self a girl begins to develop alone is a *private* sexual self; but if a partner notices or responds to such arousal, she must acknowledge her *public* sexual self. She can no longer keep her desire or physical feelings to herself. In Iris's case, once her "cover was . . . blown," she could never go back to being innocent in the eyes of others.

Given the cultural ambivalence regarding American girls' and women's sexuality, Rose's fear and Iris's embarrassment make sense. Once someone else sees them as sexual, girls must come to terms with what this means personally and what it says about their maturity and sexual development. As they recognize their burgeoning sexuality as a physical change and note that their bodies have become more complex, they begin to construct a sexual self—first in private or "back-stage" and then, as they engage in partnered sexual activity, in quasi-public or "front stage" (Goffman 1959). However, the reactions or perceived reactions of others generally inhibit the expression of sexuality and the development of sexual subjectivity. American cultural scenarios stigmatize girls who show desire, and we continue to label girls who are sexually active outside of relationships, in the "wrong" contexts, or at too young an age. Thus, they receive little validation or support for their sexual feelings (Tolman 2002). When girls feel aroused but guilty about it, they easily become disconnected from and conflicted about sexuality, which perpetuates feelings of shame and anxiety in sexual situations and hampers the development of sexual subjectivity.

Iris was far from the only woman of her generation who felt this way, although others were not as concerned about revealing their sexual selves to boyfriends or partners. Rather, they worried that their parents—their fathers, in particular—would be able to tell just from looking at them that they had been fooling around. Lori, age forty-four, spoke of the anxiety she felt about seeing her father after she had lost her virginity.

> I remember clearly going to visit my father at his job, which we did regularly. . . . I remember feeling like "Oh, my God, he's going to tell just by looking at me!" [*laughs*]. And I was worried about my father viewing me differently, and I didn't think it would be positive, by the way. . . . I was like, you know, "I'll bet you he can tell. Oh, my God, what is he gonna think?" You know? I don't

know if I consciously thought I'm not gonna be his little girl anymore or now I'm a woman or I just entered a new chapter, but I remember having this feeling he was gonna know something was different.

Although privately Lori felt good about this sexual experience and did not regret it, the idea that her father might somehow know and see her differently was of great concern.

The change that happens at this time is not just about sex. It is also about growing up and becoming autonomous and independent. Girls' resistance to letting parents know about their sexual awakening suggests concern about maturation and independence: now they will no longer being seen as their parents' pure little daughters. When girls at this stage begin to imagine themselves through the eyes of their parents, they must reconcile a new image with how they used to see themselves. Because American cultural scenarios dramatize adolescent sexuality and parents feel responsible for preventing teenage sexual activity by monitoring it and warning of its dangers (Schalet 2011), girls face pressure to break away from their parents and hide their sexuality. Amy Schalet (2011) has illustrated the way in which coming of age for American girls is a "vehicle to engage in a psychology of separation, bifurcating sexuality and family life" (21). Once they become sexually active, girls distance themselves from their families, sometimes with reluctance or guilt, because they know their behavior is not accepted. This is a further strain in their transition to adulthood and their development of sexual subjectivity because they need to hide a burgeoning aspect of their identity.

FIRST SEXUAL EXPERIENCES

Given the ambiguity of defining sex (Christina 1992), I asked women what they considered to have been their "first sexual experience." Although virginity loss was the most common response (thirty-six women defined it as such), more than half of the women I interviewed considered either kissing (twenty-three women: "French kissing," "making out") or sexual touching short of intercourse (twenty-six women: "petting," "second base," "getting felt up," or oral sex) as their first sexual experience. Women in their twenties and thirties were more likely than older women were to name intercourse as their primary sexual encounter. No woman in her thirties identified kissing as a first sexual experience, but several women in their fifties and sixties did. Because Laura Carpenter (2005) has already released a compelling study on motivations for and interpretations of virginity loss, I focus here on how women felt about having sexual contact for the first time and how it affected them going forward in their sexual lives. Rather than looking at these early experiences as independent episodes, I attempt to understand their role in the development or inhibition of sexual subjectivity.

Fumbling in the Dark

After I asked women how they became aware of their sexuality, we discussed when they began to act on their desires. For most of them, these early encounters were learning experiences, often described as "the blind leading the blind." As with feelings about arousal, girls described their first forays as fraught with fear, anxiety, and often ignorance. For example, Charlotte, a thirty-six-year-old self-described late bloomer, became aware of her sexuality when boys started to pay attention to her. She said she was very naïve in early sexual encounters. Because she had no understanding of boys' bodies, she was quite frightened by her first encounter with a penis. "I remember the first time I felt someone's erection, I was scared shitless because I didn't know what was happening and he looked really freaked out and kind of hurt. And I was all concerned that I hurt him somehow. . . .'Cause I just had no idea what was happening until like—because we were dating at the time and I think it came out a couple of weeks later what had happened. And he had to almost explain it to me because I was like 'What happened? Did I hurt you?' He was like 'No.'"

Charlotte initially viewed sex as bad, a stance influenced by her mother, who had insinuated that nudity was shameful and who did not talk about sex. At Catholic school she received no formal sex education, which added to her confusion about both sex in general and her own involvement in it. Although her boyfriend explained that he was experiencing pleasure, not pain, she felt awkward and insecure in sexual encounters going forward. Partly due to lack of information, partly due to a fear of sex influenced by her upbringing as well as a friend's unexpected teen pregnancy, Charlotte developed little confidence or agency during her early sexual experiences.

Nadia, age forty, a student, and a married mother of four, also recalled being ill-informed about sex as a teen. She summed up the sentiments of many others when she said she had learned about sex through "trial and error, honest to goodness."

> [The] first time [a guy] put his tongue in my mouth, I thought there was something wrong with him. Like I—after that I didn't want to be anywhere near him until somebody explained to me that's called French kissing. And then they were like "You gotta do it like this." And I remember a girlfriend kind of just showing me what you were supposed to do with your tongue, and I was like "It sounds kind of gross." But every part of your adolescence, it seems like, . . . it's like blind people trying to show each other where the doorway is. Nobody really knows. You're just stabbing in the dark.

Previously, Nadia had known little about sex. She had adopted a "sex is taboo and bad" stance when she was younger, largely influenced by her Catholic upbringing, and had had little discussion with her parents about sex. Although her mother told her to ask if she had any questions about puberty, she was put off by her mother's clinical approach, which she found confusing and unenlightening. She believed she was dying when she first menstruated and recalled learning only the basics of puberty during sex education class at school. At about the age of sixteen, she became aware of her sexuality when her father expressed concern about the attention she was attracting from older men. Nadia's early experiences—what she called "stabbing in the dark"—gave her opportunities to explore her sexual feelings, yet they rarely helped her develop sexual subjectivity because she was anxious, scared, and ignorant about sex. At the age of nineteen, she had her first experience with sexual intercourse when a boyfriend drugged and raped her, an event that exacerbated her disconnection from her sexuality. She became pregnant by that boyfriend, who she soon discovered was cheating on her with multiple women. Consequently, Nadia became promiscuous because she already saw herself as damaged and afraid to trust men.

Nadia felt least comfortable with her sexuality between the ages of nineteen and twenty-one because she was in a relationship in which she was insecure and she did not know her wants or needs. She felt little self-worth after the rape and unplanned pregnancy and thus lacked sexual subjectivity. "Just everything at that point was just, I wasn't comfortable with me. I didn't—I don't think I really knew who I was, so I think that that played a factor, too. If you don't know who you are as a person, you sure as heck aren't gonna know yourself as a sexual being or in your own sexuality. I think you need to really know you first."

In subsequent relationships, Nadia focused on pleasing her partners and had no idea how to achieve sexual satisfaction, nor did she feel entitled to it until she was in her thirties. She pretended to climax in her early sexual experiences because she did not really know what an orgasm was or how it should feel. "In my twenties you always had to fake it, like I didn't know what the hell I was faking [*laughs*]. But I hit thirty and all of a sudden I had one, and I was like, crap, well, I ain't faking that again. I need that. I mean there's a difference, like you really—in your twenties you really don't know what it's—it's almost like you're playing, what is that?—Marco Polo, where you're, like it's you have no idea what's really out there."

For Nadia, negative experiences, lack of self-awareness, and lack of information about sex during her formative years inhibited her development of sexual subjectivity. Her first experience taught her that sex was something taken from her, and she went along with this view as a means of numbing herself to the emotional intimacy she craved. As she matured, she accepted herself more, and this sense of self-worth and desirability fostered sexual subjectivity. Later in life, after she married and started the process of sexual self-discovery, Nadia built sexual knowledge and subjectivity through experience. As she said, once she realized what it felt like to climax, she would no longer allow herself "to fake it": she acknowledged that she needed that release and satisfaction. The more experience she had, particularly with a supportive partner, the more self-assured she became and the more clearly she defined her sexual self.

Experiences That Inhibit Sexual Subjectivity

Retrospective Regrets: "Letting People Down." Initial stances on sex influence girls' feelings about sexual activity. Many women in their twenties and thirties expressed remorse over their decisions to have sex, particularly those who did so with boys or men outside of serious relationships. Several burst into tears immediately after losing their virginity. Although this may have been because they viewed virginity as a "gift" carelessly given away (Carpenter 2005), some felt as if they had let their parents or themselves down because they had failed to follow their initial stance on sex. They had to come to terms with the emotional transition to independence, of no longer being the "good little girls" they believed their parents wanted them to be (Schalet 2011). Marcia, age twenty-two, for example, explained that she felt terrible after losing her virginity because she feared how people would view her. Moreover, the incident failed to live up to her romantic expectations.

> Well, after I had sex for the first time, I cried. I felt really bad. Like I felt dirty, I felt like a slut, you know, even though it was with like my boyfriend. . . . Like, I felt horrible about myself. I would like not talk to him for like two days because I just didn't know what to say. Like, this *happened*. It was influenced by alcohol, too. So that was worse because it's like "How can I do that?" You know? When you were younger—when I was younger something like rose petals, candlelight, you know? The sweet romantic music—like television would show me and now it's, I kind of lost it on his futon. . . . It was definitely different [from] how I viewed it from back when I was an adolescent, how I imagined it compared to reality, and how fast it's gone. I didn't know how to feel. Even though it was my boyfriend at the time—like he tried calling me, like trying to console me, but I still felt like really dirty and just disgusted with myself, like how can I do this.

Marcia felt ashamed because she had internalized sexual scripts that told her sex was about the expression of love and romance and that good girls do not do it outside of serious relationships. In retrospect, she believed she was too young and not ready for the emotional experience of virginity loss. Though she cared about her boyfriend, she was not sure her feelings were love, and she certainly was not ready for marriage. The experience inhibited the development of sexual subjectivity because she believed every aspect of it was wrong.

Pressures and Pleasing Boys. Most women I interviewed described their first sexual experiences as focused on their partners' satisfaction, not their own. Girls rarely described situations in which their sexual pleasure or climax was of concern. Many communicated feeling emotionally distant or disconnected in these early experiences because they were just going along with what boys wanted—or what they believed boys expected from them. Girls often felt more like objects for someone else's pleasure than subjects entitled to their own gratification in these early encounters, a reaction that is consistent with much of the research on adolescent girls' and young women's sexuality (Dunn 1998; Gavey, McPhillips, and Dougherty 2001; Martin 1996; Thompson 1995; Tolman 2002).

Bridget, a graduate student, age twenty-five and single, observed that in early experiences among her peers girls frequently performed oral sex yet rarely received it. With passion, she said, "I think what's interesting—and this goes on for a lot of girls—their first sexual experience is about the guy, he'll be the one that gets the hand job or the blow job or whatever. I mean, I'd be really shocked if a girl's first experience was a guy going down on her, like that would blow my mind and I'd want to meet that guy. So I think for me that was kind of ingrained. It's easier to do things for the guy because you feel self-conscious or you feel you should have to make the guy happy." Bridget's assessment that girls' early sexual encounters were usually other-directed paralleled the stories shared by many interviewees. Like those interviewed by Nicola Gavey and her colleagues (2001), most of the women in my study remembered that boys' sexual gratification and pleasure were imperative. These early experiences stifled sexual subjectivity because they reinforced sexual scripts that deem girls' or women's sexual satisfaction to be secondary.

Furthermore, women noted considerable pressure to engage in sexual activities that they did not want or feel ready for. I repeatedly heard stories in which girls felt coerced into sexual situations. Sex was defined by both boys and girls as a boy's experience. Chloe, age twenty-four, recently married, white, and a full-time college student, described falling into a routine in which popularity and recognition felt contingent on hooking up with boys and being willing to do whatever they wanted. Having been sexually molested by a family member when she was a preteen, she had learned that compliance would yield acceptance and attention. She had also found that resistance rarely stopped sexual encounters from happening: ultimately she would give in to the incessant cajoling and convincing. With a tone of regret and sadness, she explained:

> In my early experiences it was, for me, it was always about doing whatever they said, because that's what happened in the past. It's like if they were telling me to do this, I can say no, but it doesn't matter, you know, I'll still end up doing it. So there was a lot of pressure, and eventually I stopped saying no. So it may have seemed like I wanted to do it but I didn't, you know, and how were they supposed to know? . . . Sometimes I'd say it like this—*someone would be having*

sex with me because I don't feel like I wanted to. I would zone, I'd try to zone off into like a different area to not think about it, you know? Especially if I was drinking I would get taken advantage of more. And I thought that was okay, I thought it was completely normal. I didn't think there was anything wrong with this because that's like what I knew to be correct.

The absence of sexual subjectivity in Chloe's narrative is dramatic. She had no voice to say no, to refuse participation in sexual encounters. Given that her initiation to sex was nonconsensual, she came to believe that no one would listen to her protests and found it easier to go along physically and to detach mentally. When she told me that "someone would be having sex with [her]" rather than phrasing the experience as having sex herself, she communicated a lack of agency and emotional presence. To her, this attitude was *normal*. That is, it was normal for girls to give in to boys; it was normal in her high school to participate in sex as a recreational activity devoid of emotional depth and respect. Her words tell us not just about Chloe but about the gendered cultural scenarios and interpersonal scripts (Simon and Gagnon 1984) that mediate contemporary sexual interaction. The boys she was with also went along with this view, showing little interest in or regard for her as a subject during their encounters.

Women in their twenties were not the only ones with these experiences. Women of every generation told stories that reinforced the "male sex drive discourse" (Gavey et al. 2001, 922) and the lack of a discourse of desire for girls and women (Fine 1988). Sara, a white, married, full-time executive and mother of two, born in 1959, described her first sexual experience with a guy she had been attracted to in college. She almost immediately regretted it because she realized how self-centered this man was and how little he cared about her.

I think of my first sexual experience not as losing my virginity but with this guy that I became friendly with in a bar that I was working at to support myself when I was going to college. And that involved oral sex for him, and that was really my first experience, my first sexual experience. . . . It was a bad experience. I just didn't feel good about it. He wasn't—I didn't even know why even in my mind I actually even thought this guy was attractive. It was completely, you know, it was completely for his benefit. So I felt completely—I felt degraded by that experience, actually, I really did. When I reflect back on it, it's just distasteful to me. Not that oral sex is distasteful to me, I know that guys like it and I don't actually have a problem with it, but it was just this one guy—and I don't know if I was that desperate that I wanted to be with this guy, but I couldn't figure that out.

Sara's remorse over this experience is linked to her realization that sex should not be just about men's gratification. She was embarrassed that she was so willing to please this man when he so readily dismissed and disregarded her and her sexuality. Yet her behavior, like that of Chloe and a number of other women I spoke with, is not unusual. Sexual scripts fortify gender inequality in sexual interaction in American culture. The "male sex-drive discourse" and "coital imperative" argue that "men are perpetually interested in sex and that once they are sexually stimulated, they need to be satisfied by orgasm" (Gavey et al. 2001, 922). Thus, women are encouraged to engage in sex even if they do not necessarily want to.

This is not to say that women do not have desire or that some do not actively seek sexual gratification in every sexual encounter. But the lack of a *women's* sex drive discourse perpetuates the notion that men are more sexual than women are and that they have sexual needs that must be satisfied once they become aroused (Fine 1988). This "phallocentric, goal-oriented," heteronormative conception of sex reinforces men's necessity in women's sexuality as well as an implied power imbalance associated with sex (Daniluk 1998, 5). Sexual subjectivity is predicated on feeling in touch with one's own sexuality and acting on the basis of one's own desires, which clearly does not happen when girls are pressured into sex or their primary focus is on pleasing someone else.

Learning the Hard Way: Molestation and Sexual Assault. For some women, coercion into a sexual relationship—particularly under threat or fear—yields a lifelong struggle with sexual subjectivity. I interviewed seven women who were sexually abused or molested as children or teenagers. Like Chloe, they labored with feeling in touch with their sexuality and maintaining mental focus on the sensual experience of sex throughout their lives. Sexual assault or molestation often leaves victims disconnected from sexuality, and sometimes childhood sexual abuse has lifelong costs: women never feel fully comfortable with their sexuality. Kristin Carbone-Lopez (2012) has noted that childhood victims of sexual assault are more likely to experience sexual assault and domestic violence as adults as well as a greater number of relationships and relationship breakups compared to those who were not abused. Their difficulty in sustaining relationships may be due to a confusing and painful introduction to sex that keeps them from experiencing deep intimacy.

Several women in my study told me they had been molested by family members. They noted that their awareness of sexuality happened gradually as they went from a normal physical relationship with a family member to one in which they realized that their bodies were desired commodities. This complicated sexual development magnified their insecurity and unease. Georgia, for instance, was sexually abused by her stepfather between the ages of twelve and sixteen. When I asked about her first sexual encounter, she said, "The first . . . sexual experience, was a day that [my stepfather] and I were home watching baseball or something—it was the World Series—and having a fine old time. And then he lifted up my t-shirt and started caressing my breasts. And it was like 'Something just got different.' And what happened was I got this feeling that I didn't know what it was or where it came from. And I spent the rest of the day trying to figure out what that—like what just happened here. And that's one of the things that's been difficult."

Georgia tried to make sense of why their relationship had transformed, what she had done to make things different. One minute she felt like a girl spending time with her father; in the next the atmosphere had changed dramatically. At twelve, she was beginning to feel confused about sexual activity and what it meant. She had been thinking about whether or not it was something she wanted to do. "So it's all during that time when you're kind of figuring out what your boundaries are, 'Do I want to kiss him? Do I want to make out? Do I not want to make out?' You know? Where you're saying, yes or no. There wasn't a no." Georgia's stepfather did not ask her if she wanted to be touched, the mood was not sexually charged by her assessment, so she had no opportunity to think about what she wanted and what was happening because it just happened. Because it continued to happen for several more years, Georgia had great difficulty developing sexual subjectivity. She believed that compliance was important because it meant that she was loved, that this was a way to prove her worth. Yet she lacked control over her body and found herself emotionally wandering during those encounters because she knew they were wrong.

Furthermore, as a result of the sexual abuse, Georgia became pregnant as a teenager, which she did not know until the morning of her abortion. Her mother had taken her to the gynecologist because she had been missing periods. The doctor told her mother that Georgia was pregnant, but no one told Georgia. It is no wonder that she lacked a sense of control or ownership over her sexuality when such critical information and decisions about her own body were kept from her.

After four years of molestation, Georgia told her mother about the abuse. Though she did not fully believe her, Georgia's mother told her stepfather to move out. Georgia described the emotional and sexual repercussions of those years.

> So when I did finally make it stop, I was sixteen, almost seventeen, and going to college. Well, you know, I was still kind of stunned by everything and at that point I think my thought was "Okay, I have to prove that I can do this with somebody else." So I wasn't making the best decisions. It was just "Okay, I have to do this because I have to show that I can." And in a lot of ways I think that I wasn't really thinking about the sex, it was like, okay, in order to be liked and loved, then I just have to give that part up. So it was a—it was not a place or a time when I had a real firm idea about even what pleasure was. It just was all very messy.

Because Georgia learned to define sex as a physical experience during which she needed to be emotionally absent, she had difficultly connecting in subsequent encounters. She had sex when she went away to college, not because she felt desire but because she wanted to prove her ability to have "normal" sex. What she learned through doing was to disconnect, to be an object for someone else's gratification. If she just went along with it, everything would be okay. She would be accepted; she would be loved. As for Chloe, also sexually molested as a girl, sex was an activity that involved body but not mind, and pleasure was a foreign concept. Sex was an instrumental activity, not something in which Georgia was emotionally invested.

These experiences profoundly affected Georgia's sexuality and sexual relationships going forward. Since then, she has never been able to feel fully emotionally present during sex.

> Just being in the moment, in the experience, was always very hard, you know? And my archetypical story for all of that is—this was when I was married to

my first husband and we were having sex—somewhere in the middle of it I said, "Did you hear Norman Rockwell died?" And he like flipped out [*laughs*]. It's just I couldn't figure out why, why is he so pissed off? And it was like I was just not there. And I—it was only kind of hindsight and thinking about it then when I realized, "Yeah, you were not there and this is not really a good time to be talking about Norman Rockwell," even if he was still alive. And there's always been that kind of triangle, having to fight being elsewhere. . . . For me I think that it was always a difficult area of my life, and at some point it's—I'm just tired of wrestling with this. . . . And then it gets easier and easier not to be sexual and it's like okay—but I don't want to forget, either. And so it's been kind of a wrestling match. . . . I have always had trouble having orgasms, and on some level it's like I'm tired of like working. It's becoming a job and then it's just not fun anymore. . . . There is a level of frustration at not being able to find a way that is natural and to get out of my—it's, to get out of my head and into my body, a very difficult transition.

Georgia relied on a mind-body split when enduring sexual molestation as a child because she was very confused about her stepfather's actions and how she should respond or understand sex going forward. The repeated sexual abuse, combined with a "sex is confusing" stance, made it difficult for her to perceive physical intimacy as a means of emotional intimacy. When her former husband "flipped out" because she was talking about Norman Rockwell during sex, she realized that he had expected that she would be enjoying the sensuality of the encounter and caught up in the moment. But Georgia had to battle to be both mentally and physically present during sex, even when it was consensual.

As she told me about her repeated sexual molestation and its effects, I remember feeling angry on her behalf. Georgia recalled, "In some ways I felt more like an observer than so much of a participant." How unfair it was that she could not take pleasure in her own body. Georgia was indifferent and almost resigned to the situation, clearly having struggled with her inability to relax and experience sexual pleasure throughout her adult life. But I felt deep sympathy for her. Other women had also had negative experiences as children; but for many of them, subsequent positive experiences had offset or mediated the childhood damage. In Georgia's case, even a loving marriage of twenty-one years had not taught her to be mentally present during sex or to find sex pleasurable. She could not figure out how to talk herself into pleasure, given so many years of trying not to feel or think about what was happening to her body. Such experiences dramatically inhibit the development of sexual subjectivity; and those that happen in the early years, when one is still trying to "figure it all out," are especially detrimental because they stifle self-discovery and feelings of control over oneself and one's body.

Experiences That Encourage Sexual Subjectivity

Taking Control: Waiting, Planning, and Getting Ready. Although most women's early sexual experiences did little to bolster their sexual self-confidence or encourage sexual subjectivity, some girls felt relatively powerful and confident about sex and took charge in decision making. A number of the women I interviewed thought carefully about when and how they wanted sex to happen and maintained control over their bodies until they felt ready to go further. For some this was due to a fearful stance cultivated in childhood, which they followed closely because they believed they would be sinning if they had sex. Others seemed to think through the consequences of sex and waited until they felt they could handle it. They watched friends or siblings deal with emotional turmoil or teen pregnancy and deliberately decided to wait until marriage or until they felt sure they were ready. To withstand advances, some even prepared speeches for insistent boys.

Autumn, a forty-one-year-old married mother of one, had been raised in a liberal environment in southern California during the 1970s. She recalled that her parents were completely open about sex and their own sex lives.

> My family was the family of totally inappropriate behavior and conversations from the beginning. And certainly there were few boundaries, they were terrible with boundaries. So I knew about my mother's sex life so inappropriately from such a young age. I knew about my grandmother's sex life. They talked about their sex lives with each other, in front of me as a kid. I didn't know about my dad's sex life so much because my dad was separated from my mom when I was eighteen months [old]. But my mom would tell me about my dad, how he was in bed. It's like, you know [*sarcastically*], "Great."

For Autumn this hyperexposure was too much. She decided that, when she had sex, it would be a meaningful, clear-headed experience and that she would wait until she felt ready. Uncomfortable with the rampant casual sex she observed in her own home and among peers, and well aware of the pressure on girls to become sexually active, she wanted to maintain control over her body. So she crafted a script to use when such situations arose.

> I really knew that I was gonna decide, and I was gonna be very clear about when I had intercourse for the first time. And I remember, maybe not too [long] after getting my period, . . . I remember deciding that—I came up with a blurb. I came up with what I was going to say to boys or men who wanted to have sex with me and how I was gonna say no, . . . I remember, and I loved my—I remember doing it over and over again with different guys, because I had twenty-two-year-old guys asking me out when I was fourteen because I developed early. And I'd go out on a few dates but I figured it was too freaky for me, you know? I'd have my little blurb and I'd say, "I'm not gonna have sex until I'm with somebody for a long time and I know that they are in love with me and I'm in love with them." And I'd make it so boring and annoying that they would lose interest in me [laughs]. And it worked. I gave my little speech many times. But I thought—I knew that that was necessary . . . and I really did want to be in a relationship I felt pretty secure in [when I first had sex].

Unlike girls whose first experience was focused on pleasing a boy or having sex because they felt someone else wanted them to, Autumn demonstrated sexual subjectivity by developing strategies to maintain control and set limits in sexual situations. When she felt ready, she maturely and carefully planned for the experience.

> I started dating this kid when I was a junior at the public school, and . . . I'm telling my mom that I've started to date this guy and I really like him. And I think I was fifteen or sixteen, probably sixteen. And she said, "Oh, should we go get you a diaphragm?" And I was like "No, that's okay, no need, I'm good" [laughs]. But then when I actually met my true love of high school—it was probably six, seven months later, I took myself to Planned Parenthood and got myself a diaphragm and it wasn't a big deal. And the night I lost my virginity, everybody in my family knew. I was like "I'm gonna, this is the night!" Everybody was like "Oh, great!" Now this I know is not common [laughs]—and I was even at home because I lived with my grandmother at the time and my room was actually separate from her house. There was a deck and then there was like this back cabin that had its own bathroom and had an outside shower and it was very groovy, very nice little scene back there. And so we just had sex

back there, and it was like "Okay, bye" [*laughs*]. So it was . . . totally open—I told my dad that I [had sex] . . . and everybody was very supportive, and they probably also couldn't believe I waited so long [*laughs*].

Among my interviewees, Autumn's experience was atypical. It was, however, consistent with the experiences of contemporary Dutch teenagers (Schalet 2011) in that her parents not only supported but encouraged her sexual activity. In Autumn's family, and in the time and place where she came of age, sex was viewed casually and openly. This normalization and positivity fortified her sexual agency. She had the resources to be educated about sex and birth control, people she could go to with questions, and a carefully thought-out plan and stance on her participation in sex. Only one other woman whom I interviewed—a woman in her twenties who had been primarily raised in Europe—noted that her parents supported or condoned teen sex. Although Autumn's experience was unique in my study, I might have heard similar stories if I had interviewed more women with a similar background.

Though they kept their experiences secret from parents and acted without their approval, several older women also exhibited sexual agency in early sexual encounters, thus bolstering their sexual subjectivity. Sandra, age fifty-eight and a professional, married, African American mother of two, also carefully planned her first sexual experience. Raised by a mother who talked openly about sex (though not quite as openly as Autumn's parents did), Sandra developed a "sex is natural" stance. Becoming sexually active was not a difficult a transition because she did not see sex as a bad thing but as an exciting and special secret. When she fell in love as a young teenager, she and her boyfriend discussed sex and planned together for the right time.

It was a great experience and I felt like I had the best secret in the world. And I couldn't tell [anyone], but the guy I was with, he and I had talked about it, we had set a date. . . . I was actually, I was in the ninth grade and so I was fourteen because we waited until my birthday. And I had a big heart on my calendar that said love, and my mother said, "What does that mean on your calendar?" and I said, "Oh, nothing, it's just my birthday." And he and I had been, we were in school together, and we had been building this relationship slowly over a couple of months at school. . . . He had arranged his sister's apartment where we could be alone, he had condoms. Everything was like—it was not spontaneous in the backseat of a car. It was planned. We were going to cut school that day, you know, we had everything all figured out and we never got caught. And so it was just like this wonderful secret that probably only his sister knew, from evidence, or whatever. But it was very nice and—it's still nice, thinking about it now. . . . I guess I learned that it was very positive and it was something that I would want to do again. . . . So I just felt good about it and I felt more sophisticated than the rest of my friends because I had done this and I knew something they did not.

Sandra's forethought and agency were rare among the women with whom I spoke. Her first sexual experience was positive because it fit with her expectations of what sex should be like. In contrast to women such as Marcia, who "lost it on a futon," Sandra's strong feelings for her boyfriend and their effort in planning, waiting, and feeling ready enabled her to feel good about the experience. Nor was she the only woman who talked about sex with her boyfriend before having it or who discussed together whether or not they were ready. A few other women, mostly those in their twenties or thirties, and mostly those with "sex is natural" stance, described early experiences as mutual decisions that they felt good about and prepared for.

For other women, determining they were ready for sex was an independent decision. Some grew tired of waiting for the right moment or person and sought out a friend or guy they knew for a casual sexual encounter. As for some of the men and women whom Laura Carpenter (2005) interviewed, virginity was a stigma. Eve, age forty-eight, white, and married, told me this story about the first time she had sex:

I hope you don't think horribly of me, but it was like I did it just to get it out of the way. I had had this boyfriend in high school for the majority of my senior year and we had, you know, like made out a lot, you know, done a lot of stuff but we never had intercourse, I did not want to. And then when I was a freshman in college I was dating this guy, I wasn't that interested in him but I just said, "Oh, let me just get this over with, I'm just tired of. . . ." There just weren't any boys that I was that interested in and I just was like—I just want to know what it's like, you know? There's so much talk about it. . . . And it wasn't like I felt, I never felt any peer pressure, like that I had to do something because people were pressuring me, but I just kind of felt like, well, I want to see what it's like, everybody's talking about it. . . . And while I'm having sex for the first time with the "boyfriend," [a friend] is knocking on the door, "Hey, there's an outdoor concert, do you want to go?" And I said, "Yeah, I'll be there in a minute." So we finished what we were doing and then I went [out] . . . and that was the end of that. . . . I just wanted to get those first times out of the way.

Eve approached sex pragmatically. She wanted the experience so she could learn more about what sex was and how it felt and so she could catch up with her peers. She was less interested in having sex as a means of expressing love or solidifying a relationship. This is a clear example of how *learning through doing* can enhance sexual subjectivity, as it also did for Sandra. Both women had sex because they wanted to know what it was like, and they planned purposefully to make it happen. After they had sex, they felt more confident going forward. They felt good about sex because they had decided when they wanted it and were ready for it.

Courtney, an extroverted thirty-one-year-old, was a single African American woman who was pursuing a graduate degree. She, too, had a positive first sexual experience. As an adolescent and into her teens, Courtney had held a "sex is taboo" stance, only expressing her sexuality privately by reading suggestive books or watching racy films. But when she went away to college, her perspective changed. She started to think about sex as an okay activity and then suddenly decided she was ready to do it herself.

Teenagers when I was in high school, they were—they definitely were having sex. They were making out and I think that a lot of that put me off as well. It's just that I didn't want—it seemed like it complicated things and I didn't want to get involved with that. My film watching and my TV habits didn't change during that time, I just had no interest whatsoever. I was like I see it on TV, I see it in the halls, I don't need to get involved with that. . . . And I didn't actively seek it out but it kind of just like fell in my lap and I ended up having a boyfriend for three and a half years in college. When I was nineteen, I literally woke up one morning and I was like "I want to have sex today." . . . And I just want to say like that was like the best experience ever having him for my boyfriend because I was a virgin when we had sex, which he didn't know, like I told him I was but he didn't believe me because I talked about sex like all the time. And so it was like—he just made me so comfortable in my own skin, and was just so like open-minded and just so nurturing and just so great and it's like I heard so many women be like "My first sexual experience was horrible, it was awful!" and I'm just like "Mine rocked! It was awesome!" You know? And so I think that my sense of my sexuality kind of developed over those three and a half years, I really came into my own.

Both Eve and Courtney expressed curiosity about sex, knew others were doing it, and wanted to do it, too. They were not pressured by boyfriends; they felt prepared and acted assertively. Although Courtney says she did not "seek it out," she did initiate sex with her boyfriend one day after years of dating, when she felt ready, on her terms, not after acquiescing to his coaxing. She chose not to be sexually active as a teen because she found it complicating and distracting. She waited until she felt confident she would not regret her decision and then went forward with excitement and positivity. For Courtney, a supportive and encouraging boyfriend, as well as the fact that she felt in control of her sexual encounters and choices, enhanced her sexual subjectivity and gave her advantages in subsequent experiences.

Learning and Liking It: First Experiences with Sexual Pleasure. Early sexual experiences gave a few of the women I interviewed a new understanding of their bodies and an enjoyment of the physical pleasures of sex. Such feelings allowed them to rethink negative stances they had had before becoming sexually active. For those who viewed sex as a mystery, becoming sexually active allowed them to put the final pieces of the puzzle together. Emily, an engaged, white, thirty-three-year-old editor, for instance, said, "I was a little—both nervous that I was doing something wrong but at the same time it was fun and I wanted . . . to do more, so I guess it made so it seemed not so bad. Like I'm not doing a bad thing, not so wrong. It's enjoyable, and I like who I'm with and I like being with him, you know? So I was kind of thinking like 'Hey, what's so terrible about this? I'm not a slut. . . . I'm doing everything carefully,' so I guess that made me feel like it's not a bad thing."

Emily initially viewed sex as a mystery to investigate, though she knew others expected her to see it as bad. Through her own experience she developed the understanding and confidence to reject that perspective. She liked the way she felt, the closeness with her boyfriend, and the fun of sex; and it was only by actually doing it that she was able to feel more assured about her perspective and more assertive in her sexual decision making. Having sex and realizing that many of the things she had heard were not true enhanced her sexual self-confidence.

Joan, age sixty-six, was so taken aback by her first real kiss that she felt ashamed to have gone through with it. "I remember this guy kissed me in the movies. He sat next to me and, you know, I just felt dirty and disgusting afterward because that was just like 'What was I doing? Why did I let him do that?' And, uh, yeah, I was, it's a shame but that's kind of—it was, it was the aura around sex [then]—that it wasn't going to make you happy. It didn't feel good to you. There was no talk about women getting pleasure or anything about it the way there is now." Joan felt disappointed in herself because she was not acting like a good girl; clearly the burden of regulating sexuality was on her. Women of her generation, born in the early 1940s, were expected to resist the advances of boys and to at least publicly maintain the image that they were not sexually available.

However, as Joan had more experiences within the socially approved format of a committed relationship, she decided that sexual interaction was enjoyable. She recalled dating her first boyfriend and what she learned from that relationship. "We went to the movies together and dances and stuff and, you know, sat in the car out front and kissed a little bit and that was—I guess it was a way of learning. . . . I learned that sex is stimulating and the potential for sex is stimulating and fun." Before kissing boys she saw sex as taboo, but with experience she began to recognize its benefits and develop a sexual self. Being able to enjoy sex and see it as exciting helped Joan sow the seeds of sexual subjectivity. Although she truly came into her own much later in life, after her divorce, these early experiences allowed her to see herself as sexual. They were critical in the development of sexual subjectivity.

Though she was only twenty-one when we met, and relatively less experienced than many of the other women in my study, Kendra, a single African American college student, also enjoyed the physical aspects of sex and found that engaging in it when she was about fifteen made her feel better about herself. Describing the first time she had sex, she commented, "It increased my curiosity and it was a positive experience because it made me aware of sexuality in general. And it was something I wanted to explore. . . . It kind of made me feel desirable and made me feel like a woman and encourag[ed] me to explore myself and my sexuality, not even in relationship to another person. . . . I felt like it was something that completely opened me up—not just sexually but to life, I guess. Wanting to know things and learn things and learn my body and myself, so in that way I think it was positive. I think it was completely positive."

Kendra's mother was open about sex with her daughters, and Kendra's stance as a girl, which she still maintains, was that sex is natural. Although her mother objected to her early start and sent her to live with family in another state to try to remove her from temptation, she still instilled the belief that at the right time sex is a beautiful and normal activity between consenting adults. A feminist intellectual very interested in art, literature, music, and poetry, Kendra was more self-aware and self-possessed in terms of her sexuality than were many other women in my study, including those who were ten or twenty years older. Because she viewed sex as a good thing and because her experience had reinforced that sentiment, she acted very much as a subject in sexual encounters and engaged in it with a clear-head and a consciousness of her limits and desire. "I guess I would consider myself a sexual person but I would never need to use that term. Because it's like the quote, 'a revolutionary woman doesn't have to say she's a revolutionary woman, she's being revolutionary so she doesn't have to say it.' . . . [Being a sexual person means] being open about my sexuality. Being comfortable with myself and my body and being able to express my sexuality, whether it's with myself or with another person. Not being afraid to talk about it or to get other people to talk about it. Just being open to things." Kendra was by far the youngest woman I interviewed with a strong sexual self. Her early views and experiences will likely enable her to move into her sexual future feeling confident and in control and thus to have encounters that reinforce her sexual subjectivity.

CUMULATIVE ADVANTAGES AND DISADVANTAGES ASSOCIATED WITH LEARNING THROUGH DOING

The stance that women adopt as girls influences the degree to which they feel good about early sexual experiences. Girls with a "sex is taboo or bad" stance were less inclined to see early sexual activity as enhancing their sexual identity or improving their sexual self-confidence. Rather, they often felt uncomfortable, guilty, or inhibited and not entitled to sexual pleasure. In contrast, girls with "sex is natural" or "sex is for marriage or love" stances and even some with a "sex is a mystery to investigate" stance found that sexual experience bolstered their sexual self-esteem and thus their sexual subjectivity. For such girls, sex was not something that just happened to them; it was something they *made* happen. Such early experiences, coupled with a positive view on sexuality, created a climate of cumulative advantage that benefited (or will be likely to benefit) many of these women as they moved through the life course. Generation influenced not only girls' stances but also the likelihood and amount of early premarital sexual experience. Women born before 1960 fooled around less and were more stymied by proscriptive stances that elicited guilt when they were learning through doing outside of marriage. Thus, older women were less confident and generally disadvantaged in the early years because they had less experience than did women born in or after 1960.

4 ❧ VALIDATION, AFFIRMATION, AND ENCOURAGEMENT

Sexual Relationships of Consequence

I think maybe ... it helps a lot to be dating someone or to have someone who likes you because it almost brings it out even more.... I think if you're not seeing anyone and you're just living your life, doing your everyday thing, I think [sexual desire is] kind of dormant. And maybe you do kind of think about it—but it's just not, it's just not really burning.

—Tara, age thirty-one

On a rainy fall day I met Tara in a hotel lobby in a large north-eastern city. A single Asian American woman who works in real estate, she was raised in a conservative household in a conservative southern state and received little direct information about sex during her formative years. Yet she was curious and sought out clues. She recalled feeling "mesmerized" when she stumbled across one of her father's *Playboy* magazines. As she matured, Tara had crushes on boys and thought about kissing them but felt unsure of how to go about it. By the time she went away to college, she was still inexperienced. However, she then felt liberated to seek informa-tion, particularly as peers became sexually active. "I'd ask friends like 'Oh, how do you . . . ?' I asked them their advice on sex, like 'How do you kiss somebody? How do you move into having sex? How do you—how does that work?' So maybe I'd have them kind of describe it to me—maybe they would try to. I was fascinated by it all. I think I was really curious, I think I was really wanting—I was wanting to try it out."

When she did have sex, during her college years, she felt a boost of confidence as men's interest validated her appeal. "I think initially it made me feel good. Like, this is what it is, this is what it's about. This is what it feels like to feel desired or be liked, that sort of thing." Yet when we specifically discussed her intimate relationships, Tara saddened. As we talked, I realized that the failure of these relationships had made her more confused about sex, love, and her sexual desirability. Influenced by her father's infidelity and her parents' subsequent divorce, she viewed relationships not only cautiously but as likely to result in devastation. Tara felt particularly distraught when her most recent serious relationship ended; and, in retrospect, she lamented its intimacy. "I wish I had never [had] sex with him or even [knew] what sex in general is like because it just kind of—there's too much pain involved. Because you're also missing the person and there's too much pain in the relationship and . . . maybe if sex was never involved . . . that would kind of remove a certain factor and would help me get over things more." Tara implied that by having sex she gave away too much of herself. For her, sex intensified familiarity and vulnerability, and she regretted having allowed another person to get that close.

Not in a relationship at the time of our interview, Tara felt unsure about her sexuality, including what it takes to attract and keep a boyfriend and how sex should or should not be used at the beginning of a relationship. When she is in a relationship, she feels more sexual because her desire can be directed toward the specific person who helps elicit it. Feeling wanted by a partner makes her feel more interested in sex and more sexually appealing. But when she is single, her sexuality is "dormant, . . . not burning." After this last breakup, she felt even less sure about her sexuality, both what she wanted and what someone else might want in her. She questioned whether she had done the right things sexually and wondered what makes partners stray.

Although Tara replied affirmatively when I asked if she considered herself a sexual person, her response did not seem confident. Her concern about how partners view her makes her hesitant to communicate what she wants. "Maybe with certain guys or relationships they'll view it as 'Oh, is she being too?—maybe she's too easy if she's showing it too quickly or too much.' So maybe I hold back 'cause I don't want to get that viewpoint from him." She also confided that at times she finds herself playing into the image she perceives men want or expect from her. Tara's sexual self-image and sexual self-confidence hinge on validation from a partner. Although she holds back from communicating sexual interest if she feels her partner will think she is "easy," she is more assertive when she feels that this is what her partner wants. When her desire and sexual expression are affirmed, she is more confident about communicating her sexual feelings. In other words, Tara's sexuality is externally driven, and she remains unclear as to what she, as an individual woman, wants.

When I began this study, I wanted to know if women saw sexuality as only or primarily expressed with others or if desire was unrelated to relationship status. One of the most striking findings in my research is the role of relationships and significant others in encouraging or discouraging sexual subjectivity. Time again, I heard that significant others had been instrumental or detrimental in the women's ability to understand their sexual selves. As Frida Kerner Furman (1997) also noted when interviewing older women on the subject of aging and beauty, validation is critical.

Validation, affirmation, and encouragement form the third phase in the development of sexual subjectivity. Validation occurs when women receive verification of their worth as both sexual partners and women in the relationship market. Relations with significant others often follow interpersonal scripts that inform intrapsychic scripts (that is, our internalization of cultural scenarios and norms) and sexual self-image. As William Simon and John T. Gagnon (1984) noted, "interpersonal scripting serves to lower uncertainty and heighten legitimacy" (54–55). Women's self-perception of attractiveness was linked to whether they believed that others saw them that way. When women's desirability or desire was affirmed by partners, they, like Tara, felt more confident about expressing sexual agency and wishes. Male partners who followed gendered sexual scripts that mark men as sexually aggressive and women as passive stifled the development of sexual subjectivity when they failed to encourage or support women's desire. Most of the women whom I interviewed had an other-oriented, externally driven sexuality. Rather than understanding their sexuality as based on their own wants, with or without a partner, most thought of sexuality and desire as reactions evoked by someone else. Until women cultivated sexual subjectivity, they rarely imagined a sexuality of their own that they could express independent of relationships or that was based on their personal construction of desire.

Although media present images of girls and women as hypersexual and glorify women who present their bodies in ways that highlight their sexual appeal (Jhally 2007; Sarracino and Scott 2008; Siebel 2011), girls and women know that such presentations are not reality. They are well aware of the judgment and derision reserved for those who display their sexual assets or eagerly act on sexual desires (Hamilton and Armstrong 2009; Schalet 2011; Tanenbaum 2000). For women to feel like sexual subjects rather than the objects portrayed in media and gendered sexual scripts, they often look to significant others to tell them that it is okay to be sexual or confirm that they are sexual and entitled to sexual pleasure (Simon and Gagnon 1984). Supportive partners in serious relationships—first boyfriends, sexual partners, or spouses—play a critical role in evoking sexual confidence and self-assurance as they allow for exploration, discovery, and validation of the sexual self that begins to develop during early experiences. Within the comfort of these relationships women may experiment with different sexual scripts and learn new ways of expressing their sexuality (Simon and Gagnon 1984). At the same time, partners who devalue or discourage women's sexual assertiveness, decision making, or power stifle sexual subjectivity.

Furthermore, contemporary gender norms reinforce a relationship imperative for women. That is, women are expected to confine sexual behavior to monogamous relationships or to view sex as a vehicle to commitment (Bogle 2008; Holland and Eisenhart 1990; Martin 1996). Even women who reject a relational imperative are well aware of expectations to express their sexuality only in that context and anticipate judgment from others if they violate gender norms (Hamilton and Armstrong 2009). The sexual is social, particularly for women. Women learn and internalize sexual scripts that cast them as more receptive than active and stigmatize the expression of lust or sexual interest outside of committed relationships. Given this, most understandably have difficulty conceiving their sexuality outside of relationships.

VALIDATION OF DESIRE: MARRIAGE AND
PARTNERS WHO ENCOURAGE AND AFFIRM

Women from all generations indicated that knowing they pleased or attracted their partners made them feel better about their sexuality and more comfortable with their bodies. For example, Adrianna, age thirty-eight, white, and single, noted that when she's in a relationship she feels more self-assured in general. "Sometimes when you are in a relationship, because you have that confidence of having that sexual partner, it helps you to embrace your sexuality outside of the relationship, too. So you feel more sexually attractive—you carry that outside of the relationship. I noticed that being in a relationship, it impacted me because I felt more sexually attractive. I didn't have as many insecurities about my sexuality or my attractiveness." When a partner saw Adrianna as sexy, she felt sexier and carried herself with more confidence. Her relationship status influenced her sexual self-image. This is a classic example of Charles Horton Cooley's (1964) looking-glass self: when they are in a relationship, women such as Adrianna imagine themselves through the eyes of their partners and feel more desirable and less insecure.

When I asked them about their experiences before marriage, most women over the age of fifty reported few sexual experiences and little awareness of their desire or of how their bodies could afford them pleasure. Thus, the few who later had partners who encouraged their sexual experimentation and normalized their lust were pleasantly surprised. Among this cohort, Delia was unusual. She was a striking sixty-year-old, self-employed, single African American woman and one of the most self-confident women I interviewed. She was one of only a handful of what I call "lifelong sexual subjects": women who had generally positive early experiences and received relatively straightforward, nonjudgmental messages about sex as they grew up. As a child, Delia knew she could ask either of her parents about sex and believed that sex "wasn't a big deal. It wasn't ever something that I thought was dirty or wrong or bad, it was a part of things that you do when you get older." She knew exactly what to expect when she first menstruated because her mother had prepared for that event. Yet she and her friends believed in saving sex for marriage. "All throughout high school all of my girlfriends were virgins. And it's not just an assumption. We just were really all good girls, that was what we did. And . . . sex was something that you had when you got married."

However, changing times brought a rising acceptance of premarital sex. In the mid-1960s, Delia watched with shock and awe as girls, including the class valedictorian, became pregnant during her senior year of high school. What was bad to Delia was getting pregnant, not sex, because pregnancy meant an altered course of life events. So she continued to wait until she felt ready. For her, readiness was not about feeling love but feeling interested enough and self-confident enough to experience sexual intimacy. But in college, when the time felt right, she had a disappointing first sexual experience. "I thought it was kind of a yawn, like 'Oh, that's it?' And the reason that I picked the guy that I picked was because he was supposed to be the hot guy. And I remember going to his apartment, because he lived off campus, which was a very big deal those days, and I just thought, 'This is what everybody's been talking about? This is not that great.' It was not actually that painful, it just wasn't rewarding in any way. And maybe it was because I really didn't have any feelings for this boy at all, he was a tool for me." Unlike other women whom I interviewed, Delia was not disappointed because of rejection, hurt feelings, or sex that did not lead to a relationship. Rather, she had expected to enjoy sex physically. She was looking for pleasure and gratification and was disillusioned by its absence. It was not until she later met her husband, who supported her interest in sex, that she discovered carnal bliss.

Delia was married only for a short time but emphasized the significance of that relationship in solidifying her sexual self-confidence. Although she was just twenty years old when she married, she explained that "a lot of my sexual identity was formed in that relationship. We were married six years and in a lot of ways it is the one thing for which I thank him, because he allowed me, he taught me how to feel what I was feeling and not to be embarrassed by it. That it was perfectly okay, it was perfectly natural, and to be comfortable with being sexual. . . . I learned what I liked. I learned what I didn't like. I learned what I wanted more of, what I wanted less of. I learned how to say what I wanted." Delia's former husband helped her become more comfortable with her body and her desire to achieve sexual pleasure.

Delia had an open-minded mother who influenced her adolescent daughter's "sex is natural" stance. Along with a determination to experience sex on her own terms, this history made it easier for Delia to accept and go along with her husband's encouragement. Although, as a child, she did not receive strong negative messages about sex, neither did she have her sexual desire stimulated. In her first experience, her partner was unconcerned about her sexual gratification and left her disenchanted. Yet during the years she spent with her husband, she learned to relish sex and feel entitled to sexual gratification. His confirmation of her desire helped her feel more confident and allowed her to realize that she not only enjoyed sex but also saw it as a critical aspect of intimate relationships.

Delia's husband delighted in her curiosity and inspired her sexual exploration. Unlike women whose husbands focused on their own sexual gratification or who were less interested in sex than the women had expected, Delia had a partner who encouraged her. Thus, her marriage was an advantageous step in her construction of sexual subjectivity. As Judith Daniluk (1998) has asserted, "the opinions and values of someone with whom a woman is highly invested in an intimate relationship will likely be more influential in how she experiences and makes sense of the focus of her erotic desire than the opinions of a stranger" (14). In other words, a spouse who appreciates and emboldens his wife to be sexually assertive or who is focused on her sexual satisfaction is likely to have a great impact, one that may inspire changes in stances on sex or counter negative messages received from less significant sources.

Delia's first marriage ended in divorce, and she eventually remarried. However, her second husband had a lower sex drive than she did and failed to bring out or support her desire. When she realized this was not going to change, she knew the relationship would not last. "In my thirties . . . I was married again and this time I ended up marrying someone for whom sex wasn't all that important, which was a problem because for me it was very important. So for most of my thirties I was fairly unhappy sexually because I was not having sex to the extent that I wanted to have it. The relationship was okay, but that was a problem. So what had been a pretty active appetite in my twenties kind of almost went dormant in my thirties." Delia was not willing to stay in the marriage and compromise her sexual self, so that relationship ended in divorce. Since the breakup, she has had a number of relationships and partners and, when I met her, seemed perfectly happy about not being married and instead dating and having affairs with men far and near. She was clearly comfortable with her body and her sexual desire, regardless of her marital status. In her case, her sexual relationship with her first husband shaped her sexual self-image going forward, providing an advantage that many women of her generation or age did not have.

Marriage among Older Women

As a society, we place significant value on marital relationships. The fervor and expense of weddings serve as evidence of how much we celebrate and revere marriage (Geller 2001; Ingraham 2008; Montemurro 2005, 2006; Otnes and Pleck 2003). Although specific partners influenced my interviewees' sexual subjectivity when they encouraged women's desire, for some women getting married inspired new sexual confidence. Especially among women born before 1960, marriage marked them as "chosen." Many commented on the feeling that marriage proposals had confirmed their attractiveness.

According to Dorothy Holland and Margaret Eisenhart (1990), women are "educated in romance" and socialized to believe that finding a long-term partner is a chief concern. Comments from older women reinforced this argument. For example, Joyce, age fifty-seven and white, told me, "I felt because I was married and was in a relationship—I think I might have felt a little more self-assured and a little more that I was desirable enough for somebody to have wanted me as opposed to before, when I was sort of looking for somebody to want me, as you do when you're a teenager. . . . I think I would have felt a little more comfortable in my sexuality after I got married than before." Stacy, age sixty-four, who married in the 1960s, also said that marriage made her feel "much more confident" because she felt "validated."

Heterosexual relationships bring status (Dunn 1998; Holland and Eisenhart 1990; Ingraham 2008; Martin 1996; Montemurro 2006). Coupled with the excitement of being able to be sexually active without fear of violating cultural, religious, or familial mores, this increase in status made the transition to marriage momentous. It helped older women feel more comfortable with sex because sex was an expected part of marital relationships. Marriage allowed these women to see their sexual interest and activity as acceptable.

Joan, a divorced white woman in her sixties, felt differently about sex when she first got married because she knew what she was doing was no longer deviant, though it took a while for this freedom to fully sink in. She recalled that feeling of liberty. "I'm allowed to express it now. I don't have to be a good girl anymore. I could do the deed! It took a long time before the deed got to be a good thing." Even two women in their mid-forties who married in the new millennium noted that getting married enabled them to feel free from internalized judgment. One said, "I felt like whatever was transpiring was fine because we were married. There was no embarrassment or any kind of uncomfortable feelings or concern." The other told me, "I lost a lot of the guilt." In all of these cases, sexual desire and activity produced anxiety among unmarried women. Because parents, religion, and peers had repeatedly reinforced these sexual scripts, women felt conflicted or guilty about feeling desire or engaging in sex. Such feelings inhibit sexual subjectivity. Freeing women from this stigma, marriage allowed heterosexual women to take more ownership of their sexual feelings by affirming them as appropriate.

Marriage among Younger Women

Women born after 1970 were less likely to feel conflicted about premarital sex. Many had lived with their spouses or had sexual experience with more than one partner before marriage; thus, generational norms regarding premarital sex seemed to mediate the impact of marriage. Although cultural taboos did not weigh as heavily on these women as they did on women of previous generations, several did grow up in conservative Christian homes with parents who had expressly prohibited sex before marriage. Thus, marriage was liberating because it lessened the need to hide sexual relationships. Misty, age thirty-one, white, and divorced, was one of these women. Although she did not feel that getting married changed the way she personally felt about sexuality, she noted that she had married at a young age due to insistence from her family. "It certainly pressured me to be interested in getting married at a younger age. Because in my mother's mind that was the only way you should be having sex. . . . [Afterward] I got a lot of—tended to get a lot more respect from people because I was married and [they were] condoning it more that way."

In addition to providing legitimacy for sexual activity, marriage affirmed younger women's sexual self-confidence when they believed that it conferred stability. Charlotte, age thirty-six, white, and married for six years, noted that the permanence of marriage made her feel more secure in her sexuality. "I guess in a way it was kind of freeing. 'Cause I felt like it was stable and I'm not just with someone who's potentially not going to be around. . . . Trust for me was the biggest thing. Especially with my [divorced] parents—I think that has kind of screwed me up a little bit. . . . But I trust [my husband] completely—I'm not at all concerned about other people with him." For women such as Charlotte, marriage gave her a new level of respect for and confidence in her partner, which in turn made her feel more confident. Despite her insecurity about fidelity, the power she attributed to marriage indicated her cultural faith in both the institution and its protective elements in contemporary society. Even though Charlotte's parents had demonstrated that marriage is not always a binding contract, she clearly believed that her own marriage had made her relationship stronger and less fallible, which made her more comfortable about expressing her sexuality.

Past experiences affected whether or not women marked marriage as influential in their sexual development, as the Gendered Sexuality through the Life Course (GSLC) model I discussed in chapter 1 also stresses (Carpenter and DeLamater 2012). This was particularly true among those who lacked trust during previous relationships or whose parents had dealt with infidelity. If these women could define marriage as a safe place, they increased their comfort with sex and sexual expression. Sex can make us feel vulnerable when we expose ourselves physically and emotionally, and women are socialized to see sex as both an expression of love and a means of securing a relationship (Bogle 2008; Martin 1996; Thompson 1995). Thus, it is logical that the more they feel loved, the more vulnerable they are willing to be. Research links sexual activity to overall happiness or fulfillment in marriage: the greater the satisfaction in marriage, the more sex couples have (Blumstein and Schwartz 1983; Call, Sprecher, and Schwartz 1995). When a woman feels that she can trust her partner and that her partner respects her, she is likely to be happier in her marriage than will a woman who feels the opposite and may thus be more comfortable sharing fantasies or communicating her sexual needs.

Among younger women, marriage also enhanced sexual subjectivity when it allowed them to see married sex as different from single sex, a reconfiguration that gave them a way to reconstruct their sexual self-image. In these cases, partners affirmed wives' worth beyond sexual prowess. The most salient examples came from several women who had had adventurous sex lives before marriage. They explained that their perception of a wife's appropriate sexual behavior, in contrast to a single woman's, had led them to redefine their sexual self-image and sexual expression after marriage. In other words, cultural scenarios had influenced intrapsychic scripts (Simon and Gagnon 1984), which in turn had affected interpersonal interactions with their husbands.

Leann, age twenty-nine, white, and married for seven months, was conflicted when she got married. On the one hand, she enjoyed sensual pleasures; on the other, she saw sex as heavily imbued with shame. Leann had been raised in the south in a religious community. As a child, she "wasn't heavily exposed to sexuality," but "in [her] church [sex] was viewed very negatively, almost like an outcast if you were to exhibit that for a woman." The only sexuality she saw was in the soap operas she watched with her grandmother after school. Messages from family were "to behave. Church was a very dominant force in my life, so it was to be a lady, cross your legs, watch your language." Like many other women I interviewed, Leann rarely discussed sex with her parents. They simply told her, "Don't get pregnant." She explained, "They wouldn't tell me why, they wouldn't go through the whole birds and the bees. So I kind of knew what was going on but I really didn't know how it related to me."

As she got older, she became curious about boys and kissing; but she quickly learned the consequences of sexual expression. In tenth grade, when she and her boyfriend were caught fooling around, she was stigmatized and realized that others saw sex as dirty and shameful. "I was dating this guy and we were on the back of the bus and he felt under my shirt and that was more of a sexual experience to me because it was something that was mutually wanted. It wasn't like . . . Spin the Bottle or Truth or Dare. It wasn't innocent, I want to say, although it was my first sexual experience. And then people found out—the important part of this is that people found out and my parents—my mom got yelled at by my [teacher]. And from then on I kind of got the sense that it was a dirty thing to do." In her small southern town, Leann was embarrassed when people learned of her behavior. People's reactions were strong and judgmental and led her to believe sexual activity was bad.

Soon after this incident, her family moved north. There, Leann discovered that boys were charmed by her southern accent. She started to think about what sex might be like for her and sought their attention. "I joined the cheerleading squad, so not only was I southern, I was a southern cheerleader. It was almost an addiction, like I kept going with it. Like, whatever the next step I could do to get more attention, I would do it. I was so nonsexual [where I used to live], and all of a sudden I was getting this attention." Leann knew that winning boys' interest ensured popularity, and this made her feel good about herself and her worth. Yet she was also conflicted when she remembered her early stigmatization. Her negative experiences continued as she progressed through her teens. At the age of eighteen, she was raped, and she believes this painful experience set her on course of promiscuity. She said that after the rape she was "desperately trying to find love, . . . desperately trying to connect with someone and trying to erase that image." Although she attempted counseling, she did not feel it helped her heal and continued seeking attention from men as a means of trying to find acceptance and approval and to rid herself of harrowing memories. She continued on a path of risky casual sex throughout her twenties, until she met her husband and marriage allowed her to reframe sex and her sexuality.

Leann had had many sexual partners before meeting her husband, and she had engaged in what she described as alternative sexual practices, often accompanied by copious amounts of alcohol or drugs. She viewed her former self as reckless, but her image of sex as a wife involved unsullied, responsible fidelity. So when she married, she started to re-create her sexual self-image. She viewed sex with her husband as different from what it had been with previous partners. "Lovemaking with him is very innocent—not innocent but pure. I almost still have the view of sexuality as dirty, and . . . you don't need to be that way in marriage."

Leann's perception of marital sex as "pure" and unmarried sex as "dirty" calls attention to the way in which marriage and the role of the wife is con-structed in American culture. As John Mark Dempsey and Tom Reichert's (2000) research has demonstrated, we generally perceive sex within mar-riage to be predictable, responsible, and infrequent. For women such as Leann, getting married and assuming the role of wife necessitated a trans-formation in sexual behavior. Marriage chastened and changed sex. The way in which her husband viewed her—as deserving of tenderness, as pure—allowed her to see herself in the same way. Leann could have sex with her husband without feeling guilty, which increased her confidence.

For women such as Leann, the stigma associated with being promiscu-ous (Tanenbaum 2000) and the shame linked with being the victim of sex-ual abuse often manifest themselves in a negative sexual self-image before marriage. Kristen Carbone-Lopez (2012) has noted that early sexual victim-ization may inhibit sexual agency and make it difficult for adult women who have been abused to trust their partners, even within marriage. But as I have mentioned, cultural scenarios about marriage affect intrapsychic scripts (Simon and Gagnon 1986). Leann tried to model her sexual behavior on her image of how wives should behave, which she saw as less sexual or adven-turous than she had been before marriage. In her eyes, marriage correlated with respect and partnership, whereas her past negative experiences had led her to associate sex with dirt, shame, and stigma. At the time of our interview, seven months into her marriage, she still was trying to "learn the rules of marriage" and figure out how to express her sexuality and reconcile her image of a sexual woman and a married woman.

Negative or stigmatized experiences generate disadvantage while positive experiences or socially valued transitions generate advantage (Browning and Laumann 1997; Carpenter and DeLamater 2012). Thus, while marriage as a culturally sanctioned institution in which sex is expected and normalized provides an advantage in the general cultivation of sexual agency, women's premarital experiences influence the degree to which they see marriage as a turning point in their sexuality. Though Leann believed that sexual activity was less important in marriage than it had been when she was single, this transformation nonetheless gave her the means to enhance her sexual subjectivity. Marriage brings status elevation for women and confers a positive sexual self-image, both of which counter negative feelings associated with the stigma of sexual abuse or promiscuity. Having less sex and feeling less sexual may increase comfort. Rather than feeling ashamed about sex, women who have less sex or "pure" sex in a committed relationship may feel more confident than they did when having more sex or engaging in risky casual encounters. During our interviews, most women in their twenties and thirties used words such as *trust* and *respect* to differentiate committed relationships from previous relationships. For them, feeling safe meant that they were less motivated to use sex as a way of gaining attention or validation because marriage itself verified their value. This validation increased sexual self-confidence as did the fact that sex had less weight or significance in their marriages than it had in previous relationships.

PARTNERS WHO STIFLE THE DEVELOPMENT OF SEXUAL SUBJECTIVITY

Women born before 1960 remarked on inadequate sex education in school and taboos against discussing sex, even with close friends or family members, which disadvantaged them going into adult sexual relationships. For them, no discourse of women's desire was taught or even acknowledged (Fine 1988). As I've discussed, most of my interviewees with a "sex is bad or taboo" stance were from older generations. They modeled their behavior after their perceptions of how wives were "supposed" to act, modeling themselves on idealized and unrealistic media depictions of marriage, watching their mothers' attentiveness to their fathers, or drawing conclusions about their partners' expectations.

Older women were not the only ones who entered marriage sexually inexperienced. Their husbands were also naïve, even those who had had premarital sex. Many women, particularly those born in the 1940s and 1950s, expressed disappointment with their husbands' sexual abilities. They had expected their husbands not only to know what they were doing in the bedroom but also to please them and take the lead in sexual experimentation, which was the sexual script of the time. According to Sinikka Elliott and Debra Umberson (2008), married couples are more likely to understand conflicts in sexual relationships when these align with their understandings about the sexual natures of men and women. In general, we expect men to be more interested in sex and pursue it more frequently than women do because, as many believe, this is how they are biologically wired. Given this expectation, what actually happens during marriage affects how women see themselves sexually. When recalling the early years of their marriages (and sometimes an entire marriage), many of the older women I interviewed recalled their husbands' lack of communication or their ignorance of women's desire or sexual satisfaction.

Shirley, age fifty-six, white, and recently remarried, described the messages she had received as a young woman about her place in society. When she was not allowed to go to college but her brother was, she learned that girls were inferior, which she believed has had a lifelong influence. Her father made it clear that "women are subservient to men. Women should please men. We don't talk about sex." She became aware of her own sexuality at adolescence when flirtation began. She recalled, "Maybe you kind of wanted to talk to the boys, or maybe not. . . . 'Is he going to look at me?' You know? A kind of self-conscious interaction. . . . It made me feel sexier because this guy wanted me, you know, and it was fun, I guess you could say, to kiss and . . . it increased my feelings of sexuality." She was excited by attention from boys and the feelings it created. But sexual double standards and complicated expectations perplexed her. "People made fun of the girls who were easy or loose or whatever. That that wasn't what you should do. They also made fun of the girls that wouldn't kiss anybody so it was—you were made fun of whether you went too far or not far enough and it was very confusing. I remember being very confused."

Although she kissed boys and "fooled around" before marriage, she was admittedly naïve and focused on following her former husband's lead after they wed. "I still was learning a lot. Still in . . . the experimental stage, you know, I wasn't comfortable with it. I related to myself the way he saw me. I used him as a mirror of my sexuality. You know, if he thought something was attractive, I would wear that. If he thought I should do this in bed, I did it. So it was more a mirror of what he was feeling." Shirley sought confirmation that she was satisfying her husband, which was how she perceived her role. Though she was uncomfortable, she thought, as a wife, she should be focused on her husband's sexual needs. "I was married . . . for twenty-three years and he was only interested in pleasing himself. I mean, that was his main goal. . . . I was looking out to please him sexually. I was being the nurturing person, I was being other-centered, where it turns out that he was being totally self-centered and he was manipulating me and taking advantage of me." Shirley connected her willingness to devote herself to gratifying her husband with her childhood messages about girls' subservience. She had little awareness of her own desire: which feelings were authentic and which were driven by her need to meet her husband's expectations. Not until she was well into her forties did she realize that she did not have to tolerate her husband's selfishness. She left him.

Shirley was far from the only woman of this generation who suggested that marriage had fostered an other-oriented sexuality. Joan, age sixty-six, white, and divorced, said that with her former husband "sex became an obligation as a wife. I don't know how you kind of prevent that. . . . You don't have to go up to bed at ten o'clock every night and be ready. It should be something that, you know, you want to do together and somehow you figure that out. We had no words. We had no ideas. What did we know? Nothing."

Leslie, age sixty, white, and divorced, described participating in objectionable sexual acts with her former husband because she thought she was supposed to. She had had only minimal sexual experience before meeting her husband and viewed her short marriage as eye-opening.

> Sex for me was probably a lot more traditionally based than [it was for] my husband. He was into some things that did not appeal to me, and it was a little bit difficult for me because I had the mind thing of "I am a wife, I'm supposed to

love this person. I'm supposed to do that." But I also had the "I don't like this, it's not pleasurable." I was not the lady that was gonna be the, you know, the lady that was gonna be there with the whips and chains and the high heels and everything else. It just wasn't the way I saw myself and I did not feel particularly seductive or sexy that way. I was self-conscious and I didn't like it. It wasn't a turn-on for me as it was for him. . . . I didn't, I just didn't know. And so that was hard and it's hard to maintain your level of feeling for someone at that point when you know that you're going to be asked to do something that you're not comfortable with, yet you do care for this person and you care for their pleasure and their feelings, but it's hard to compromise yourself a lot of the times, and it was for me.

Leslie learned that being a good wife meant responding to her partner's sexual needs and interests, even if they made her uneasy. She tried to ignore her discomfort because she wanted to please her husband and felt it was her duty. Clearly, this experience stifled the development of sexual subjectivity. Yet as the relationship unraveled, her husband's lack of concern for her sexual preferences or comfort spurred her to make different decisions going forward. "I learned that there were certain things in my life I would not do ever again, no matter what I felt for a partner. And there were certain things I liked, so it was a learning time. And I guess it would have been a lot better to learn it before I was married, but it's okay because I did learn it." Thus, in some cases, partners who failed to affirm ultimately did inspire women to seek something or someone different and act as subjects in subsequent relationships.

Some women lacked the ability to communicate their feelings with their partners. As Joan said, "we had no words." Though this was not an issue unique to women from older generations, it was much more common among them. For women coming of age in the 1950s and 1960s, lack of public discussion of women's sexuality and lack of resources for learning about sex disabled interpersonal dialogue. Women coming of age in the 1990s and later had media that promoted (even if in an empty way or without acknowledging the consequences) sexual expression, desire, and premarital sex as normative. Self-help books, suggestive advertisements, and sexualized films are readily available in today's society (Rutter and Schwartz 2012). But older women were less equipped to discuss sexual concerns and thus felt less entitled to seek sexual gratification.

To offset feelings of undesirability gained from previous relationships or experiences, some women sought validation of their worth through sexual relationships. One of them was Sherry, age forty-seven, white, and divorced, for whom negative encounters as a girl and young woman had made sexual subjectivity unattainable. Given religious proscriptions, her family upbringing, and a clear "sex is bad or taboo" stance as a girl, Sherry had internalized the idea that sex was sinful. Early sexual experiences intensified her uneasiness and confusion about sex. In her teens, she went to parties with her much older sister, who was supposed to be taking care of Sherry but did not want to miss out on anything. As a result, Sherry often found herself in dangerous situations.

> We went to a pool, like [a] middle-of-the-night kind of thing, late at night. It was somebody's house they knew and . . . then they all start skinny dipping. And then this guy took me up on this roof and had me start feeling him and I don't remember—I was somewhere in my teens—I don't think I had done anything like that. It started raining and that's the only reason we left and I remember going back to [my sister's] apartment with this whole group and I remember locking myself in her daughter's room. . . . I just remember it as scary and really kind of at the time not even understanding why it was scary, or that it should have been scary.

Describing her first intimate encounter with a boy, Sherry recalled,

> It was a little bit of a scary experience because I was down in [the south], visiting my brother and I was—I think I was just sixteen. . . . I don't even know how I met this guy—and we were walking around and he was drunk and it was really gross. And he kissed me and I didn't know what was going on. And he kept wanting me to go down to the beach—I know what he wanted, you know, I had enough knowledge to know that. And I didn't—I kind of got out of the situation and went back to my motel room, but, so that was kind of [scary].

Sherry's early experiences reinforced her lack of self-confidence and her sense that sex was about giving in to boys' pressure. Then, when she was eighteen, her first love broke up with her because she would not have intercourse with him. Sherry was devastated. On the day I interviewed her, she still regretted not having slept with him because she knew he had cared about her, as the man to whom she eventually lost her virginity did not. When reflecting on her past during our conversation, she realized that during her teens and early twenties she had internalized the message that sex would result in affection and attention, though they might be fleeting. Thus, she had often found herself trying to affirm her sense of self-worth in sexual situations rather than pursuing sexual satisfaction or pleasure. "I was never one who could be completely guilt-free or not be ashamed if I slept with this guy and he was sort of creepy, and he was sleeping around, or sleep with two people in the same day or whatever. It never, it never felt completely right to me to behave that way, for whatever reason, ingrained—whatever the messages were coming from. I guess [sex] was more need-driven than anything."

I asked Sherry to clarify if her phrase "need-driven" meant a biological need. She replied, "Biological, but I'm sure there was an emotional component to it, I would guess. I think it's hard to separate those. Whether it's wanting to be needed or feel needed or look attractive or think I look attractive." For Sherry, sex was about seeking validation and affirmation of her worth and value, both physically and, more broadly, as a woman. It was important to her to know she was desirable, as this was not communicated to her in other ways. Her father rarely said that she was attractive, and she had insecurities about that lack of praise. Unfortunately, repeated negative encounters made her quest for affirmation fruitless.

Other studies have also found that girls and women engage in sexual activity because it makes them feel loved or to satisfy emotional rather than physical needs (Bogle 2008; Martin 1996; Thompson 1995). For example, in her study of hooking up on college campuses, Kathleen Bogle (2008) noted that women engaged in casual sexual encounters with the hope that the hookup would turn into something long term and romantic. The sexual encounter was a vehicle to a relationship rather than a satisfying experience in and of itself because the relationship would provide more concrete and lasting affirmation than the sexual encounter had.

Sherry did not feel affirmed or validated in a way that enhanced her sexual subjectivity. In her descriptions of previous relationships, including two unsuccessful marriages, she made it clear that validation had been fleeting. When discussing her second marriage (the relationship in which she initially said she had felt most sexually confident), she noted that although she believed her former husband had enjoyed her body, as she had enjoyed his, he had made it clear that he thought her breasts were too small and had pressured her to do things she did not want to do. When this marriage failed, Sherry committed herself to celibacy, and she does not imagine that will change anytime soon, if ever. As a born-again Christian, she believes that if a sexual relationship is meant for her, God will lead her to it. But for now, sex outside of marriage is against her beliefs. Her string of failed relationships and partners who were uninterested in her sexual pleasure or sexual subjectivity have turned her off from men and relationships. Sherry's story is a useful example of a woman who desperately sought validation in sexual relationships. But without affirmation from the men with whom she was intimate, she could not feel good about sex or behave like a sexual subject.

DECLINING DESIRE: THE INFLUENCE OF PARTNERS' WANING SEXUAL INTEREST

The women in my study placed a great deal of emphasis on relationships as affirmation of sexual desirability. Thus, when partners' desire decreased, women questioned their own sexual appeal, particularly as they aged. Many reported feeling sexual longing throughout their lives but were stifled by husbands or boyfriends who did not have a compatible libido. Younger women were more likely to be frustrated by their husbands' lower desire because they saw it as unusual for their stage in life. Caitlin, age twenty-seven, white, and separated, noted that she was more interested in sex than her estranged husband had been. This confused her.

> I felt embarrassed in a way because he wasn't tapping me on the shoulder and I was thinking what's wrong with him? And [my friends] acted like their husbands wanted to have sex so much and I did not feel that way from my husband. . . . I kept thinking, "What's wrong with him? What's wrong with him?" And honestly I didn't even feel that way until we actually moved in together because before . . . , you know, you're busy doing your own thing and you only see each other on the weekends, so of course it is going to happen every weekend. Then you're living together and you think you're going to have sex all the time and then you're not and it's like what the heck's wrong with this picture?

Misty, age thirty-one and divorced, also questioned her desirability when her husband did not seem as sexually attracted to her as she had expected.

"My twenties sucked. My situation was probably different from most women. I got married when I was twenty-one and found out four years later that my husband was transgendered. And so . . . with the sexual relationship, that explained a lot. I didn't have a very good sexual relationship with him because of his issues, but that was a whole issue with my body image and what did I do wrong and all that kind of stuff." Though Misty's situation was unique, both she and Caitlin had images of what a normal sex life and a normal sex drive should be. Their expectations influenced their reactions (Elliott and Umberson 2008). Both women felt something was wrong with them and questioned their level of desirability because they believed their husbands should be pursuing them insistently. They were familiar with the male sex-drive discourse, which suggests that "men are perpetually interested in sex" (Gavey, McPhillips, and Dougherty 2001, 922). This knowledge influenced interpersonal sexual scripts and in turn intrapsychic scripts. As Simon and Gagnon (1984) have made clear, sexual scripts work as models of gendered patterns of sexual initiation, and they seem to play a significant role in many women's expectations—and not just when they are dating. Women carry these expectations into marriages and feel sexual frustration when they are unmet.

Caitlin, Misty, and other women also mentioned their lack of communication and confidence about expressing sexual longing. They did not talk to their former husbands about their sexual needs and satisfactions, nor did they ask their husbands why they were not more interested in sex. They may have been inhibited by stereotypes of sexually aggressive women who initiate sex or the desperation associated with a woman who has to continually pursue a man. Compared to women from older generations, they had more information about sex and had become familiar with it as a larger part of contemporary culture. Yet that information and familiarity still did not give them the resources or confidence to talk about their concerns with their husbands. There is a general stigma against discussing personal sexual matters openly which along with nontraditional gender sexual interaction and the women's weakened sexual self-image worked to stifle conversation. In other words, cultural scenarios influenced their intrapsychic scripts, which then shaped interactions between the sexual partners (Simon and Gagnon 1984).

DO I STILL HAVE IT? THE ROLE OF VALIDATION IN LONG-TERM RELATIONSHIPS

Some women who were married for many years complained that sex can become routine or boring as marriage endures. Other researchers have noted that habituation often leads to a decline in the frequency of intercourse (Edwards and Booth 1994; Rutter and Schwartz 2012). The longer women are married, the less likely they are to receive regular validation of their desirability. Because American society does not consider it appropriate for long-married women to flirt in public or dress in a way that attracts attention, they have fewer opportunities for or sources of affirmation.

Nonetheless, several women specifically mentioned that their husbands complimented them and made them feel desirable. Alyssa, a white woman who had been married for thirty-one years, told me that her marriage has had a positive impact on her sense of self. "It's huge, a huge impact, you know? I'm fortunate that my husband, even at fifty-one, still considers me to be really attractive and desirable and I think that that's not always the case for women my age. So I think I'm really fortunate in that respect." It is interesting that Alyssa feels that she is lucky and that she sees her husband's behavior as atypical. For her and for other women who made similar comments, the knowledge that their husbands still found them sexually appealing encouraged their interest in sex and generally increased their self-confidence.

Because women's sexuality is very much defined by their appearance (Montemurro and Gillen 2013b), it is important for women to feel physically desired in order to feel sexual. Thus, partners who affirm are likely to aid women in developing sexual subjectivity. Yet as time goes by, couples may not see the importance of complimenting their partners, and women may become insecure. Amanda, a white, thirty-nine-year-old single mother who works in the health field, was dismayed by her ex-husband's lack of attention or affirmation of her sexual appeal. During her pregnancy, she felt perpetually aroused but discovered that he wanted nothing to do with her. Realizing that her sexual needs were incompatible with her husband's, she eventually found herself looking outside of the relationship for verification of her appeal. "He wasn't a sexual person, he wasn't a vocal person, so I had no, no feedback, no confirmation, no 'you're beautiful,' any of that. Um, so that was crazy. Nuts. And I just hit a wall and begged to go to marriage counseling and he didn't want to. And I did the whole cougar thing, Thursday nights out at [a local bar] trying to get my confirmation or whatever I was trying to get, and I think now looking back I realize that—if I was getting it at home, you don't need, well, you need some, but not the confirmation I was getting [*laughs*]."

Nia, a twenty-nine-year-old, married, African American woman, said that she had relied on boys' and men's attention as validation during her adolescent years. She explained that her first boyfriend, when she was about age thirteen, "gave me more confidence about my sexuality and made me aware of it, I guess. That whether you realize it or not people are looking at you, or that people are admiring you, so it kind of gave me . . . a little self-confidence." During her childhood, her parents did not talk about sex, and her first perspective was that sex is taboo. After Nia menstruated, her mother simply told her to "stay away from boys." Even after her fifteen-year-old sister became pregnant when Nia was eighteen, there was still no discussion of sex in her household. Yet the dominant message from peers was that sex was important, normal, and something she should do with a boyfriend. So, as she matured, she continued to date and measured her popularity and desirability by her sexual appeal. Attention made her feel more confident because it reinforced the notion that if she was physically desirable, she was valued. As she said of the relationships she had before meeting her husband, "I think each . . . just made me more confident, also . . . made me notice myself more and made me notice other females more. It just made me more self-aware and more self-confident."

Because Nia grew used to gauging her sexuality based on the reactions of men, she has struggled with continuing to feel alluring in her marriage, given the lack of ongoing affirmation.

I think [my marriage] made me more aware and it's made me sometimes less confident than how I felt when I was single. Just there's more, for me anyway, I guess [I'm] worried more that I'm still the self-confident or sexy person that I saw myself as when I was single. Like I worry about being able to maintain being sexy enough for him because, you know, we're the only people now, like there's not any competition to base it off of, so it just made me a little more aware of it and sometimes less confident. . . . When you're dating, you know that there's always a possibility that there may be someone else, so you know, you're not gonna, there's no room for you to not be confident in yourself. You have to be confident and try to stay one step ahead of the game, if you're liking this person anyway, to keep their interest in you. And then when you're married, it's like there's not supposed to be anyone else, so—and then a lot of times you don't get the same feedback from your mate as you did when you first were dating, so it's kind of hard to tell, you know, if this is still working for them or if they would like things different.

When we spoke, Nia had spent seven years with her husband, three in a relationship and four in marriage. That habituation and a lack of competition for her husband's affection had made her feel insecure. Because she no longer had the reassurance of repeatedly being chosen by her partner, she wondered about her ability to maintain his interest and please him sexually.

Nia's sexual dependence on her partner was also apparent when I asked if there was anything she would like to change about her sexuality. Hesitantly, she said,

Maybe the ability to climax more or the ability to, I guess, know how to have control over it yourself and within the act, and not have to rely so much on your partner. Yeah, I guess, yeah, if there's a way of doing that—I mean, I think so much of it is relying on your partner, based off of what they do to get you to that point. And I'd like to be able to know how to get myself to that point within it so you're not solely relying on, you know, somebody that may not know what to do or how to do what you need them to do.

Her comments clearly demonstrate the lack of information that girls and women still receive about their bodies as well as continuing taboos against women's masturbation. At the age of twenty-nine, after having given birth to two children, Nia still does not know how to please herself. Edward O. Laumann and his colleagues (1994) found that about 50 percent of women report masturbating but about half of those who do feel guilty about it. Guilt may be related to the individualistic, pleasure-focused, nonprocreative aspects of self-gratification, which eschew the relationship imperative that characterizes American culture (Rutter and Schwartz 2012). Such taboos against masturbation and self-exploration limited Nia's level of comfort in exploring her body and increased her dependence on her husband for sexual pleasure and satisfaction, which in turn diminished her sexual subjectivity. When sexual gratification and desire are externally driven or other-oriented, women's agency is minimized.

AFFIRMATION AND AGING

Aging caused some women to doubt their sexual appeal, and they often looked to partners for reassurance. Heather, age forty-six, white, and married, noted that knowing her partner is attracted to her as she grows older has made the transition more tolerable. "He makes me feel attractive and desirable and worthy of being a person, all those things. . . . This relationship not only affirms me as a person, as a physical person just in general, but affirms my worthiness at my age. . . . His finding me desirable and attractive and the fact that we have a healthy relationship reaffirms and continues to affirm that age is not a big deal." Because Heather's husband loves her and finds her appealing, he encourages her to see herself in the same way. She feels more self-satisfied when sees herself through her husband's eyes.

Older women who were newly single also felt validated when they caught men's attention "past their prime." Leslie, age sixty and single when we met, was divorced in her twenties and always thought she would remarry. As she aged, however, she felt less confident that this would happen. Without a partner in her late forties, she became increasingly insecure. Then a relationship with a man twelve years her junior rejuvenated her sexual self-confidence.

> It was very flattering to have this guy who used to see me when he was walking the neighborhood when he was twelve [*laughs*]. . . . That was kind of cool because it was somebody who was so much younger who was attracted to me, who felt so much older. And age is a state of mind, we all know, but still twelve years to me was twelve years and I thought, well, "Isn't this curious?" The sexual part of it was absolutely great and it was just fun. It was kind of what the doctor had ordered for turning fifty. Stopping having your period, realizing you couldn't have any children anymore and realizing, hey, everything you thought was gonna happen kind of didn't, the story didn't turn out the way you thought it would. So there was that piece at the end of my forties, and it was just a surprise, a real surprise. . . . Oh, my God, I was horny as anything, pardon the French [*laughs*]. But it was great because I had a partner who was ready, willing, and able all the time and who was absolutely as interested in sex as I was. And it was fun, it was fun, and I hadn't been in that kind of situation for a really long time. . . . I felt desired, appealing. I felt like somebody else thought I was pretty cool, which was neat. I mean, you can tell yourself you're pretty cool all the time; when somebody else says it, there's nothing like it, it

just makes you feel even cooler. So it was a good thing, I think it was just a real ego boost at that point in my life when I was really feeling that there were so many endings coming along that this was, well, it's not over yet, you know? So it was fun and it was really, it was pretty exciting to know you can still function as a woman. Because when you go through a long period of time of not having a sexual relationship, even if you're masturbating, it's a little different to know "Oh, man, this is cool. I remember this. This is good." . . . I always thought it was kind of a great fiftieth birthday present, you know?

Leslie's younger boyfriend's infatuation jolted her sexual self-confidence, which increased her overall feelings of well-being. He came along at a point in her life when she was feeling unwanted and skeptical about ever having another intimate relationship. He validated and encouraged her desire; the relationship, the sex, and his attraction thus enhanced her sexual subjectivity. She felt more confident about wanting and having sex than she had for many years. He also helped her accept herself and her body as it was, at age fifty.

In a way, this experience mirrored Leslie's early experiences as a teenager, when she was also feeling unsure about her sexual appeal. Back then, boys' attention had boosted her sexual self-esteem.

I felt different because a boy was turned on by me or wanted to be with me or wanted to touch me or kiss me. I felt like I probably looked pretty, I felt that I was not necessarily sexy but sexual because I was experiencing those things with a boy that only a man and a woman . . . were experiencing together. . . . And that was always, it was exciting, it was new, it was, of course, stimulating, and it was always cool because you knew you could make somebody else feel the same way. . . . It wasn't just "This is the way I feel" but "Whoa, look at the effect I have on somebody else." That's pretty cool.

In both cases, her partners' vision of her and her ability to please them enhanced Leslie's sexual self-confidence. Knowing that she had aroused her partners, that they wanted her and liked it when she was sexual, underscored the notion that sex is a good thing—not just in general but for her in particular. Although Leslie also had early experiences and partners who were less affirming, her story illustrates the power of relationships and the degree of influence a partner can have.

CUMULATIVE ADVANTAGES AND DISADVANTAGES ASSOCIATED WITH VALIDATION, AFFIRMATION, AND ENCOURAGEMENT

Desire and desirability, as well as expectations for the initiation of sex within relationships, are significantly influenced by cultural scenarios and gendered sexual scripts (Elliott and Umberson 2008; Simon and Gagnon 1984). Sexuality is deeply personal and private to many women, but it is equally social. Although women feel desire, concerns about its legitimacy and appropriateness constrains their comfort about expressing sexual longing. Thus, sexual partners and marriage as a social institution can validate and affirm desirability and sexual worth.

Younger women, those born in or after 1960, were more likely to view marriage as a turning point that enhanced their understanding or security in their sexuality when they felt a greater level of commitment from their partners or when they were able to shed the stigma associated with premarital sexual promiscuity. In contrast, many women born before 1960 were disillusioned by the reality of marital sex because neither they nor their partners had had much prior experience and there were few options for discovering or enhancing their sexual selves. The role of partners' expectations and the recurrent implication of privileging men's sexual drives over women's show that sexual relationships are a means through which gender inequality is constructed. Prioritizing men's sexual satisfaction underscores men's power in relationships as well as the idea that men's sexuality is active and women's responsive. This undermines women's sexual subjectivity.

Initial stances on sex influenced women's feelings about sex in marriage. For many older women, marriage gave them an opportunity to shed negative beliefs and see sex as legitimate and appropriate for the first time. This made such them feel more confident. For younger women and those who had already had favorable ideas about sex as girls, marriage was simply another steady step on the road to sexual self-assurance. When partners affirmed desire or desirability and women were able to see sex as appropriate, they gained confidence, which helped them as they moved on to other role changes, such as motherhood or divorce.

5 ⑥ SELF-DISCOVERY THROUGH ROLE AND RELATIONSHIP CHANGES

Divorce

I think someone in my position—I'm freer to be who I am right now, especially since I don't have the inhibiting husband. I'm free to be who I am, that if I want to go to a swinger's party, I can do that and not feel like "Oh, this is gonna get back and there's my chance for promotion" or whatever. If I want to go to a nudist beach, I can do that.... And I think these past couple years have really helped me to grow to be who I am, to not have to suppress who I am, I can be me.... Since being separated now over a year, I've been able to meet people that were more on the same level as I was sexually wise. Also to know ... that I've done nothing wrong, you know? What has happened has happened. And you tend to blame yourself for a lot of things that go wrong. And I understand I've done nothing wrong.

—Jacqueline, age forty-four

Jacqueline, an energetic, petite, African American woman, walked into my office with many stories to tell. As a military wife, mother of six, working full time, and pursuing higher education, she had had a lot on her plate before her marriage began to fall apart. She had long been dealing with issues stemming from not only her childhood sexual assault (described in chapter 3) but also her roots in an ethnic group, a religion, and a family in which sex was taboo. Her mother never talked to her about sex or her body, and Jacqueline now feels this did her a disservice. Like many of the women with whom I spoke, she regretted her first sexual experience, wishing she had waited for a relationship in which there were strong mutual feelings. She felt that losing her virginity had propelled her into adulthood. "It did change me to the aspect that—how can I put it?—I wasn't a little girl, that innocence was gone, you know? And I did wish I would have waited." Furthermore, the cumulative disadvantage of her childhood sexual assault made it difficult for her to enjoy early sexual experiences (Browning and Laumann 1997; Carbone-Lopez 2012). "I think a lot of times that when at a young age you've been violated, sex doesn't have that specialness, you know? So for me the first time with this young man, it was like [*in a matter-of-fact voice*] 'Oh, so this is what everybody's talking about.' It wasn't how you hear it's so special, I think, because that was gone already."

The pain of her first experience and a few other empty premarital encounters did little to enhance Jacqueline's sexual self-confidence. So when she married at the age of twenty, she did not have a strong sexual self-image or an understanding of her desire. Like other women I interviewed, she was concerned about her husband's sexual satisfaction. "When I met my husband and married my husband and we became intimate, it was like 'Okay, gotta please him. Gotta please him.'" She became pregnant shortly after her marriage and spent her twenties having kids and feeling insecure about her appearance and desirability. "Between raising children and being home alone and moving all around the country, it was very hard for me. I was not in tune with my sexuality. Even though I was having these children, you know, me—myself—I was not in tune with my sexuality." The frequent separations associated with military life "strained that intimacy because now when [he was] here [he] expect[ed] me to be all about [him], but we still have these six kids running around. They still need to be fed and taken care of and the attention and the homework and everything and you want me to be just you and I? It can't be just you and I, you know? And so that intimate part of our relationship became robotic."

As she and her husband began to grow apart, Jacqueline started to think more about her sexuality and what she preferred as an individual. She began to write erotica and even had a story published in a magazine. She was proud of her accomplishment and enjoyed the self-discovery associated with fantasizing and learning about her longings. "In my writing I think it was a way for me to get my desires out, what I wanted, you know? And the fact that I found out I was very, very imaginative and very creative, I started appreciating the sensual part of me more, which I have always suppressed because I didn't want to be perceived as the bad girl. . . . It enabled me at a time [when] I could not express myself physically, to express myself within my writing, to free—to be who I wanted to be, how I wanted to be."

Even though her sexual relationship with her husband was tense and inconsistent, Jacqueline was able to use writing as not only a sexual outlet but also a means of discovering her sexual identity and understanding her desire. However, when her husband came across Jacqueline's stories, he immediately imagined that his wife was writing from experience. It seemed incomprehensible to him that she had created these stories from her imagination. He tried to shame her, saying, "'Go ahead. Keep writing all your dirty little secrets.' And I'm like 'What are you talking about? I wish I would have done half of the stuff that I write about.'"

By the time Jacqueline had turned forty, the marriage was essentially over; and separating from her husband inspired her to further explore her sexuality both physically and emotionally. She began to see herself once more as a woman, not as a mother or a wife but a person with sexual yearnings and needs. She continued writing, started dating, and began to feel renewed and refreshed as if she were starting a new chapter in her life.

For Jacqueline, the role change from married to single woman was inspiration for the new sexual self she could not be in her marriage. Single Jacqueline was "no longer the [military] wife, no longer the kids' mommy. I was no longer [my husband's]'s wife. . . . I was starting to claim who I was, the dynamic Jacqueline, the outgoing Jacqueline." This dynamic Jacqueline did things the old Jacqueline would not have, such as visiting a nude beach. Although the end of her marriage did not cause her to be more sexually subjective, the demise of the relationship stimulated self-discovery because it gave her a newfound sexual freedom. She began to see herself differently because she no longer felt constrained by someone else's perception of her. This led her to become more confident and to act and feel like a sexual subject going forward.

BREAKING UP

As women move through adulthood, most experience several significant role and relationship changes that influence their sexuality. In this chapter, I discuss the fourth phase in the development of sexual subjectivity, *self-discovery through role and relationship change,* with a focus on how the dissolution of relationships affects the way in which women feel about their sexuality and precipitates a new understanding of the sexual self. Although other scholars have studied divorce as status transition, most have concentrated on the process of uncoupling (Amato 2000; Vaughan 1990) or how sexual attitudes and behaviors change after divorce (Wade and DeLamater 2002). In contrast, I examine the degree to which divorce acts as a catalyst for sexual self-discovery and precisely how women's sexuality and sexual subjectivity are affected.

For most of the women I interviewed, divorce or separation marked a pivotal moment in their sexuality. The realization that they would once again have the opportunity (or burden) to seek new sexual partners spawned reflection and growth. Being single for the first time in years was at once eye-opening, anxiety-producing, and exciting. However, the initial ending of a marriage and acceptance of its finality often triggered feelings of depression, which inhibited sexual desire during the period of crisis and separation. Even when sexual relations with their spouses were strained or nonexistent for months or even years, some women resisted acknowledging their marriages were over because they did not want to put themselves or their children through the pain of divorce. Despite acknowledging how much happier she is out of her marriage, Jacqueline tearfully told me,

> Well, I knew things were kind of done, I would say, a year before we actually separated. We had stopped being intimate with each other. I can honestly tell you the date, you know, and I would recoil every time he would come near me or touch me. I didn't want to be with him. Like I said, I'll always love him because we share something that two people don't often share—we have six beautiful children—but to be in love with him, no. . . . I think my stubbornness not to fall into the stats kept me going. I didn't want my children to be from a broken home.

Though ultimately better off and far more in touch with her sexual self, Jacqueline needed time to accept divorce as the next step.

The End of Sexual Days: When Breakups Suppress Sexual Subjectivity

The acrimony and stress associated with the termination of a legal or long-term relationship and the tension of sorting out the practical and financial aspects of uncoupling can have a broad impact (Vaughan 1990). Debra, age fifty-nine, related how she felt during that period:

> I was too stressed at that point to feel sexual. . . . I mean there's no such thing as a good divorce but there's bad, badder and worstest, and this was a bad one. And very bitter and very acrimonious and there was no time for feeling sexual because all my emotions and all my thoughts and feelings were all wrapped up in this situation that I was in. And . . . my daughter was twelve, my son was in his mid-teens and I was dealing with that, too. You know, my son was hostile and difficult, my daughter was withdrawn and needed therapy, and [my ex-husband] was obnoxious and he refused to leave that house. That was part of the problem. . . . So I had to stay there whether I liked it or not because that's where I had to be. And he would not leave—he would not even leave the bedroom. So like I threw out the king-sized bed, I got two twin beds, put them on either side of the bedroom. So as far as that's concerned, that was—and there was just no time or energy for sexuality. You know, I always used a vibrator and I always had some expression of my sexuality to myself, but those were kind of low days and they were not supercharged for sexuality, let's put it that way.

Debra was unique in her ability to separate her sexual dissatisfaction in the relationship with her personal sexual self-image. Though her dispassionate marriage left her unfulfilled and weakened her desire, she still sought out occasional sexual satisfaction through masturbation. Yet she felt less sexual than she would have under normal circumstances because she was focusing all her energy on trying to deal with the emotional fallout of divorce for her children and herself.

Miriam, age sixty-one, also experienced a difficult divorce. Although she acknowledged that menopause may have contributed to the absence of desire that preceded the end of her marriage, her husband's lack of communication and respect had a more significant impact. "At one point we had three stepchildren living here. . . . Not supposed to happen, not in our plan. He lost his job, all kinds of things were sitting here with us, and I was not a happy lady. And I was not the person who initiated these things. I was not a participant in these decisions so I didn't feel very validated. And don't ask me to go to bed with you if you're treating me like that. So I lost interest, I guess you could say." Without an emotional bond, physical intimacy was not an option for Miriam. Sex was not just about sensual pleasure, physical

release, or marital obligation. When her husband disregarded her as a partner in their marriage, she lost interest in being intimate with him, which
eventually spurred her to initiate their separation.

Many of the women I interviewed connected sex and love. Though some
felt able to separate emotion from the act and enjoy the physical experience
of sex, none suggested they could do so with partners they had once loved.
Virginia Rutter and Pepper Schwartz (2012) affirmed this point, conclud-
ing that women's desire is more likely to focus "on a specific person and
is ratified by love and mutual passion more so than men's. . . . A woman's
sexual desire increases (or her inhibitions decrease) when she is focused
on a person who cares about her rather than a person who can simply fill
an immediate sexual need" (59). Miriam's husband still pursued her during
their period of disharmony; but even when she craved sexual intimacy, she
had no interest in seeking it with a partner who, in her eyes, did not love
or respect her.

According to Wendy Watson and Charlie Stelle (2011), some older
divorced or widowed women in their study were not open to dating because
they felt as if that chapter in their life was over. This was also true of several
of the women whom I interviewed. Some were newly single in their late fifties and sixties, while others had been divorced more than once. Sadly or
with relief, they told me that they were finished with being sexually active.
Debra, for instance, said that after her divorce she decided that she was only
going to be intimate with herself. "At that point I was like I don't want anything to do with a man. . . . I was so off of men, you know, they're disgusting.
I don't want anything to do with them, I don't need a guy. I don't need to get
out there. It really was fear but at that time that's how I saw it—I saw it as
yuck. And I expressed my own sexuality to myself but I just had no interest
in getting out there and meeting a guy and going out. . . . That lasted a long
time, a really long time, because I was burned so bad . . . through the marriage as well as during the divorce."

Alice, age fifty-five, white, and a mother of three, was married to man
who had an affair when she was in her late forties. Soon after she discovered his infidelity, they divorced, but she continued to feel a strong sense
of rejection and could not face the thought of dating. As a single woman
in her fifties, Alice saw her future as uncertain, and she struggled with self-
confidence and her image of her sexuality. Like the majority of the women
in this study, she placed desirability before desire. She did not see herself as

appealing because her self-image was based on her perception of her husband's view of her, not her own.

One deterrent to dating or rediscovering sexuality after divorce is women's concern about the caliber of available men and their fear of failing at another relationship (Watson and Stelle 2011). In her study of dating after divorce among midlife women, Bronwen Lichtenstein (2012) found that the women she interviewed feared "risky" dates. Like Debra, they worried about "repeating past mistakes" and unsafe partners, whom they characterized as "abusers, losers, and addicts" (189). Another study, which focused on women between the ages of fifty-seven and eighty-five, found that unpartnered women were about twice as likely as partnered women to report disinterest in sex, noting not just a dearth of desire but also lack of opportunity, religious proscriptions, and, most often, not having met the right person (Waite, Laumann, Das, and Schumm 2009).

Given men's penchant for dating younger women, older women's choices are limited (England and McClintock 2009). Moreover, many are reluctant to pursue new relationships because they are less interested in sex and in going through the work of finding a new partner. Miriam, for example, who was in the process of ending her third marriage at the time of our interview, explained matter-of-factly that her plans for her future did not include a partner. She did not want to go through another breakup, even though she still considered herself a sexual person in theory.

> I'm not interested in engaging with a guy right now. Like I just bought a new bed because [my ex-husband] and I had been talking about how our bed . . . had seen better years. . . . And I decided to get a double bed instead of the queen-sized bed that I've always had for years. And so I told my ex, soon to be, that I got a new bed, and he goes, "Oh, did you get a queen or a king?" And I said, "I got a double, why?" And he goes, "Well, what happens if you meet somebody?" . . . That didn't even enter my mind. Like it's much more fun to romp around in a queen-sized bed than in a double bed, but right now I don't know that that's something that I would be interested in doing. That just sounds very alien and weird to me. . . . Right now I'm not interested in sex, and I haven't been interested in sex for a while.

Miriam's marital experiences made it difficult for her to believe in the reality of a successful relationship, and she was uninterested in putting forth an effort to make one happen. Similar thoughts also deterred other older women from dating, some of whom believed that their luck may have run out and that it was easier to be alone (England and McClintock 2009; Gott and Hinchliff 2003; Lichtenstein 2012; Watson and Stelle 2011). The physical satisfaction, experience, or pleasure that can result from sex was not enough of a reward for them to take the risk or make the effort. Like Miriam, many women did not imagine sex outside of a committed relationship. Furthermore, as other research has documented, our culture does not perceive older women as sexually desirable (Carpenter, Nathanson, and Kim 2005; England and McClintock 2009; Gott and Hinchliff 2003; Montemurro and Gillen 2013b; Tally 2006). Older women are well aware of this assumption and may be hesitant to attempt dating for fear of rejection (Lichtenstein 2012). Cultural scenarios that imply asexuality among those over forty influence intrapsychic scripts and imagined sexual futures. Moreover, given women's greater life expectancy and men's propensity to marry younger women, the pool of available partners is limited (Carpenter et al. 2005; England and McClintock 2009; Sassler 2010).

Better on the Other Side: Divorce As a Catalyst to Sexual Subjectivity

Though it may seem logical to expect marriage to bring greater sexual subjectivity and divorce to bring sexual insecurity, overall the pattern was the opposite among the women I interviewed. After grieving over a marriage that had ended, they had the opportunity to reflect on their sexual desires and make different choices in subsequent relationships. Marilyn Meadows (1997) noted a similar pattern in her study of midlife British women: relationships affected women's sexual self-image, and new relationships inspired more sexual self-confidence. Women who discovered greater sexual subjectivity in the aftermath of divorce were generally those who had divorced in their twenties or thirties and found the search for new partners exhilarating and fruitful. The same was true for women in their forties, fifties, and sixties who had left sexually unsatisfying marriages. Given generational changes and the greater cultural openness that began in the 1980s, older women found they had more freedom of sexual expression and more power in sexual interactions. Although divorce itself was usually a shock, the experience shook women's vision of their imagined futures. In this new anomic state they felt free to write a new story and make new rules.

Divorce in the Younger Years. For women who experienced a divorce or separation in their twenties or thirties, the end of a long-term relationship or a short-term marriage most often had a positive impact on sexuality. These women had often been unhappy with the sexual aspects of their relationships or had focused on their partners' pleasure rather than their own. As relationships dissolved and they spent time being single, they often took the opportunity to reflect on what they wanted in their sexual lives and needed to feel sexually satisfied. Amy, a thirty-four-year-old white woman who had married her high school boyfriend when she was in her twenties, described sex with him as "monotonous. I guess that's the only way I can put it. It was almost like a schedule. I think that's what it became, . . . maybe that's what happens when you're with someone for ten years. . . . There was no passion. . . . I think it had to do with me not having that experience before I got into that relationship in order to know what I really like. I wasn't able to explore what I liked or anything else." Once the couple had established a routine of when and how they had sex, and because neither had had much experience before their relationship, they found it difficult to change.

Although Amy said their stale sex life was not the primary reason that their marriage ended after two years, she told me that only post-divorce did she really begin to know herself sexually. Amy used that time to date, experiment, and learn about herself in ways that she imagined her peers had done before they got married.

> In my twenties [after my divorce], that's when I was going out, I guess learning about sex and not really having one-night stands—but not getting serious with a boyfriend and then doing the "making love" and all that. No. We were having sex. And I think that's when I became, when I decided, like that was my sexual—that was my sexuality that I was able to express. . . . I think that's really when I blossomed . . . because I never went out to bars [before]. So it was really in my twenties when all that was happening and I would meet someone at the bar and maybe go back to his place. . . . I was definitely insecure with myself, but I think it definitely got better as I progressed and maybe that's just from experience.

Through dating and casual sex, Amy realized that she enjoyed sexual variety and could have sex for sheer pleasure without looking for a long-term commitment. The more experience she gained, the more comfortable she became with her desire and her positive view of sex.

Reflecting on the impact of her divorce, she said, "I think I definitely changed, I definitely progressed. . . . Just to not go back to that same old same old kind of missionary style, okay, that's it. I don't think that I would go back to that. I would hope not." Getting divorced gave Amy the opportunity to have new sexual partners and experiences that led her to better understand her body and sexual preferences and ultimately enhanced her sexual subjectivity. Divorce provided perspective, which was an advantage for Amy and other women in her situation (Gott and Hinchliff 2003).

Divorce in Later Years. For older women, such as Joan, born in 1942, the feeling of freedom and liberation after divorce was even more acute. Joan had married at the age of twenty-one and divorced twenty-three years later. The sexual climate in 1963 for a single woman in her early twenties was different from the one she reentered in 1986 as a new divorcee in her mid-forties. "Because now, you know, you had the availability of sex with anybody who struck your fancy! It was a new world, a whole different place, it was—oh my God!" When I asked how she felt about dating, she replied, "It's scary, it's like I'm a grown up finally. . . . Since I never had an opportunity to ever be with somebody else, ever, ooh, it was very scary. Did I know how to do it? Had I learned anything? What was expected? Oh, all those things. . . . You know a man took you out to dinner and expected sex. And did you want to or didn't you want to? Should you? Shouldn't you? Was it a good idea? Are you going to feel bad if you never saw him again and you gave him this gift of your intimacy?" Although she found post-divorce dating tricky to navigate, in due course the experiences helped her learn. "That was a whole new bag of tricks. I just think everybody has things to teach you, and you know it's just all good—the more you know the better. Could I get a job as a hooker? No! Do I know enough stuff? No." But after divorce, "I was much more uninhibited then I could ever imagine I would be."

The majority of older women I interviewed who divorced in their forties or later felt liberated by the separation and the opportunity to rediscover their sexuality. Iris, age fifty-eight and white, divorced in her early forties. She noted that the relationship she began when her marriage ended was exciting and gave her the chance to explore her sexuality in ways she never had before.

I was a little bit anxious about it just because my husband had been the only man for nineteen years—in my entire life—that I had ever had sex with. But at the same time I sort of felt that that was a good thing, I felt that that was a strong thing. Because women of my generation had a lot of sex with a lot of men when we were young, but I hadn't. . . . I was so crazed with [this new relationship], like trying—having sex anywhere-anytime kind of thing, that I was more—what's the opposite of cautious?—foolhardy, daring. So my sexuality, I guess I was just happy that I—like can still have a good time and stuff.

Iris's new partner and experiences made her more confident, and she felt lustful as never before. For her, the "crazed" feeling of wanting sex all of the time and trying new things invigorated her. As with the women interviewed by Dennis Waskul and his colleagues (2007), her sexual subjectivity followed sexual experimentation and encounters. Iris began to see herself differently after participating in a highly sexualized relationship, and she became more confident with more experience.

Another older woman who found greater sexual subjectivity after divorce was Celeste, age fifty-eight and dating at the time of our interview. Although she described the idea of dating in her fifties as initially "really scary and risky," after years of being sexually unfulfilled in marriage she eventually felt "reborn, almost. There's a renewed interest in sex and I feel that I have good sexual relationships. I have been in a few relationships since I separated and I feel very positive about that. . . . I feel in the sexual realm that I'm pleasantly surprised. It's like a renewal." Celeste also emphasized the importance of casually dating or "putting herself out there" as a means of reviving her sexuality and gaining self-confidence. Not feeling pressure to be in a relationship and reconciling her guilt about sex outside of marriage (influenced by her Catholic upbringing and her childhood "sex is bad " stance) made her more comfortable with her sexuality and spurred excitement about her sexual future in her fifties and beyond.

Celeste turned a bad situation into an opportunity. After mourning her marriage and reflecting on what she wanted in her life going forward, she was able to feel entitled to and comfortable with her sexual desires. "It was sort of like a gradual epiphany for me when I was separated and then starting to get myself back to normal again after the really horrible part. And then just kind of like understanding myself, finding out more about myself. I was trying to—I was reading a lot—I was doing a lot of introspection. And part of that whole discovery was discovering my sexuality again, and so I felt like I was becoming more aware of my sexuality. And now that I have been in a relationship I value that, you know, I feel, yes, I am more interested in my sexuality."

Celeste entered into marriage with little sexual experience and the belief that sex was for marriage and primarily procreation. However, after divorce, like some of the women interviewed by Wendy Watson and Charlie Stelle (2011), she set aside religious prohibitions and developed a fresh perspective on the significance of physical intimacy. Celeste's use of the word *reborn* indicates the magnitude of this transition. Divorce enhanced her sexual subjectivity because it catalyzed her sexual desire and brought her more in touch with her sexuality.

When most women marry, they believe their husband will be their last sexual partner and often resign themselves to the sex life, good or bad, they've had since the marriage began. Liberated from unsatisfying relationships and inspired by anomic sexual possibility, the newly divorced women with whom I spoke tended to approach sex with a different level of consciousness than did any other group of women. Rather than focusing primarily on the love relationship or basking in the feeling of being chosen, they acted decisively and judiciously, rejecting partners with whom they did not feel sexual chemistry.

New Partners, New Relationships: Living Lessons Learned

Post-divorce relationships with partners interested in satisfying them helped some women gain sexual confidence and enhanced sexual satisfaction (Gott and Hinchliff 2003). Similar to the findings of Waskul and colleagues (2007), who noted that some women's boyfriends "discovered" their clitorises for them and awakened a whole new level of pleasure, I learned that new partners who encouraged sexual assertiveness sometimes increased women's sexual subjectivity. Given the male sex-drive discourse and the commonly held definition of sex as penetration and men's ejaculation (Gavey, McPhillips, and Dougherty 2001), such partners were novel to women who had been in sexual relationships that had centered on their former husbands' gratification. The notion that some men thought women should also experience orgasm as a regular part of sex was a revelation. As Tiina Vares and her colleagues (2007) also found, several women reported that they had never climaxed until their thirties or forties because their partners had never made attempts to satisfy them beyond intercourse. An example was Shirley, a fifty-six-year-old woman who, throughout her verbally abusive marriage, focused on pleasing her husband and trying to be a "good wife." Leaving that relationship and starting one with a partner with whom she shares equal status allowed her to discover her sexual voice.

> I carried my beliefs about sexuality through until I was like in my late thirties and then I started questioning because my marriage was falling apart. I started questioning everything and among that was my feelings about sexuality. And once I divorced him and I got my act together, then my attitudes changed and it was reading . . . and just thinking I'm going to make life better for myself. And part of that is accepting everything about me and sexuality is a part of myself. . . . I am in a very sudden relationship and I am very comfortable in it but it's because I am comfortable with who I am and he's comfortable with who he is, too. He's a little character, but it's fun . . . and sex is great. . . . I'm not devaluing myself in any way. I'm not changing myself in any way to please him. This is who I am. Take me as I am. . . . Sex with him is, it's more about me and I'm totally not used to it. I'm used to being about the guy and here [my partner] is like "How many times did you [climax]? . . . Was that two or three times?" "I don't count! I'm not going there." . . . But he's interested in [my satisfaction].

Shirley grew weary of tolerating a controlling and selfish spouse and suppressing her feelings and desires. When her marriage ended, she engaged in a process of self-discovery and gained self-confidence, which led her to realize that she did not have to and would no longer put up with someone who devalued her. As she recognized that sex was important to her and experimented with masturbation so she could learn what worked best, her self-assurance grew stronger. She realized she could reject any man who did not care about her sexual satisfaction. The transformation from sexual object to sexual subject required more than just understanding her desire.

> More [it was] the attitude of "Well, this is the way I [am]—if you can't put up with it, I'll find somebody who can. I need certain things. This is what it is." And I think women are more comfortable with themselves [in their forties and fifties], even than they were in their thirties, and more willing to get what they feel they need at that age. Less willing to do something just to please their

partner. . . . I think more of the woman comes into it, more self-centered if you want—because I think women are very other-centered and at some point you have to realize that to be other-centered you need to be a little self-centered.

Divorce eventually brought Shirley greater agency and the opportunity to reflect on her definitions of desire and satisfaction. In new relationships, women like her pursued their desires and discovered fresh aspects of their sexuality. Shirley realized her capacity for sexual pleasure and gratification and grew more confident about communicating what she wanted and needed in sexual encounters.

Some women whose self-esteem suffered when their marriages ended found validation by dating or engaging with new sexual partners. As in marriage or other relationships, attention from men post-breakup inspired sexual self-confidence. Misty, age thirty-one, who had a brief marriage in her early twenties, noted that having casual sex with men friends after her divorce helped her gain a sense of sexual self-confidence that was missing during her marriage.

I kind of went on a little spree after I got divorced. . . . There were a couple of male friends that I had that were conveniently located and were safe bets which helped me knock the rust off. . . . I would recommend that to any woman after a divorce, finding a single guy who's a friend of yours after you're divorced. Who has no strings attached, who is a safe bet, and who will not judge you for it. That really restarted—it was like "control, alt, delete" my sexuality. It was nice to have a couple of experiences like that where I didn't have to worry "Is he going to call me tomorrow?"

Clearly, Misty was not looking for a relationship but validation that she was desirable. Men friends whom she called "vultures" because of the way they "conveniently started calling" after she had separated from her husband were "safe bets" because they pursued her and she knew them well enough to know there would be no expectations for anything more than sex. She did not have to fear that they would harm her, as a random stranger she'd met in a bar or online might. Misty's awareness of the potential judgment that generally accompanies casual sex functioned as an intrapsychic script that influenced her choice of post-divorce sexual partners. "Safe bets" were safe not only because she did not have to worry about a phone call the day after but also because they protected her from stigma. These experiences enabled her to feel more confident and adventurous going forward.

Misty also made use of the transition period for physical self-discovery. This period of personal exploration made her sex life with her current partner much more satisfying. "Buying a vibrator was probably very liberating. I don't think—looking back on it—once I've had orgasms with a vibrator, I don't think I've ever had an orgasm before. I thought I did. But once I did, I thought, 'oh, maybe I didn't.' So that was interesting because having that as a baseline to compare to was actually really beneficial in having sex with [my boyfriend]. . . . I knew what I wanted more than I did in the past in a sexual encounter with someone." Misty's self-exploration, her active seeking of a partner through a personal ad, and her casual sexual encounters with "safe bets" were all things she would not have done if she had remained married. For her, the process of divorcing led her to reflect on what she wanted sexually, and her actions to make that happen increased her confidence and her comfort with her body and sexuality.

Masturbation in itself can be an expression of sexual subjectivity. Yet among the women I interviewed, few openly discussed it. When a partner is unavailable after a breakup, masturbation allows a woman to continue to experience pleasure and feel connected with her sexual self. For women who have not previously masturbated, it can also be a way of learning and building a new understanding of their bodies. Although women's bodies may be limited by cultural discourses about them, women can resist such narratives and construct their own as they discover their bodies and have new *personal* sexual experiences that bolster sexual subjectivity (Waskul et al. 2007).

In addition to masturbation, some women pursued other new sexual activities after the end of a relationship. For instance, after separating from her husband, Adena, age thirty-one and Middle Eastern, started her first relationship with a woman. She told me she had not known she could be sexually attracted to a woman, but her desire for self-realization led her to explore the possibility. "I'm really in the place in my life that I'm discovering myself, and I feel so free to do that because of this relationship. If it was some other relationship, I think it would be a total like different environment, but here I feel more confident to discover and feel the way I want, and question." As for Misty, the end of Adena's marriage was the beginning of a period of self-examination that led to a new understanding of her sexual self. Though not all of the younger divorced women I interviewed had simi-larly dramatic transformations or actively engaged in efforts to improve their sexuality, divorce gave many of them an opportunity to validate their desirability after it had been questioned. A deeper exploration of their sexu-ality ultimately resulted in increased sexual subjectivity. Feeling desirable, feeling desire, and learning new means of experiencing sexual pleasure also allowed them to resist cultural scenarios and stereotypes that stigmatize women's sexual interests, particularly those that are outside of heterosexual relationships or among women over the age of forty. By doing and being sexual in different ways, these women learned what they wanted, not just what gendered scripts told them they should want.

Based on their analysis of data on sexual attitudes and behavior, Lisa Wade and John DeLamater (2002) asserted that age is less significant than marital status is in predicting sexual activity. Like Philip Blumstein and Pepper Schwartz (1983), they noted that older divorced and newly remar-ried individuals were more sexually active than were those who had been in long-term marriages. Sheryl Kingsberg (2002) has written, "The excite-ment of new love (or even lust), the mystery, the challenge, and the discov-ery are often the ingredients that make sex during this stage of a relationship incredibly passionate. There is much less risk of emotional dependency early on because . . . each partner's identity is still independent of the other" (432). This passion continues as relationships evolve in the early stages.

Furthermore, older women may be more likely to cultivate excitement in sexual encounters with second husbands or post-divorce boyfriends because they feel a greater sense of agency in those relationships or within themselves. When I asked about their sexuality in comparison to their peers, women who had more recently remarried generally thought of themselves as more sexual, given their experience. Camille, age forty-seven, white, and recently divorced, commented, "I think just by virtue of my situation and what I've been thrown into, you know, because a lot of them have been mar-ried for years and have—I don't think—I just don't think they know them-selves probably as well as I do now because of just it being forced upon me." Likewise, Kristen, age forty-one and remarried, told me that her first husband was much more interested in sex than she was. During our inter-view, she implied that she recognizes the importance of sex more than her friends do who have been married for many years. "I think that some of my friends who are in their first marriages, they haven't gone through what I've gone through. They're still sort of in that mode, that motherhood mode, and don't really appreciate what they have." In other words, Kristen's failed first marriage made her more aware of maintaining intimacy and not taking her closeness with her husband for granted. Merryn Gott and Sharron Hinchliff (2003) made a similar point based on their interviews with older women and men regarding the importance of sex. They suggested that old relationships help put new ones in perspective and provide a basis for interpreting the new as more satisfying. Among the women I interviewed, divorce facilitated self-discovery, and they saw themselves and their sexuality in a new light.

OTHER RELATIONSHIP ENDINGS

Divorce was not the only dissolution that inspired reflection and positive change. For some women, the end of long-term dating relationships, particularly bad ones, spurred self-discovery. Lori, a forty-four-year-old, engaged white woman, described how breaking up with a domineering boyfriend had prompted life-changing sexual self-discovery. She had grown up in a family in which sex was not discussed, and she had had few sexual experiences in her teens and early twenties. "I kind of was a late bloomer. In my twenties I will tell you that sexuality for me was about pleasing my partner, and then in my thirties I realized, 'Hey, what about me?' . . . I figured out that I had a right to it, too, and I was entitled to my own pleasure and I figured out what that meant for me and had the confidence to ask for it." This was not an overnight revelation. As Lori started to realize how oppressive her partner was, she sought therapy, which opened her eyes to the possibilities of sexual self-fulfillment.

> I went [to counseling] specifically because I was trying to get out of a relationship. I was having difficulty getting out, . . . and I just felt like I couldn't do it alone. I knew it was unhealthy and I had to get out of it, and so I went for that specific purpose, but it just became more encompassing. . . . It was life changing because [it was] one of those biggest moments. . . . I remember my counselor saying to me, "Okay, it's obvious what [your boyfriend] wants and what he needs out of this relationship. What do you want?" And I remember saying, "Oh, my God, I'm almost thirty years old and I don't think I've ever been stumped for words." And I didn't know—I couldn't even answer her

question of what I wanted out of a relationship, and I was like, wow, talk about co-dependency. But thankfully, you know, I started probing those things and figuring it out. But it was all encompassing, it was relationships, and it was life. I ultimately went back to school. I always wanted to and didn't have the confidence to do that and it enabled me to do that. So it was on many levels, it wasn't just one thing.

With newfound self-assurance and a desire to figure out what she wanted, Lori began to read and one day came across a book that helped her connect with her sexual desires. "I think it was like a self-help psychology book I found in the bookstore and it was really about feeling entitled to your own pleasure and realizing that as a woman you had that right and you were entitled to it and, you know, so it was just a change in perspective, I would say, from reading that book. . . . It was one of those aha moments, like 'Oh, yeah, why should it be all about him?,' you know?" Without that relationship, she probably would not have sought out therapy and so actively worked to acquire agency in her life. Once she began to understand and believe in her right to make decisions, she carried this confidence into the sexual aspects of her life and subsequent relationships.

Some women's relationships ended not by choice but by misfortune. I spoke with several widows, two of whom were in their twenties when they lost their husbands. Unlike late-life widows, who were usually discouraged about new relationship prospects, Stephanie, age thirty-two and widowed in her mid-twenties, found that new sexual self-confidence was a silver lining of tragedy. Her relationship with her late was husband had been good, but they had married young and she was inexperienced. She also suffered with insecurity and a negative body image and generally felt uncomfortable in sexual encounters. Her husband's fascination with pornography exacerbated her insecurity. "My late husband enjoyed looking at naked women online, which at that point in my life made me very self-conscious and [have] low self-esteem . . . because these women were, you know, beautiful and I didn't think of myself that way. . . . It definitely kind of made me feel not good about myself."

Though deeply saddened by her husband's death, in time she felt ready to date and discovered a new side of herself. "I started feeling really comfortable with myself after my husband had passed and I started dating and going out to Vegas. I had lost a lot of weight and went out to Vegas with a couple of my friends and was wearing things that I would never ever wear here or anywhere. And I think that was when I realized that I'm a woman and it's okay for me to dress this way. I feel good about myself. At that point I liked the attention that I was getting, I liked the look." As in the validation phase of the development of sexual subjectivity (discussed in chapter 4), positive attention from men (and her weight loss) helped Stephanie see herself as sexually desirable, which in turn awakened her desire.

> I guess my feelings about my sexuality changed after my husband passed because about a couple months or a year prior to that I had felt that our relationship was based on sex. And he like always wanted it and, you know, there were times where I just need[ed] a break. So I think the funny thing is after I had healed and started dating, I wanted it more. And for a while there I was like "What's going on?" I didn't know what to think about that. But I think it was just [that] I was becoming aware of myself again and on a different level because at that point I was on my own for the very first time. I had my own apartment, job, car, et cetera, so I was—it was me and it was a part of me becoming who I am today.

Stephanie's widowhood was transformative because it inspired self-discovery. Although she had become sexually dissatisfied in her marriage, given the couple's incompatible libidos, she later was able to realize that she was a sexual person. While validation from men was important in inspiring sexual subjectivity, the critical change came when Stephanie was able to control decision making and feel mature and responsible in general. Once she felt ownership of her life and had to make choices on her own, she felt more self-aware. As with many other newly single women, independence fostered her sexual subjectivity. Although she is currently in a relationship with a partner whom she described as not very interested in sex, Stephanie remarked that she is more comfortable with her body and now sees herself as a sexual person.

CUMULATIVE ADVANTAGES AND DISADVANTAGES ASSOCIATED WITH RELATIONSHIP DISSOLUTIONS

Among the women I interviewed, sexual problems were prevalent in most of the marriages that ended in divorce. Divorce gave them a chance to seek new opportunities and gain new experience. Though the initial stress of the divorce should not be minimized, ultimately it was a catalyst to greater sexual subjectivity in subsequent relationships. While women who divorced in their twenties and thirties had the benefit of youth, those who divorced in their forties or fifties had the benefit of wisdom and experience. They had spent more time in an unsatisfying relationship, and a subsequent period of independence gave these older women motivation and courage to seek a gratifying new relationship. Furthermore, many found divorce liberating: being single in the 1980s or later was very different from being single in the 1950s or 1960s. Online dating, hypersexualized media, and changing attitudes about sexual expression and women's status empowered many older women. Those who divorced when they were older were also more likely to report self-discovery or purposeful reflection about their sexual desires because they knew their own bodies better than many younger women did.

6 ❧ SELF-DISCOVERY THROUGH ROLE AND RELATIONSHIP CHANGES
Motherhood

I definitely think having children changed the way I feel about myself because I did feel less sexually inclined or interested years after they were born. . . . I worked continuously through both my pregnancies. . . . So I do feel that the rigors of just having a job and a family was completely exhausting. And I didn't feel like [sex] was all that important to me anymore. You know, sex is good; it's not that I'm saying that, you know, I'm an abolitionist now, but I just, I feel like it just wasn't really that important to me after a while.

—Sara, age forty-nine

Sara, a white, married, mother of two teenagers, told me that motherhood had complicated her relationship with her husband. After more than twenty years of marriage, she still struggled to balance the roles of working mother and wife. Sara was the family breadwinner, and she prided herself on her success and dedication. However, she also had little free time for her family, and her children took priority over her husband. Like other women with whom I spoke—both working and stay-at-home mothers—Sara felt that her motherhood role had added a new element to her identity, and she struggled to keep it from reducing her sexuality. As time went by, her relationship with her husband suffered; and when we met, she was at a crossroads in her marriage. How could she shift from her role as a mother to her role as a wife and a sexual person? How could she summon up the energy and desire for intimacy?

Motherhood is a complex subject, with social and psychological ramifications as well as physiological changes. Therefore, I've chosen to break my discussion into two chapters. Here I discuss how the social and psychological aspects of motherhood affect women's sexuality and the development of sexual subjectivity. In chapter 7, I will address the development of sexual subjectivity as the result of physiological changes associated with pregnancy, childbirth, and breastfeeding.

Although generally women have time to prepare to become mothers, they often need to occupy this new status to fully come to terms with its magnitude and its effects on sexuality. Motherhood and sexual appeal are rarely linked in western culture; instead, mothers are generally perceived as asexual or matronly (Friedman, Weinberg, and Pines 1998; Montemurro and Siefken 2012; Weisskopf 1980). Many people seem to believe that once a woman has children, she becomes first and foremost a behavioral example and must be responsible and conservative in a culturally specific way (Guendouzi 2005).

Most of the mothers whom I interviewed agreed that how they felt about sex, their sexual appeal, and their level of sexual desire changed after they had children. For some those feelings carried over from pregnancy, when they felt heavy, unattractive, and self-conscious about their bodies. Coupled with the fatigue and responsibility associated with being a new mother, such perceptions made many women feel asexual for a period of time. However, others found that the transition to motherhood gave them a new understanding of their sexuality. They learned about the capabilities of their bodies and found common ground with other mothers, which ultimately augmented their sexual subjectivity.

NO TIME FOR SEX: MOTHERS OF YOUNG CHILDREN

Overwhelmingly, motherhood inhibited the development of sexual subjectivity because the expectations of motherhood conflicted with the cultivation of sexual desire. For new mothers, the most often mentioned barriers to feeling sexual were exhaustion and time shortages (Montemurro and Siefken 2012; Trice-Black and Foster 2011). As women from all generations noted, lack of sleep or altered sleep schedules made it difficult to sustain energy for pre-motherhood activities. Danielle, age thirty-five, white, married, and a working mother of two, explained,

> The energy is just zapped from you whereas before, when we were living together and dating, we were so active. We were out and about every night. We went out dancing three or four nights a week for like three or four hours at a time. We were in tremendous shape so it was just—the energy was always there. Kids just kind of zap it from you. Between working and commuting and trying to keep my household in some sort of order, . . . it's—you have to really prioritize and the energy goes to your family, your marriage, and you kind of go from there. And sex kind of gets put lower on the priority list.

Cora, a fifty-one-year-old, married, African American mother of one felt the same way when her daughter was young. "I had the little one, so . . . I tried to balance the two, make time for [my husband], make time for her, so it really wasn't like—how can I say it? I wouldn't wanna say, 'Not interested,' but it was like 'All right, okay, I know I need to spend time, I need to do this, need to do that.' . . . By the time you get home, cook dinner, do this and make sure this is all right, all you wanna do is get in your bed and go to sleep. 'Don't even think about it.'" Cora laughed as she said this last phrase, an admonishment to her husband. Several women expressed similar sentiments: by the end of the day they could not deal with anyone else's touch or needs. They craved time for themselves and tried to establish boundaries when they could (see also Montemurro and Siefken 2012).

Like most of the mothers I interviewed, both Danielle and Cora shifted their concerns after they had children; their sexuality and sexual desire were no longer priorities. They were so busy focusing on their children's physiological needs that they usually neglected their own. Moreover, the majority of the mothers I interviewed worked full time outside of the home when their children were young (although this was truer for women born after 1960 than before). Nia, age twenty-nine, married, African American, and a mother of two, pointed out that it was not just the transition to motherhood that changed the way she felt about sex but also trying to balance that identity and her responsibilities with everything else. "[Things change] not because you have children—because, I mean, kids have a bedtime—but it's because of all of the things that go along with that. So like you're trying to work or you're going to school, in my case, you're trying to keep the house to look halfway decent, you know? You have kids and the man running around, you have to cook. And then you have just financial issues so I think all of that changes your feelings or your frequency of sex."

Nia spoke about the importance of validation and attention from her husband and how, the longer she is married, the more she questions her desirability. Having children and taking on the identity of a mother has added to her insecurity because she has less time and energy for sex, her husband sees her as a mother, and they are less intimate. This lack of security about her sexual identity and her reliance on her partner to satisfy her has made her feel more vulnerable at this stage of sexual development.

Monica, a thirty-five-year-old, African American mother of two, also addressed role conflict and the difficulty of summoning interest in sex. "More responsibilities, real life kind of sets in, you know, you have bills and children, you have to juggle, . . . you're always thinking about what's next and you never have enough to make ends meet. And . . . my husband works two jobs so . . . I'm married but I feel like a lot of times, I'm a single mother. And then at the end of the day it's like your husband comes home and then he wants to have sex and you're just kind of like [*sarcastically*] 'Great,' you know? Sometimes you're just like 'I don't even know if I have enough energy to even kind of get myself ready for the next day.'" Like Nia, Monica commented on the worries that were distracting her from sexual interest. For both women, financial pressures, managing home responsibilities, and serving as primary caregivers for their children while also working or attending college full time inhibited their sexual desire.

Many women need to feel emotionally connected to want to have sex, and this is not always comprehensible to their partners. As one husband in Lillian Rubin's (1983) study told her, "It seems to me being sexual would make us closer, but she says it works the other way—if she felt closer, there'd be more sex" (98). Many of the mothers I interviewed felt they did not have time or energy to cultivate that closeness. For women such as Nia and Monica, being able to relax enough to emotionally connect with their husbands was exceptionally difficult given the ever-present demands and concerns of motherhood and the heavy responsibility of maintaining the house and family.

Furthermore, most, though not all, of the mothers told me that they found it difficult to take advantage of small windows of opportunity for intimacy because they were too distracted by other tasks or were emotionally disconnected. Jane, age thirty-eight, white, a married mother of two, and a teacher, explained,

> I felt like before I had kids, if I were to make myself emotionally available, it was in total to my husband and it was fun and it was both an intellectual and physical experience of being really, really open. And after having kids I think, . . . uh, I don't really know how to parse it out. I feel like being open takes on a different role to [my kids], and then when I get to him it doesn't feel like—it's not the same kind of—it's not the sexuality part as much as the emotional availability. Which to me is tied to sexuality in the world of being with him. . . . I don't have problems accessing, having orgasms or whatever, but I'm often not just all there and so I am just participating in someone else's thing. And that's just the way it's had to be. In order for me to be all there all the time, somebody has to make dinner [*laughs*]. There [have] to be some other aspects to it.

Jane's comment that "somebody has to make dinner" is telling. Like most women with whom I spoke, she needed to be freed from thinking about real-world responsibilities and obligations. Before having children, she felt more able to relax and enjoyed the holistic connection with her husband during sex. But after having kids, even though her husband could ignore dirty dishes in the sink or the fact that their children might wake up prematurely from a nap, Jane could not put pressing things out of her mind and get into the proper emotional state for sex to be meaningful. She sometimes went along with sex but in body, not mind, which certainly reduced her sexual subjectivity.

Other women had desire but no time. Joyce, age fifty-seven, white, and married for twenty-three years, noted that when she had children, the gendered expectations were different from contemporary ones.

> When you have small kids, I think—I'm sure I still wanted to have sex, but I'd rather sleep. So I don't think it changed desire, I think it was more the surrounding—just the timeframe and all the things that you needed to do. And again, in my generation, back then it was, or in that marriage anyway, I was responsible for taking care of everything. You know, my husband went off to work and that was it. So I was taking care of the kid and he wasn't like saying, "Oh, let me help and do diapers and let me help by cooking dinner." And so there's that exhaustion mode when you have somebody that's under four or five years old.

Though Joyce did not think the transition to motherhood had diminished her sexual desire, she recalled the challenges associated with making time for sex. Like the working mothers in their twenties and thirties, she felt responsible for the majority of child rearing; so while sex was important in her marriage, it was low on her priority list.

Alyssa, age fifty-one, was a stay-at-home mother while her kids were young. She, too, commented on the different expectations she perceived for mothers of her generation. "I just felt like I was tired. I think it gets back to that issue of me saying that women have, or back then certainly, so many more things to think about than a man does in a relationship in that sense." More of the women born before 1960 did not work before their children began school, and a number did not work until their children were in high school. These women, like Alyssa and Joyce, felt that roles for mother and father were more clearly defined when the father was the sole breadwinner. So they dealt with fatigue—not just from the normal demands of caring for young children but because they were doing the vast majority of the care.

Women born after 1960 were more likely to mention that their partners had helped with child care tasks, though many did not get as much help as they would have liked or enough to enable them to "get in the mood" on a regular basis. Because most worked full time, even a partner's help did not open extra time for leisure pursuits, which, at best, is how they regarded sex (as a chore, at worst). Lack of time for sex and the physical exhaustion of mothering young children inhibited the development of sexual subjectivity because women had little time for sexual exploration, and many felt disinterested in sex or disconnected from their sexual self.

In the clash among the roles of mother, wife, and sexual person, mother won out time and time again. The work of psychoanalytic scholars such as Nancy Chodorow and Carol Gilligan, offers insight into this role conflict. According to Chodorow (1978), because most girls are raised by their mothers, they learn to see gender similarities and identify with their mothers rather than their fathers. They see their mothers as connected to them, as similar, and as their primary nurturers. Thus, they learn that to be a mother is to be other-oriented; to be a girl or a woman is to be connected to others and to focus on others' well-being. Gilligan (1982) built on this argument, noting that girls are socialized to see the world as a web of connections and to prioritize relationships with others over individual achievement.

These explanations extend specifically to sexuality. Sexual gratification is often viewed as indulgent. Religious taboos suggest that sex for its own sake is unnecessary and, according to some religions, immoral. Thus, those who pursue sexual pleasure can be viewed as self-focused. Furthermore, the ideal mother in our culture is self-sacrificing. Her primary concerns are her children rather than herself (Guendouzi 2005). Thus, it may be difficult for women to justify or reconcile their image of mothers with their image of sexual women, which inhibits the cultivation of sexual subjectivity.

SEXUALITY IN TRANSITION

A number of women did not view the lack of sex or a decrease in its frequency as an indication of either personal or relationship trouble. Rather, they saw it as a temporary condition that was rational for this stage in their life. Indeed, studies of postpartum sex have noted that decreases in frequency usually are temporary (Apt and Hurlbert 1992; De Judicibus and McCabe 2002; Hyde, DeLamater, Plant, and Byrd 1996). Eve, age forty and a married mother of two, said, "Ever since we had children we don't have sex as often as we did, and I feel like that's okay. Like, if we were having sex this infrequently before the kids were born, I would think there was a problem, but I think it's okay because I understand how much of our time is spent on our kids and our work, but it still remains [important]. I'd like to have sex more but I'm not concerned about it, if that makes sense." Although women who said they were not worried about this situation often noted that they wished they were having more sex and looked forward to a change, they tended to view it as something they needed to go through as a family.

According to Paula Nicolson (1986), part of the process of taking on the new status of mother is mourning one's independence while figuring out a way to negotiate new roles and old relationships and construct a new identity. Yet Judith Daniluk (1998) has pointed out the paucity of information for women about the way in which sexuality changes as they transition through life-course statuses such as motherhood: "women and their partners are faced with the absence of realistic sexual paradigms by which to reconstruct their sexual lives and renegotiate their sexual expectations once they become parents" (166). They lack concrete information or examples of how to be both sexual and mothers and thus must go through a process of sexual self-discovery postpartum. Jane, the introspective mother of two I quoted earlier in the chapter, addressed this issue directly.

I don't connect being a mom with feeling sexual, I guess. In fact, I find that they're in conflict for me. And I love being a mom but it requires a different kind of energy that zaps the other energy and doesn't contribute to it, I guess. . . . Being a mom, that space that was occupied with "how am I doing as a sexual person?" now is knocked down really far [compared] to being a mom and taking care of [children]. Especially early on when they're toddlers and they're sick and stuff like that. And that's so . . . very asexual. So you have to take parts of your body that you see sexualized and not even purposefully become very asexual for a while and then resexualize them. And I think the resexualizing stage is not easy to accomplish. I found it very hard to get back into the swing of things. I did but it wasn't just a "oh, now that I'm all healed up and feeling better, let's go do it." It wasn't—my emotional experience was very different.

Paralleling her earlier remark about the difficulty of feeling emotionally present given the responsibilities of being a working mother, Jane noted the difficulty of mentally transitioning from her identity as mother to her identity as wife and lover. Now that she was using her breasts to feed her children and viewing her body functionally, she had a hard time reorienting and redefining her sexual relationship with her husband.

This reorienting and redefining process continued throughout motherhood. As their children aged and even as they approached independence, women noted a need to adjust to being couple-focused again. More opportunities to be intimate did not automatically result in more sex. After years of prioritizing the mother role, women needed to figure out how to be alone with their spouses. Some were anxious about the empty-nest phase for that very reason. Brenda, age fifty-one and a full-time working mother of one, said,

As I got into my early forties [sex] was just not a focus, I mean I wasn't as frustrated as I was when my son was little but I was busier with him with outside stuff. . . . When your kids are teenagers I think it's more emotionally draining and you're running them around to a lot of different activities and you just kind of lose track of yourself. . . . My husband would be running with my son to hockey tournaments and doing stuff and I'd be home or vice versa, so we weren't together as much. So it just kind of—not that it wasn't important but it—the word *numbing* kind of comes to mind. You just kind of get numb about it. And then you kind of, I kind of woke up and went like "wait a minute, you know, he's gonna be going to college in four years and we're still gonna be here and we've got to start thinking about other things that are more couple-oriented."

In Brenda's case, as her son grew more independent, he also became more active and their family became busier, making it even harder to find time to focus on her relationship with her husband. Her use of the word *numb* indicates the level of dissociation she felt after years of orienting her family life around her son and his activities rather than her relationship with her husband. With her son's departure to college fast approaching, she realized that she needed to invest time in her relationship with her husband so they could emotionally connect and revitalize her desire and enjoyment of sex.

Faith, age fifty-two, married, with one child in college and another in high school, also recognized it was time to start thinking about her intimate relationship with her husband in a different way. So she made an effort to rekindle that aspect as their children grew.

I think probably in my early thirties I wasn't putting as much effort into my husband as I was my children. And by the time I was in my forties my children were more independent so I was able to put more of my focus back on my husband and doing more things [like] going out without children and being more back into feeling like you're doing things as a couple and dating, rather than feeling that you're doing things always with your kids. So it allows you ... when you have that opportunity to be like more in a dating environment or a couple's environment. Of course, it makes you maybe more interested in sex.

For Faith, making an effort to emotionally connect with her husband and focus on their relationship as a couple, not as parents, helped her reinvigorate her sexual desire. Although the timing of empty nests often corresponds with menopause or other physical changes that complicate sex, older women met this period of transition with excitement and anxiety. For couples who cultivate and want to maintain intimacy, the empty-nest period can enhance women's sexual subjectivity because it allows extended time for sexual exploration and activity when women know themselves and their bodies better than they did in their pre-motherhood days.

SETTING A GOOD EXAMPLE

As I have noted in previous research (Montemurro and Siefken 2012), most women are concerned about appropriate displays of sexuality in front of children. Sexual expression is suppressed for mothers when they fear that showing sexuality is setting a bad example. Women are aware of negative reactions to mothers who talk about sex or dress in provocative ways (see also Montemurro and Gillen 2013b). As the mother of teenagers, Sandra, a married, fifty-eight-year-old project manager, pondered the hypocrisy in her directives to her children, given her strong desire for passion in her relationship. "It's hard being the parent and telling my children [not to do] these things and wanting my husband to be doing things with me down the hall. You know, I haven't given up that feeling of wanting to have fun sex. And it's hard to say to them, 'Yeah, it is fun, but you have to be careful,' you know? 'Yeah, it does make you feel good but you should wait.' It's very difficult."

Sandra's question about boundaries and honesty sheds light on the secrecy of women's sexuality. Sex, even among married people, is constructed as private. There may be no need for Sandra's children to know about her sexual desires or their parents' intimate life, yet there may also be benefits from a frank discussion or the normalization of sex (Schalet 2011). Sandra felt the need to compartmentalize this part of her identity; and when kept private or suppressed, sexual self-discovery and growth are limited.

Single mothers described role conflict as they negotiated dating while raising children. Given cultural assumptions about single mothers and sexual responsibility, these women, even more than married women, expressed deep concern over how to balance sexual desire, relationships, and the messages they sent to their children. Amanda, age thirty-nine and a divorced mother with two children, noted that she had recently been reflecting on whether it was possible to be a mother and a sexual person at the same time. "You feel like you shouldn't be doing it or you shouldn't be feeling those things. . . . It's as if a responsible—I was just having this conversation with my sister last night—it's as if a responsible person or a good person, a good adult doesn't have sex." What it means to be responsible, Amanda implied, is to avoid any behavior that children should avoid. Her strategy for dealing with this conflict was to parcel her identity. "There's mom me and dealing with all the questions my kids have about sex and how much they know and how much they see and their questions. And then there's single me with [my boyfriend] and we're out at dinner."

Based on a review of the literature on mothering, Jacqueline A. Guendouzi (2005) sketched the characteristics of a good mother: protective, nurturing, caring, organized, and socializing—that is, "instilling good social and moral values in [her] child" (20). Successfully reproducing this image requires a focus on caring for others before (or instead of) oneself, which is counter to expressing sexual agency. The single mothers with whom I spoke had internalized these instructions, and some resorted to lying to avoid letting their children know they were pursuing new sexual relationships. For example, Jacqueline, age forty-four, had been separated from her husband for about a year but still did not feel ready to tell her younger children she was dating.

> We've had the conversation, [the youngest daughter] and I, and she flat out told me, "Mom, I don't want you dating. I don't want a stepfather. I don't want a stepmother. I want you and daddy to get back together." And I kept saying to her that "Your father is happy, your father is dating someone." And she was like "No, no, no." . . . And so I'm like, how much do I expose her to? How sensitive am I to her feelings? But yet I have my girlfriends telling me, "Jacqueline, you can't deny you, you can't put you on the back burner for her. She'll eventually have to get over it."

Though she felt very sexual and excited about dating, Jacqueline decided to keep that part of her life private and told her children she was going to meetings in the evening. This deception made her uncomfortable. "After work I may go out to dinner or catch a movie or something, but to say that I'm going out on a date, no. . . . I'm tired of sneaking around. I mean it makes me feel like I'm doing . . . something wrong." Although, post-separation Jacqueline was one of the most sexually self-assured women with whom I spoke, she continued to minimize this part of herself around her children. She did not want to be a bad example, nor did she want to tarnish their image of her as a mother by showing them she had moved on before they were ready for that knowledge. Yet hiding her sexuality made her feel deviant. She had emotionally and physically moved forward and was confident in herself as a sexual person. But she was prevented from fully embracing her newfound sexual self-confidence because she was concerned about her identity as a mother.

Likewise, Celeste, a fifty-eight-year-old administrative assistant who told me she felt "reborn" after divorce, has had a hard time facing her teenage and adult children's awareness of her sexuality as a single woman.

I was asked by the gentleman that I'm seeing now to go on a vacation and he was sort of like encouraging me to do it and I was, you know, dragging my heels a little bit because I had never done that, you know? I only went on vacation with my husband. And I felt funny about going away with a man that I wasn't married to on a vacation. And maybe that's a generational thing but it was something that I thought, "Okay, I have to tell the kids." You know? . . . I don't think they—they don't think of mom as being a sexual being and it's difficult for me to play that part with my sons, you know? And it was a transition from being a parent as a couple to being a single parent and then having them see me as somebody who was going to date. I do draw the line, I'm very careful about, . . . I would never have, I wouldn't sleep with someone when they were around.

When women feel conflicted about expressing sexuality, then they are less likely to feel confident about it in general. Like the American teenagers in Amy Schalet's (2011) interviews, who felt they needed to hide their developing sexuality from their parents, mothers who feel their sexuality should be concealed turn it into a separate aspect of their identity. Although Celeste was more open than Jacqueline was about dating—that is, her sons knew she was doing it and generally supported her—she, too, struggled with how to be both a good mother and a sexual person. She did not want to alter her children's image of her, as she feared might happen if they began to think of her as a woman with sexual interests.

CUMULATIVE ADVANTAGES AND DISADVANTAGES ASSOCIATED WITH MOTHERHOOD ROLE

For the women in my study, becoming a mother influenced the lifelong process of developing sexual subjectivity. In their early years of mothering, they lamented lack of time, exhaustion, and their inability to connect emotionally, all of which impeded their sex lives and their enjoyment of sex. As their children grew, women had to work to redefine their relationships with their husbands. It could be a challenge to sexually reconnect because their focus had long been on their children, not on their relationship as a couple. Mothers struggled with balancing their identities as wives or sexual people with their role as caregivers and models for their children.

Though becoming a mother rarely enhanced the development of sexual subjectivity, women with strong sexual relationships with their spouses before having children were less disadvantaged by the transition than were women who had been married for longer periods of time and whose sex lives had focused on conception. Women born before 1960 who had had children soon after getting married or whose early perspective on sex tied it to procreation often experienced a cumulative disadvantage associated with motherhood because they had not had a chance to develop their sexuality or learn about the pleasures of sex. The same was true of women who were less comfortable with their sexuality because they lacked experience before marriage. Once they took on the asexual role of mother, they had trouble thinking about their sexuality and sexual pleasure, which did not benefit them going forward.

7 ◈ SELF-DISCOVERY THROUGH EMBODIED CHANGES

The Physical Experience of Motherhood

On the one hand ... I was maybe losing parts of the perfect body thing, which is part of sexual appeal ... [that] I kind of identified with. But at the same time, this is like the real sexuality, in a way, manifested. So I was realizing that, too. And then it was after that when I realized all the power of myself, of my body—that I could actually like make this person and give birth, the whole thing, you know? Really it was after that that I first experienced orgasm during sex with another person. I had never before.... It did something freeing for me and something that made me feel powerful, something that gave me the confidence.

—Alice, age fifty-five

Giving birth was a turning point for Alice, a white, divorced, mother of three. Becoming a mother dramatically changed how she both saw and experienced her body. Partly biological (recognition of her body's strength and its reproductive capacity) but largely social (because physical changes allowed her to appreciate rather than police her body), her new awareness allowed her to lose "the perfect body thing" while further exploring its sensual possibilities. She began to see her body and herself as formidable, a new view for her. In her words, "this is ... the *real* sexuality."

Having sex to become pregnant and using one's body for childbearing are socially constructed as the main purpose of intercourse. Alice's comments, like those of other women in my study, reinforced this idea. Her discovery of this innate power was freeing; it made her feel more confident and comfortable with her body and finally able to relax and enjoy the pleasures of sex. "I really didn't get it about fulfilling sexual relationships until after I had my first child. I just didn't, I don't know why. . . . It just really didn't seem like such a big deal, so much fun or anything." Having a baby thus inspired sexual self-realization.

The fifth phase of the development of sexual subjectivity is *self-discovery through embodied changes.* In this stage, sexual subjectivity progresses when women learn about themselves through physical changes such as pregnancy or menopause. As women's bodies change, they may recognize their strength and feel empowered or accomplished, which brings them greater self-confidence. When women experience pregnancy and motherhood, many realize the commonality of their sexuality, and their shame or embarrassment about sex and bodies is reduced. For other women, however, these body changes diminish their strength and thus decrease sexual agency. They may become self-conscious about weight gain or breasts that sag after breastfeeding. The more alienated women become from their bodies, the less comfortable they are with their sexuality (Daniluk 1998; Langer 2000).

Sexual activity plays an essential role in motherhood and life, and it is also linked to health and relationship benefits (Hinchliff and Gott 2004; Rutter and Schwartz 2012). Yet public expression of sexuality is still primarily associated with women who are young, childless, and unmarried (Daniluk 1998; Dempsey and Reichert, 2000). People rarely discuss the topic of mothers' sexual desire and desirability, an indication of the degree to which *mother* and *sexual person* are separate identities in western culture (Daniluk 1998; Friedman, Weinberg, and Pines 1998; Montemurro and Siefken 2012; Oliver 2010; Trice-Black 2010; Trice-Black and Foster 2011). Consider a recent *New York Times* column in which reporter James Braly (2012) suggested that breastfeeding past infancy leads to the sexual neglect of fathers. Arguing that nursing mothers turn off their partners and threaten a couple's sex life and relationship, he took issue with his wife's attention to their child and contended that supporting breastfeeding was tacitly agreeing to "sexless fidelity," which leads some men to adultery.

Braly's article was published in July 2012. In the same month, bottle manufacturer Bitty Labs initiated a Twitter campaign with the slogan "New Baby? Reclaim your wife." One of the company's sales-focused posts asked,

"Feeling like you're competing with your newborn for mommy's attention?" (Urban 2012). Such messages reinforce the idea that women's breasts are for men, who should be threatened by their use for other purposes. These sentiments construct an Oedipal competition between father and child over the mother/wife's body, underscoring its object status. Of course, not all men share these opinions; but such views do highlight the cultural dissociation of motherhood and sensuality, and they desexualize and objectify women's breasts (Weisskopf 1980). Research corroborates anti-breastfeeding attitudes. Not only do American cultural mores discourage public breastfeeding (Acker 2009), but men with traditional gender ideologies often reject private breastfeeding as well, fearing that it will interfere with relationships (Ward, Merriwether, and Caruthers 2006). Stigmatizing breastfeeding reinforces the desexualization of mothers. Women cannot be both sexual and mothers in contemporary American culture, so they need to make a choice or find ways to separate those identities.

During pregnancy some women feel concerned about potentially harming the fetus, so they refrain from sexual intercourse (Hyde, DeLamater, Plant, and Byrd 1996; Weisskopf 1980). In the first year after a birth, due to physical pain, exhaustion, stress, emotional adjustment, and in some cases postpartum depression, their sexual activity and desire often decrease (Ahlborg, Dahlof, and Hallberg 2005; Apt and Hurlbert 1992; De Judicibus and McCabe 2002; Hyde et al. 1996). As with the social changes related to motherhood that I discussed in chapter 6, when women cede control over their bodies, many of the initial physiological changes inhibit their development of sexual subjectivity. Pregnant women's bodies are objectified; they are regarded as vessels for future children. Restrictions constrain behavior. Women are supposed to avoid alcohol, tobacco, caffeine, and foods that might cause bacterial infections. Most American women undergo medically directed pregnancies in which they are regarded as wombs first and subjects second. This does not stop after birth. Breastfeeding women must share their bodies, reconceptualize or desexualize their breasts, and be cautious about their diet.

CONCEPTION AND PREGNANCY

Although many of the women I interviewed spent their premarital years fearful of pregnancy, most were happy when they learned they were expecting. A few conceived through artificial insemination, three became stepmothers by marriage, and one adopted. The vast majority, however, experienced pregnancy; and several mentioned that sex was more meaningful when pregnancy was the aim. Jessica, age thirty-eight, a white, married mother of two young children, specifically remembered the sexual encounters when she conceived. When I asked her if sex had been different when she was trying to get pregnant, she smiled. "Having sex and having a baby being the ultimate goal, those—I remember both times we had sex that resulted in being pregnant as being really beautiful—different kind of sexual experiences. And when I think about them I just kind of feel like giggling. It was like—this is what sex was supposed to be the whole time, and it definitely wasn't what it was about for the last twenty years."

Jessica's comment that "this is what sex was supposed to be the whole time" is striking. From a biological perspective, reproduction is certainly the intended consequence of sex. However, what sex is "supposed to be" is largely culturally defined and multivalent. Sex is supposed to be different things at different times for different people. Yet when Jessica acknowledged the manifest purpose of her body and identified the moments when she had used it intentionally for an outcome other than pleasure, she chose the word *beautiful*. In a way, she romanticized those sexual encounters as loving and meaningful in way that others she described had not been. Her voice softened and her smile broadened when she talked about sex for procreation. Those physical responses were a marked change from her frank discussion of her quest to understand her own desire and her exploration of the magnitude of her sexuality.

Sandra, age fifty-eight, married, and African American, gave birth to her children in her late thirties and early forties. She, too, described the decision to focus on procreative sex as a marker of the next phase in her sexuality. Unlike Jessica, however, she felt the pressure of her biological clock. Her tone was more serious, describing these attempts as goal-oriented tasks that increased her stress and may have stalled conception. "My sexuality at that point was much more about getting pregnant, having children. I had a lot of fun, knowing a lot of men, been a lot of places." Rather than seeing this period of trying to conceive as exciting, she saw it as work. She had had her fun earlier, but now it was time to get down to business. Sandra developed so much stress about getting pregnant that her doctor recommended a vacation to relieve some of the tension. This worked. Finally, she was able to unwind and appreciate time with her husband. Like Jessica, Sandra smiled broadly as she told the tale of her first child's conception. "We were away and we were having fun, we were not thinking about 'this is going to be the time.' We were relaxing and having fun. We had never been to [this resort area] before. . . . And it was just, it was a full moon, it was just romantic and very, very pretty."

Unlike many of her peers, who had married and had children when they were in their early twenties, Sandra had placed her career over parenthood and marriage. Other women born before 1960 often mentioned becoming pregnant quickly rather than specifically "trying" for it. They did not differentiate sex with the purpose of becoming pregnant from any other kind of sex. In addition, because many of these women had had little sexual experience, they did not demarcate this procreative stage because it did not follow another sexually active stage. Any change in their sexual desire came after the children were born.

SEXUALITY DURING PREGNANCY

At the end of my interview with Kelly, a thirty-five-year-old professor and the mother of a toddler, she inquired why I did not ask about sex during pregnancy. I explained my focus on feelings about sexuality, not sexual behavior. Nonetheless, she was not the first interviewee to allude to this stage as sexually different, so I began asking. Generally, women expressed extremes. Some, particularly those from older generations, had been completely uninterested in sex during pregnancy or fearful that it might cause complications, even when had doctors assured them it would not. In contrast, a sizable number of other women, mostly those born after 1960, noted that their sexual arousal and desire had been heightened, particularly in the second trimester.

Robin, age forty-eight and a mother of three, told me that she had felt anxious. "During pregnancy, yeah, it was like I was always afraid something was gonna happen to the baby. Like it was gonna hurt the baby. . . . No sex during pregnancy, just because I was always afraid." Robin had already admitted that she was generally unenthusiastic about sex and that her attitudes were influenced by Catholic doctrine, which forbids premarital sex and underscores procreation as the true purpose of sex. With this background she did not mind avoiding intercourse during pregnancy. However, her comments about protecting the fetus also show that she had shifted into her mother role as soon as she became pregnant. For her, this temporary celibacy was positive and enhanced her sexual subjectivity. She had a solid and culturally revered justification for avoiding sex, which seemed to make her feel more in control of her body. Furthermore, once she had become pregnant, she felt that she had finally had sex for what she saw as the right reasons. Because she and her husband had intended to conceive a child, she was not being sinful and thus had no reason to feel shame or guilt.

Many women happily commented that pregnancy made them feel desirable and feminine. Some, particularly those who were in their fifties and sixties at the time of the interview, recalled that being pregnant had made them feel more womanly and grown up. Their swollen bellies were evidence of their purposeful sex lives. Shirley, age fifty-six, white, and the mother of two, said, "I felt very sexual for most of my pregnancy because it was again a proof of my sexuality. . . . I was sexual up until my belly was so big that *mother* became more important than *sexual*." Her comment that pregnancy was "proof of [her] sexuality" is revealing. Shirley had entered marriage with little sexual experience and was one of many women of her generation who noted that she had learned about sex by doing it. At first this meant that she followed gendered sexual scripts that focused on pleasing her husband. However, becoming pregnant shifted the focus to her own sexuality rather than her husband's because it publicly confirmed her involvement. It was her body that changed, and she was the one who felt the hormonal shifts. In a way, pregnancy allowed Shirley to see herself as a mature woman who was entitled to have sex. She also noted a transition during gestation, when "*mother* became more important than *sexual*." Her comment acknowledged that these separate identities did not coexist during the full course of pregnancy. Even though she may have known that sex was safe, her ideas about motherhood probably influenced her sexual activity as pregnancy advanced.

Some women not only felt more feminine but also remarked that pregnancy increased sexual arousal. In their benchmark study, William Masters and Virginia Johnson (1966) noted an increase in sexual desire during the second trimester of pregnancy, although subsequent studies have failed to replicate such findings (De Judicibus and McCabe 2002; Hyde et al. 1996). My sample was too small for generalizations, but I did note that more women commented on amplified sexual desire during pregnancy and fewer reported a lack of interest in sex. I heard remarks such as "I think I felt sexiest when I was pregnant," "I liked being pregnant, and my husband . . . was turned on by me being pregnant so it didn't slow things up," "I wanted to have orgasms all the time when I was pregnant—both times," and "sex was a priority during pregnancy, that was one of my cravings." A couple of women attributed their feelings to biology, noting an increased pressure on the cervix as pregnancy advanced. Amanda, age thirty-nine, divorced, white, and a mother of two, said, "I mean, because everything swells, I would literally walk around the block and be turned on." Given their perpetual state of stimulation, a number of women also noted that climaxing was easier when they were pregnant. Nadia, age forty and a mother of four, pointedly said, "What I found was that [during the] first pregnancy I had a heightened sexual response, like I constantly wanted it. And then I could probably snap one off within like the first two seconds of starting. Like it was the weirdest."

For all of these women, the middle months of pregnancy increased sexual desire. Their partners, however, did not always welcome this intensified interest. Some feared they would injure the fetus during intercourse, while others communicated that they were not sexually attracted to their pregnant wives. This left many women frustrated. Autumn, age forty-one, a white mother of one, described her dissatisfaction with her husband's attitude. "We went through a classic—I felt very sexual and he was afraid for the baby, even before I had him. I'm like 'Let's have sex, and all the doctors said, yes, it's a good thing to do.' And it just freaked him out too much, so I was like 'Wah!'" Regina, age sixty-two, recalled, "I was very sexual [laughs]: 'Now, now, I don't care. It's not gonna hurt the baby, let's go on.' . . . The hormones were screaming and he's saying, 'I'm gonna hurt you.' 'No, you're not.'" For partners inhibited by concerns about risks to their future child, the mother identity superseded the sexual partner or wife status. Even though pregnant women such as Autumn and Regina felt highly sexual, reluctant partners stymied their opportunity to explore that desire and bolster their sexual subjectivity. As a result, partnered women's general reluctance to engage in self-gratification led to a mostly celibate pregnancy.

INFERTILITY, MISCARRIAGE, AND
UNPLANNED PREGNANCIES

Infertility

Women who had had difficulty becoming pregnant or whose pregnancies were unplanned often noted that those experiences negatively impacted their sexuality and sexual relationships. According to the Centers for Disease Control and Prevention (2013), approximately 11 percent of American women between the ages of fifteen and forty-four experience issues with conception, and women's sexual self-image and sexual desire are often transformed by such difficulties (Chandra, Martinez, Mosher, Abma, and Jones 2005; Daniluk 1998). Challenges with conception can leave women feeling ashamed or defeated (Daniluk 1998; Langer 2000). Among those I interviewed, infertility created stress in relationships, which was especially acute for women who had a deep desire to become mothers. For example, Celeste, a fifty-eight-year-old mother of three who was separated at the time of our interview, had had seven miscarriages during her life and struggled to maintain viable pregnancies. Although she ultimately did have children, the focus on conception took the pleasure out of sex and a toll on her marriage.

> I would say it was the first nail in the coffin for the marital problems that we eventually experienced. Because it really did take the love away from the marriage because sex was relegated to an obligation and a timeframe, and it became mechanical. And I guess, you know, I was very obsessive almost about having a baby and I didn't really—it was like this was the means to the end. And it was hard, well, it was hard for us to then get past that after the infertility issues were resolved, to get back then to a loving relationship, the way it was before all of that occurred. And we went to support groups for infertile couples and we weren't alone, that was very much the case with everyone else, too. It really does change the complexion of the marriage.

When sex becomes constructed as purposeful and the desired outcome does not happen, the meaning of sex can be altered permanently. Clearly, conception was Celeste's primary focus during the time she described. Because she was only having sex to conceive and felt ruled by ovulation, intercourse was stressful and enjoyment difficult. Furthermore, in the 1970s, when Celeste was dealing with infertility, she heard little discussion about the issue or its frequency. Although she and her husband did attend a support group, they did not talk about their problems with family or friends and had fewer options for alternate forms of conception than contemporary women do. So her experience minimized sexual subjectivity because she felt powerless over it. "I felt like . . . there was something wrong with me that I wasn't able to have a baby easily, the way other people did. And that was something that used to drive me crazy, and it still does to this day." As their sexual relationship disintegrated, Celeste and her husband grew apart. Without physical intimacy, emotional intimacy faded, and they lived together as parents rather than sexual partners. Eventually, when their third child was a teenager, they separated.

Sandra Leiblum (1997) has found that sexual satisfaction decreases when couples focus on trying to conceive. After becoming pregnant or accepting infertility, most are not immediately able to redefine sex as fun and pleasurable. Unless couples make a conscious effort to change their focus, this phase can have deleterious consequences on sexual relationships, as it did for Celeste. Most of the women with whom I spoke discussed the importance of love in sex and viewed it as a means of affirming their connection with their partners, of expressing intimacy and closeness in a way they did with no one else. Lillian Rubin (1983) has also noted that most women need to have an emotional bond in order to want to have sex. She traced this need back to childhood and adolescent socialization, which requires girls, but not boys, to suppress erotic attachment to their mothers and privilege emotional connection. Thus, when sex is primarily functional rather then emotional, women such as Celeste may have a hard time putting the passion back into their relationships.

Among my interviewees, even those who had relatively brief struggles with infertility often said that focusing on conception had made sex less spontaneous and less enjoyable. However, a few did not believe that it had changed how they felt about sex or their sexuality. For example, Brenda, age fifty-one and a successful executive, adopted a child after she was unable to get pregnant. Although infertility was stressful and frustrating, "I just had to accept it. And I don't know if this could be different for a lot of people because there's a lot of different reasons why you can't get pregnant. I just—I mean it didn't affect our sex life or—there was nothing physical in that way that prevented it. It was other issues." Brenda and her husband had tried to conceive for a few years in their early thirties before pursuing adoption, and they continued to maintain emotional intimacy throughout these events and beyond. Given Brenda's executive abilities, she may have been more accustomed than other women to dealing efficiently with problems and finding alternate solutions. Moreover, she clearly derived self-esteem and self-confidence from work that was not motherhood, unlike Celeste, who married young and whose chief focus in those early years was on becoming a mother. In other words, being a mother was only one of many things that Brenda wanted to accomplish, so she seemed to have less at stake. I am not minimizing her emotional pain or frustration, but I do interpret her experience as different from that of other women.

Miscarriage

Miscarriages also affected women's sexuality. Eight of the women in my study had had miscarriages, and several had had more than one. Generally, miscarriages negatively influenced sexual subjectivity because, as with infertility, women felt a lack of control over their bodies. Jeanne, age sixty-six, white, and married for forty years, had had a miscarriage before giving birth to children in her mid-thirties. "I was really upset that my body didn't work—I was worried about whether my body would function as a good female body. That was one concern in addition to just the other sadness and difficulties and all that kind of thing. But I think it made me doubt—am I able to do this? Am I, you know, like a good normal person?" Throughout Jeanne's life she had known that being a mother was something women were supposed to do, and she had never anticipated difficulties. So after the miscarriage, she began to doubt her femininity and lacked confidence in her body.

Amy, a thirty-four-year-old college student and retail worker, had been unaware of her pregnancy when she miscarried. Yet she, too, questioned herself and her body, initially believing the loss was her fault. "The only reason I knew is because I thought I was dying. I felt like something happened . . . and the [doctor] said, 'You know, you were pregnant, you just lost it.' But I didn't even know I was pregnant. . . . Like, how could I have not known that I was pregnant? . . . Aren't women supposed to know?" After experiencing the physical and mental pain of the surgical removal of the fetus, Amy felt alienated from her body, as if it had somehow betrayed her. With emotion, she said, "I didn't want to have sex because I didn't want to get pregnant and have to lose another. . . . That definitely has an impact on—you don't want to have anything to do with sex or anything after that."

Both Amy and Jeanne had high expectations for their bodies. Socialized in a culture in which motherhood is expected and encouraged, they were frustrated when their bodies did not work as anticipated. Jeanne wondered if hers was "a good female body," a clear indication of her view of what women are supposed to be. Her phrase echoes Alice's statement that motherhood "is . . . the real sexuality" and Jessica's remark that conception is "what sex was supposed to be the whole time." When Amy lamented that she "should have known," even very early on, that she was pregnant, she also implied that a woman's intuition or maternal instinct should have kicked in after she had conceived. For both Jeanne and Amy, the heart of their frustration seemed to lie in their inability to control their bodies and their lack of power over their pregnancies. They did not have subjectivity because they could not control their bodies, which can be an alienating experience that reinforces mind-body dualism (Hesse-Biber 1996).

Unplanned Pregnancy

Unplanned pregnancies also marked turning points in women's sexuality when they called attention to problems in relationships or brought shame. Jennifer, a forty-year-old mother of four, confided that her first pregnancy had been a surprise. Raised as a Catholic, she was embarrassed that she had conceived before she was married because now everyone knew she had had sex. She felt redeemed by marriage, however, when she and her husband made the decision to wed before she gave birth.

Caitlin, a white, twenty-eight-year-old professional who was separated from her husband when we met, had had a different experience. Also raised as a Catholic, she had grown up with a "sex is for love or marriage" stance and felt conflicted about premarital sexual activity. Although she took charge and went to Planned Parenthood to get birth control pills before having sex, she knew her parents would strongly disapprove so did her best to hide her sex life. Caitlin had also had negative experiences. As a teenager, she was date-raped, which made it difficult for her to trust men. She believes this history is one of the reasons why she sought out and stayed with her passive and less passionate former husband.

When she was nineteen, Caitlin became pregnant unexpectedly and chose to have an abortion. She knew that she and her boyfriend were not ready to have a child, and he left the decision in her hands. She described that episode as humiliating and traumatic.

I really felt like "I'm going to go to hell for this" and was really upset about it, but I really felt like I didn't have an option. I was actually with my [future] husband, and I felt like there was no way he was going to be there for me and support me or anything like that. And I knew my family would blow the lid and my mom would probably tell me give it up for adoption because she doesn't believe in abortion. And I just felt really alone and I felt like I had to do it for myself. I had just finished my first year of college and I knew I would be the one stuck with this baby and—I hate to say it like that, but it's like it would be my burden for the rest of my life and he could walk away free of everything. And even my parents—we didn't have the room at the house so I felt like I had to do it and that I couldn't tell anyone because it was so shameful and I actually got really depressed. And that was part of the reason I had to [come] home and I had to see a therapist and had to get sleeping medicine because I was so upset about it.

Caitlin's situation stunted her development of sexual subjectivity. Because she felt depressed and ashamed after terminating the pregnancy, she lost interest in sex, which she saw as having led to this catastrophic event. Like women who had suffered miscarriages, she did not feel desire, nor did she feel powerful or in control of her sexuality or her body. Her body was no longer part of herself but something she needed to act on.

In her study of adolescent sexuality, Karin Martin (1996) described the connection between sexual agency and self-esteem. "If one feels helpless, unable to act, as if he or she has no ability to affect his or her own life, then one will feel poorly about his or her self. Sexual subjectivity is a necessary component of agency and thus of self-esteem. That is, one's sexuality affects her/his ability to act in the world and to feel like she/he can 'will things and make them happen.' One must experience a link between agency and body/ sexuality" (10). In this view, Caitlin's depression was linked to the lack of governance she felt over her body and her feelings of shame associated with violating religious taboos. Because she felt helpless and pressured to make a choice that she did not want to make, her self-esteem plummeted.

Three of the women in my study told me that their unintended pregnancies expedited the demise of their marriages or relationships. Sherry, age forty-eight at the time of our interview, was in her early thirties when she married for the second time. Soon thereafter, she discovered she was expecting. She and her new husband had not discussed having children, and he became enraged when he heard the news. Because of his reaction, she felt coerced into making a choice that went against her values. With tears in her eyes and an expression of shame, she said, "Shortly after we got married I got pregnant and he was just furious, basically. And I basically allowed him to talk me into it." Her voice dropped to a whisper. "An abortion. And I don't know if it's typical or not, but it was certainly the beginning of the end of our relationship and it certainly majorly affected our sex life. And he was to the point of like begging [for sex] or whatever and we just kind of started like sleeping in separate rooms and eventually separated and divorced." Sherry was devastated by the experience of the abortion and felt deeply disgraced, given her religious upbringing. She also felt remorse and loss of control because the abortion was not her decision. When her former husband gave her the choice of continuing to be married or terminating the pregnancy, she succumbed to his demands. Afterward, however, she lost interest in sex and could not bring herself to be intimate with him. Their marriage soon ended, and Sherry has not had a serious relationship since, nor does she imagine one in the future.

Miriam, age sixty-one and separated from her husband, described a similar situation.

> When I found out that I was pregnant for the second time, it wasn't supposed to happen and he asked me to have an abortion, and I said I couldn't do that. And so I think we probably were intimate maybe twice in the nine months. He was full of anger and resentment, and that was—I'm surprised that my children were born normally because that was a very stressful time for me. So that really was a big shift—that was the shift in terms of my marriage because I thought, "Okay, better or worse, you're supposed to take it as it comes." He could have taken precautions to make sure that we didn't have any more kids. I would have been fine with that. But I was not—because I really wanted to have more children—I was not okay terminating my pregnancy. . . . So after that, sex became a very different issue.

As Sherry's husband had done, Miriam's husband pressured her to end her pregnancy. Although Miriam did not succumb to his wishes and the couple did stay married for some time after their children were born, he emotionally checked out of the relationship and that, in Miriam's mind, was the downfall of their marriage. He left her the lion's share of the parenting and household care, an indication that she should reap the consequences of the extra labor. So because Miriam had gone through with the pregnancy against his wishes, sex became a bargaining chip for negotiating with her husband. She no longer felt sexual desire for him but knew he was still keen on intimacy. When she needed his cooperation, Miriam found herself initiating sex because she knew this was one way to get him to help. "And so I would ask him, 'Well, can you do such and such?' And he'd go, 'What, you didn't get to do it? You wanted all these kids, this was your dream.' And it would be like that. So that was his thing. . . . And so you asked what about the sexual piece, well, that was a way—he was like a sex machine [*laughs*], so that was, like I'd engage with him and then I'd say, 'Well, how about if we do such and such?'"

Thus, sex changed considerably for Miriam after she became pregnant. She knew that, after sex, her husband would be susceptible to her requests for help with tasks or parenting, so she used it as a way of soliciting his involvement. Although this was not the only friction point in her marriage, it did shift her perception of the purpose of sex. It may have been less about emotional bonding or forging intimacy, but she still found it satisfying.

Sexual subjectivity is not just about using one's body to experience pleasure. It also means feeling in control and making choices that fit with one's sexual desires, which may include acting in control of one's body, not having sex, or having sex on one's own terms. In this sense, Miriam's decision to have her children despite her husband's resistance as well as her use of sex as a tool provide evidence of her sexual subjectivity. She maintained control over her body by going through with the pregnancy and then used sex in a way that was effective for her. Miriam was raised to see sex as natural, had had positive early experiences, and had felt confident before this episode in her life. Women like her, who had developed sexual agency before an unforeseen event, were aided by previous experiences. Sherry, in contrast, was not.

Only one other woman's discussion of an unplanned pregnancy or infertility communicated sexual agency. When I met this woman, she was in her early forties, and she told me this anecdote after our recorded interview was over, as an afterthought. In her college years, she said, she had aborted a pregnancy, and even then she knew her decision was right and she felt confident about her choice. Rather than being haunted by it or ashamed, as Sherry and Caitlin had been in their situations, she told me that afterward she had heard a voice whispering, "Thank you, thank you, thank you." Raised in a liberal family by a young, inattentive mother, this woman did not want to have a child she would be unable to care for. Unlike Sherry and Caitlin, she was not worried about sinning in the eyes of the church, and she had never had a "sex is bad or taboo" stance. For her, making this decision confidently and independently was a means of exercising the sexual agency she had cultivated throughout her life.

CHANGES POSTPARTUM

Physical Recovery

Given the pain of delivering a baby and the time needed for recovery, most women told me that sex had been the last thing on their minds during the early postpartum weeks and months. Though Janet Shibley Hyde and colleagues (1996) found that women report having the same level of sexual activity four months after giving birth as they did during the fifth month of their pregnancies, I find it more probable that sex was less frequent than it had been before the birth. Like other women I interviewed, Angela, age sixty-two, white, and married for forty-two years, put off her husband as long as possible. "After she was born I was just dreading [sex] because I hurt so badly that I didn't want him to touch me. It took a long time afterward and I would just cringe because it hurt." Monica, a thirty-five-year-old mother of two, talked about a similar anxiety. "After I had kids [things changed]. You know, your body is going through all kinds of changes, emotions and, yeah, after I had kids it really changed. Even from the first time you have sex after you have a baby, it's just kind of like 'Oh, my God.' It's like tense and you're nervous and it takes a while before you feel comfortable with having sex."

Fear associated with sex can cause women to resist sexual intimacy for an extended period of time (De Judicibus and McCabe 2002), which may eventually decrease relationship satisfaction. Those whom I interviewed noted that this protracted period without sex presented a challenge when they were transitioning back into a sexual relationship. Even when they were physically ready, many were both consumed by new responsibilities and emotionally distant from their partners, sentiments that quelled their desire or gave rise to a new sense of asexuality.

Breastfeeding

Today most American women at least attempt to breastfeed their children. But even though rates of breastfeeding have increased in the past decade, fewer than half of nursing mothers continue past six months, and only about 16 percent still exclusively breastfeed at six months (Centers for Disease Control and Prevention 2012). Many women must deal with practical barriers such as working away from home, or they may have physiological difficulties associated with nursing. However, reluctance to breastfeed may also be motivated by both social rejection and the sexual nature or potential arousal of the experience (Acker 2009; Weisskopf 1980). Because women's breasts are hypersexualized as objects to entice men, the shift to viewing them as functional pushes many women think differently about their sexuality (Acker 2009; Ward et al. 2006).

I was curious about not just how the experience of breastfeeding influenced women's sexual self-image but also how they felt about transitioning back and forth between practical and sexual conceptions of breasts. Some women completely compartmentalized this process: they said there was nothing sexual about breastfeeding and seemed perplexed by my question. Others showed discomfort, as if they thought I was asking if they had found nursing sexually stimulating (which I was not), although other studies document that this reaction is common (Kitzinger 1983; Rich 1976; Weisskopf 1980). Several expressed relief because they had not felt aroused.

Not only do many North American women resist acknowledging that the physical aspects of mothering can be sensual, but their feelings of embodied pleasure may elicit shame or guilt (Daniluk 1998; Oliver 2010; Rich 1976; Weisskopf 1980). Most of the women I interviewed felt uncomfortable thinking of their breasts as sources of sexual inspiration or pleasure during the months they were nursing. Danielle, a thirty-five-year-old working mother of two, for example, had boundaries. "It was like 'work zone only.' Those orange cones. 'Cause anything could . . . let your milk let down." Monica, also a thirty-five-year-old mother of two, remembered shying away when her husband attempted to touch her breasts during foreplay. "I do recall moments where I didn't really want my husband to even like touch me, you know, there. And when he would. It was just kind of like 'Oh, like how do I tell him to stop?' [*laughs*] . . . I guess subconsciously I kind of forget about that, but there was a period where I was just kind of like—I would kind of cringe and not really tell him because I didn't want to put him off in any way." But even though Monica was uncomfortable with the way her husband was touching her body, she continued to feel that it was important to please him. She saw his sexual needs as primary and went through the motions to satisfy him. Her breasts were for others, and during this time she suppressed her own anxieties to make sure her husband's and child's needs were met.

Camille, age forty-seven and recently divorced, also struggled with idea of involving her breasts in sexual interactions with her husband. "That was kind of weird, having sex while you're still breastfeeding your children, because . . . the breasts took on a different . . . definition to me then because of feeding my children. So they became less sexual. . . . It was hard getting back into it. It was hard letting him touch them after I had babies and was breastfeeding because it just felt weird. I'm like 'No, wait, this is what your, this is—they shouldn't be part of sex because they're feeding my children.'" Yet trying to discourage her husband from touching her breasts did inspire Camille to try new methods of sexual interaction and stimulation. "I just was keeping him away from my breasts, you know? Like 'these are my kids' food,' like 'let's try something else,' you know?"

Women who had trouble thinking of their breasts as sexual while they were breastfeeding were concerned about lack of control over their bod-ies and the embarrassment of letting down milk when they were aroused. Moreover, the overlap between motherhood and sexuality and the col-lective awareness that arousal resulted from touching or suckling breasts made them uneasy. When women felt these sensations with partners, they worried about also feeling them with their nursing children (Rich 1976; Traina 2000; Weisskopf 1980). Would responsible mothers use the source of their children's sustenance as part of sexual play? Clearly, breasts become objects that were both part of and separate from a mother's sexual self. They were hers to control, but only as regards a partner's or a child's access.

When the women in my study could not integrate mother and sexual-person identities, breastfeeding inhibited sexual subjectivity. However, a number of women did derive power from their ability to nourish and sup-port life (Oliver 2010; Rich 1976). As with sex for procreation, nursing made these women see their breasts differently. They acknowledged their "real" purpose and became more comfortable with their bodies. Sandra, age fifty-eight, reflected, "I started thinking, well, this is what breasts are for, they're not for ogling and squeezing, they're for nursing. That's what they're for. That's why they're here. I didn't think about that before. Probably at eighteen I would have thought nursing was disgusting. . . . And then later on I thought, 'Well, this is very satisfying.' I found it very satisfying, very relaxing you know?"

Several women made mechanical or bovine comparisons. Although Alyssa, age fifty-one and a mother of three, agreed that she felt like a machine while she nursed, she also told me, "You definitely feel differently about your body, and that there's a real purpose for the female body the way it is and what you can do with it. And then the pleasure part comes back in, but for a while there you're just thinking about the utilitarian aspect of it." As nursing mothers, neither Alyssa nor Sandra viewed their breasts as sexual. Yet they saw breastfeeding as a purposeful stage and were gratified to be able to sustain their children.

Research suggests that the physical experience of breastfeeding causes the secretion of oxytocin, a sensation similar to that associated with sexual climax (Rich 1976; Rossi 1973; Traina 2000). Several women talked matter-of-factly about the sensual aspects of nursing; and Misty, age thirty-one, a divorced mother of two, said that she was able to adjust to the feeling. "It was a little odd. But because I nursed both of my kids and I'm still nursing [my baby], the first time I had sex after her, because [my partner] is very much a boob man, . . . I just kind of warned him to be careful in case something were to happen, but he didn't seem to mind when things shot—sprayed out at him, which has happened a couple of times. . . . It's weird to have the same kind of feelings of pleasure when I'm nursing my baby as I associate with sex with him, so that's kind of odd. But I think I'm pretty much used to it now." Misty's comfort with her body and the erotic sensations of mothering was unique among women I interviewed. After divorcing in her mid-twenties, she had been inspired to engage in sexual self-discovery. Not only was she in a fairly new relationship when we spoke, but she also possessed greater sexual subjectivity than did most of the other women of her generation.

Debra, a fifty-nine-year-old retired teacher whose divorce had also inspired sexual self-discovery, agreed that nursing was stimulating. "I'm not saying I had orgasms from breastfeeding, but . . . sexuality and sensuality are really two sides of the same coin and there was a very sensual feeling about it, you know? Just when you feel the milk let down and you have the baby snuggled up against you and they're sucking. It's not so much sexual as sensual. And it makes you very aware of your body, and anything that does that is gonna be sexual." Debra's attitude was consistent with research that underscores the view of mothering as a sexual experience, but few of the other women in my study acknowledged this position. Most were uncomfortable with the idea of eroticizing motherhood (Oliver 2010; Traina 2000; Weisskopf 1980). Because Debra and Misty were more sexually self-aware, they may also have been better able to reflect on the complexity of sexuality or more comfortable about discussing maternal sexuality with a stranger. For these two women, and for other women with greater sexual subjectivity and sentience, becoming a mother had less influence on sexuality.

The physical transformation in lactating breast size was a temporary boon for small-breasted women and often inspired newfound confidence in their bodies. Shannon, age sixty-four, told me she was flattered when someone complimented her chest for the first time in her life. Stacy, age sixty-two and the mother of one, said that enjoyed the change in her appearance. "I loved the fact that my breasts were bigger, just for those few months. It was just so neat to put on a tee shirt and have breasts, you know? [*laughs*]. There was something there, which is obviously a sexual reaction to it. But I really liked presenting myself to the public and having breasts. It was fun while it lasted."

However, more women said that post-nursing sagging damaged the appearance of their breasts and made them feel old (Montemurro and Gillen 2013b). Jane, a thirty-eight-year-old teacher, told me, "They changed totally. And after the second time they changed again. So they're different things to me now. . . . And they're—I don't feel at all about them the way I did in my twenties. [In] my twenties they were something that I thought could be part of a certain game of fun and now they've been neutralized. I don't know—and that's another thing about aging. It's not like they're going to perk up and go back to their pre-baby world." Robin, age forty-eight, was also disappointed. "Like, I had like an all-right chest and all of a sudden it's saggy, yeah, yeah, horrible-looking, you know?" Because breasts are symbols of femininity and sexual desirability, many women view them as central to their sexual self-image. Thus, sagging breasts decreased sexual self-confidence because women associated them with aging and undesirability.

SELF-DISCOVERY THROUGH THE PHYSICAL EXPERIENCE OF MOTHERHOOD

Though many of the changes associated with reproduction limited or inhibited sexual subjectivity, a number of women said motherhood enhanced their sexual self-confidence and experiences. Adrienne Rich (1976) noted the power in women's bodies and the ways in which sensual aspects of reproduction can, when affirmed, improve women's sexual self-image. Others have argued that linking motherhood and sexuality is critical to women's understanding of their sexuality (Oliver 2010; Rossi 1973; Traina 2000). In other stages in the development of sexual subjectivity, women's agency is bolstered by affirmation from or experiences with others. But despite the significance of these social transitions, the women in my study really began to understand their sexuality as they experienced pregnancy, childbirth, and breastfeeding. In this stage, they learned about their bodies and their potential from within.

Motherhood heightened not just sexuality but also sensuality. After conception, several women found different parts of their bodies stimulating or experienced new levels of sexual pleasure. For example, Holly, age twenty-three and the mother of a toddler, noted, "During the pregnancy I was pretty active sexually and it wasn't until after I had him that I just—I didn't like the same things. I had different hot spots. I just felt different because I was a mother. And over the last two years I have come back into my own in a different way now. I'm a lot more mature and I know what I want and I am in control of my sexuality. Because I had a baby I had to kind of re-explore everything and accept myself for who I am now." Like women who were more physically aroused during pregnancy or experienced stronger orgasms, Holly learned that sex now felt different, and this excited her and enhanced desire as she rediscovered sexual pleasure postpartum.

Dawn, age fifty-four, white, married, and the mother of two adult children, explained why having children was so significant in her sexual development. "I think that having children changed things for me. Doesn't necessarily for everybody, I'm sure. But it did for me. But I think it also made me more comfortable with my body. . . . You learn things about yourself being pregnant and giving birth that you wouldn't have known, that you can't possibly know otherwise. And I think that for me sexuality and having children are very closely tied because obviously you can't have kids without having sex, but it's not that simple. . . . It's the connection between body and sexuality, I think, the physical [act] of having a child." Though she found the change difficult to articulate, Dawn's physical experience of childbirth deepened her understanding of her sexuality. She recognized her physical strength and endurance and, like other women I interviewed, discovered that sex now made sense for her in a way that it had not before.

Motherhood As an Accomplishment

When women learned that they were good at a task or when their success was measured, validated, or rewarded, they were inclined to feel greater subjectivity in general and sexual subjectivity in particular. Motherhood was one of these accomplishments because it allowed many to realize that they possessed unexpected physical and emotional power. Alice, the divorced mother of three whom I quoted in the chapter epigraph, explained how motherhood enhanced her feelings of self-worth.

> I had . . . two kids and a third by the time I was thirty-two so, you know, that whole experience definitely was kind of a confidence-building thing because it's like a big job, and if you can do that pretty well, then you must be good enough to do other things well for yourself, I guess. Probably that whole experience of pregnancy, delivery, childbirth, raising people is, you know, such a confidence builder. That probably made a big difference, to me. . . . To handle like three people that you have to take care of in your whole life, . . . that definitely made me feel like that, and more like accomplishment of something that gave me the right or something to like control my own life.

Motherhood presents daily challenges and dilemmas. For Alice, feeling skilled at responding to the demands of motherhood increased her self-confidence and sense of control. This self-assurance carried into other areas of her life, making her feel more comfortable with her body and about seeking or asking for what she wanted sexually. Trusting her body and feeling more relaxed during intercourse, she achieved new levels of sexual pleasure after having kids. Her conclusion that motherhood gave her "the right or something to control . . . [her] own life" was powerful. By experiencing motherhood, she learned about her physical and emotional strength and felt surer about making decisions.

Confidence through Commonality

During pregnancy, labor, and delivery, women's bodies are constantly monitored and examined by relative strangers. This may press modest women to come to terms with their embodied sexuality. As Jamie, age forty and a stay-at-home mother of two, commented, "Surviving motherhood—if you could get through being a new mom, you can do anything [*laughs*]. It's true. . . . After giving birth, like everybody touches you. Like, the doctors touch you, the person who helps you breastfeed touches you. . . . So you really lose a lot of modesty, . . . and you kind of realize, well, maybe it is a little bit more common or . . . I don't have to be so modest." Heather, a forty-six-year-old married woman with one daughter, also said that her sense of sexuality changed when she realized the essence of her femaleness in her reproductive capacity. "My sexuality became more normal then, like more just a part of who I was. Like, it wasn't some secret special thing [in which] everybody talks about sex all the time and stuff. . . . It was more like 'Wow, I'm female, I have these parts. Look what my parts did. This is amazing.' I mean, when I had my daughter it was like a parade of people kept coming in and out of—I had no shame, no, you know, it's like 'This is it, this is who I am as a person.'" Both Jamie and Heather were late bloomers with little sexual experience before marriage. Jamie had grown up in a conservative Chinese family that did not talk about sex and advocated virginity until marriage. Sex was a private topic, and modesty was very important in both her ethnic culture and her religion. When she gave birth to her son and recognized how regularly bodies are exposed and how nurses and doctors regard sexual body parts, she was able to accept her own more readily.

Eve, age forty-eight and the mother of twins, said that her "maternal instinct" kicked in after she gave birth and she lost her previous self-consciousness. "I was just like whipping them out and breastfeeding from the minute—I mean, and I have pictures of me holding both [babies] at the same time in the hospital room, and you see all of my—my father-in-law—all these people. And now I'm like 'Oh, my God, what was I thinking?' But when you're in that mode you just do what you have to do, like I just did it. I can't believe how unselfconscious I was about it. I didn't give a shit about what anybody thought or what they saw." Kristen, age forty-one and now a mother of teenagers, explained, "I've become more accepting of my body since giving birth. I don't necessarily know why that is. I think, like it's never—I was very self-conscious of being naked or anything and now I'm not as much. [When you have a baby,] it's like a zillion people are in the room and they've seen you, and . . . after a while it's like everyone's got pretty much the same parts, what's the big deal?" All of these women related the same sentiment: pregnancy and childbirth required repeated monitoring and exposure; and the more often women's bodies were revealed, the more comfortable they became with them. They likened having a baby to joining a club in which women learn self-acceptance.

As Danielle, age thirty-five, noted, becoming aware of the commonality of body parts and feeling less modest made some women more comfortable talking about sex. "I see myself as being more free with my body now that I know it can do what it was truly meant to do, have children. I guess that's kind of opened up new avenues of discussion and things like that." Charlotte, age thirty-six, observed that having a baby established new common ground with co-workers, who now began sharing stories of labor and graphic discussions about bodily functions. These comments suggest that, for some women, motherhood gives them a deeper understanding of their sexuality and their bodies and thus yields positive changes. Such affirmative experiences can benefit women's sexual subjectivity.

CUMULATIVE ADVANTAGES AND DISADVANTAGES ASSOCIATED WITH EMBODIED CHANGES OF MOTHERHOOD

Pregnancy generally led the women I interviewed to feel more feminine, more libidinous, and better about having sex. Because procreation is culturally perceived as the manifest and primary purpose of intercourse, even women raised with strong cultural or religious proscriptions felt more liberated about having sex when they were trying to get pregnant. For the women who experienced them, infertility and miscarriage generally weakened sexual subjectivity. They described feeling a lack of control over their bodies and an alienation from their sexual selves. Women with less sexual confidence before pregnancy and those who had initially viewed sex as taboo, bad, or confusing were more likely to be disadvantaged by these situations. In addition, older women recalled that they did not have adequate resources or support for dealing with the aftermath of miscarriage or infertility.

The embodied changes associated with becoming a mother usually enhanced sexual subjectivity. Women also became more comfortable with their bodies when they recognized the commonality of body parts and felt less shame associated with nudity. Most of the women I interviewed felt that pregnancy and childbirth taught them more about themselves and their bodies and enhanced their sexual self-confidence.

8 ⊚ SELF-DISCOVERY THROUGH EMBODIED CHANGES

Aging and Menopause

Menopause, it's brutal. . . . I have no mojo right now. And I never thought I would ever be without my mojo [*laughs*]. . . . And the last thing you want to do is say to your husband, 'I'm sorry, honey, you're just not doing it for me anymore.' So—I mean as far as my husband goes, things are fine. But I feel bad because I just feel—I feel guilty. It's like, oh, gosh, you know, he's my husband, I love him to death, why don't I—it's like I just don't feel like it.

—Paula, fifty-three

In a study of Americans over the age of sixty, researchers found that 66 percent of women said sex was an important part of their relationships with their husbands and that 70 percent of sexually active women were either "as satisfied or even more satisfied with their sexual lives than they were in their forties" (Kingsberg 2002, 432). According to a more recent survey, 41 percent of women between the ages of forty-five and fifty-nine rate their sexual relationship as "extremely pleasurable" (considerably less than the 60 percent of men who say the same), and about a third of women in their fifties report that they have sex at least once a week (Fisher 2010). However, this same survey finds that just 43 percent of older Americans are satisfied with their sex lives, and other stuies note a decline in frequency of sexual activity and interest and an increase in sexual problems associated with aging (Fisher 2010; Waite, Laumann, Das, and Schumm 2009). Women report less interest in sex as they age, which appears to be related to the fact they are less likely than older men to be in a relationship (England and McClintock 2009; Waite et al. 2009).

Sexual dissatisfaction and decreased frequency of sexual intercourse are consequences of physiological changes associated with aging and menopause. Women such as Paula, who is an active professional, must deal with fluctuations in their bodies and libidos. It took Paula a long time to embrace her sexuality. As a child, she believed that sex was taboo and heeded her mother's advice about abstinence well into her twenties. Overweight during her adolescent years, Paula could not imagine that anyone would find her desirable. But when she graduated from college without ever have been involved in a sexual experience , she decided she wanted to have sex for the purpose of learning. She sought out someone for a casual encounter so she could "get it over with." Paula told me, "I was never in a serious-enough relationship and I had issues. But finally I got out and I was like 'Oh, jeez, I've got to.' It's sort of like facing your fear because I think I knew part of my issue was my weight and that I was afraid of it for so long. So I needed to do it just to find out what all the talk was about. So I think I was really disappointed because 'Oh, this is it?'"

Sex failed to live up to Paula's expectations. Until her mid-twenties, when she finally experienced sex with a boyfriend, she did not understand why others thought it was such a big deal. "Getting into a relationship where you really cared about the person made me realize that this is not something that's bad, it actually is something that is good. And I think . . . I had a better understanding of what it meant. It wasn't just raw sex or whatever, there was a lot more to it." Whereas most of the women I interviewed recalled feeling aware of their sexuality and sexual desire during their adolescence, for Paula it happened when she began this relationship and moved from feeling innocent crushes to true sexual longing.

In her early thirties Paula lost a considerable amount of weight and began to feel "comfortable in her own skin" once she saw herself as "normal." Like most other women for whom desirability preceded desire, when Paula made peace with her negative body image and low self-esteem, she became more self-assured. In her forties she met and eventually married her husband, and in that relationship sex took on a new meaning as a way of connecting, showing love, and maintaining intimacy. Aided by sexual experience and her feelings for her husband, she accepted herself and acted with sexual confidence.

I think I had experience, I kind of knew myself. I think we're all projects and it's a lifetime thing. I was a late bloomer so I think I was experiencing in my early forties what most women probably experience in their thirties. . . . But I felt comfortable with myself, career-wise. You knew . . . kind of where you were gonna be or you were kind of more settled is probably a better word. I think I knew myself, I knew what I liked, and I think it was really more about being happy with me. And it definitely affects me, it affects my sexuality. If I'm happy with myself and I feel good about myself, I'm more open about that.

Given Paula's later sexual start, the onset of menopause was both awkward and unwelcome. In a relatively new relationship and finally living with a partner, she had expected regular sex and scoffed at friends' suggestions that sexual frequency would decrease after she married. But with the reality of physiological changes and symptoms of menopause (and responsibility for washing copious loads of laundry and other mundane household tasks that stifle romance), Paula worried about whether her desire would return and she and her husband would be able to get back on track. "It's only been five years and all of a sudden like he's dealing with me throwing off the covers in the middle of the night and sticking a leg out, you know?" Menopause suppressed Paula's sexual desire, and she almost felt cheated because it had taken her longer than most women to become comfortable with her sexuality. She told me that, at fifty-three, her strength is not what it once was and that aging influences how she sees herself and her sexuality. "My lifestyle is changing drastically because . . . my knees are really giving out on me. I used to [exercise] a lot, and I think as a result of that I'm starting to feel old. Like the things I used to do to get the endorphins going I can't do as much anymore, and there are things I still am trying to keep in it, but I think it is having an effect on me. . . . I think it's making me feel older, and it probably is having an effect on how I feel about my sexuality."

Other studies have noted the conflation of sexuality and youth and the desexualization of older women (Carpenter, Nathanson, and Kim 2005; Furman 1997; Gott and Hinchliff 2003; Gullette 1997; Lichtenstein 2012; Montemurro and Gillen 2013b; Montemurro and Siefken 2013; Twigg 2004, 2007). For Paula and many of my interviewees over the age of forty, aging and menopause, as a continuing part of *self-discovery through embodied changes*, generally inhibited the development of sexual subjectivity. Some women felt less confident about showing their sexuality because they were aware of the judgment against doing so. Yet I want to emphasize that lack of sexual desire or sexual activity does not automatically correlate with a lack of sexual subjectivity. Sexual subjectivity is about feeling in control of one's body and sexual decision making. Several women in their sixties told me that they are celibate and content. They do not imagine a sexual future but believe their lives are full and rich or satisfying without sexual intimacy. They are happy or at least comfortable with their bodies and their nonsexual relationships with family and friends. Some women who have considerably less sex than they did in their twenties or thirties also showed strong subjectivity. They felt sexually confident because, when they did have sex, it was intentional and meaningful. It became one of several ways to connect with a partner. As Penny, fifty-one and married, remarked, "I've gone through menopause. . . . The physical nature of it isn't there as much anymore. I would be just as happy lying on the couch with a blanket and a movie with him next to me. But it's not that I don't like [sex]—that I dislike it—it's fine. But I don't get the physical arousal anymore." Penny communicated the normality of the transition. The satisfaction of partnership allowed her to appreciate sex when she had it and her relationship more generally when she did not feel like having sex. A couple of women, particularly those who had never really shed their "sex is taboo or bad" stances, felt better about their disinterest in sex as they aged because a slower libido is consistent with sexual scripts for older women (Gott and Hinchliff 2003; Gullette 1997; Montemurro and Gillen 2013b; Twigg 2007).

MENOPAUSE

As women age, estrogen levels decrease and women begin to experience menopause, which can have acute effects on sexual organ functioning (Rosenthal 1987). Menopause follows the final menstrual cycle in a woman's life and can last up to one year (Daniluk 1998). Among western women it typically occurs during their forties or fifties (Dillaway 2012). A number of women in their late thirties and early forties told me they were experiencing perimenopause, when hormone levels fluctuate, causing symptoms such as hot flashes, depression, night sweats, or irritability as well as changes in menstrual cycles (Daniluk 1998). Although still menstruating, women were attuned to these early alerts of menopause.

For some, particularly those who felt vital and energetic in their early forties, the realization was devastating. Joan, age sixty-six, lamented, "Your whole focus from the time you're ten is that you can reproduce. And I remember when I was like about forty-four and I went to the doctor and he said, 'Oh, you're in perimenopause.' And I thought, 'Oh, my God, I'm dead.' . . . Yes, [the end of my reproductive cycle] was just a thrust to the heart." Nadia, at age forty, also felt something shift. "Right now I'm still in that—I'm still capable. . . . I still have a menstrual cycle and there's that feeling that you're still very much a woman. But when you start to go through the change it does put into question your sense of being a woman because you're no longer of childbearing [age]. And I think that that impacts how you view yourself." Menopause signals the end of fertility; and because women are socialized to see motherhood as an ultimate calling and source of identity (Rich 1976), some struggled to come to terms with this transition and felt less sexual (Dillaway 2012).

When Menopause Stifles Sexual Subjectivity

Menopause was a turning point for many women (see also Daniluk 1998) because, like no other experience since first menstruation, it dramatically marked a stage in life. Many of the menopausal and postmenopausal women with whom I spoke were saddened by the passing of their youth and their status as sexually desirable or viable women. Although they often remarked that menopause was natural and accepted the transition, they still saw "the glass as half empty" rather than half full. For example, while Jeanne, age sixty-six, remains interested in and enjoys sex with her husband, menopause has made her aware of her age and how part of her sexual life has changed. "I guess I've had a pretty long run with that. . . . I guess in my fifties . . . I realized that with menopause you've kind of hit the end of some road. I mean, it's not that I became uncomfortable but you realize that that ain't where it's at so much anymore. And so I guess it was up and then a peak and then sort of a slow slide."

Most of the women experienced menopause in their fifties or sixties, though a number did experience it earlier after hysterectomies. While most women discussed a decrease in sex drive or the cessation of spontaneous sex, others noted a sense of freedom associated with not having to worry about menstruation. A few even said menopause did not affect their sexuality at all.

Angela, age sixty-two, who had a hysterectomy in her forties that induced early menopause, said, "If you're going through menopause and you're having hot flashes, you could care less about some guy hitting on you, like 'Get that thing away from me.' You're not interested because your body is undergoing so many changes you don't know where you are. . . . I couldn't wait until it was over [*laughs*]. Oh, it was horrible! It was the worst time in my life." In her forties, during the worst parts of menopause, Angela had no interest in sex. And because her husband is older and has had health problems, there has been little rejuvenation of their sex life since.

Faith, age fifty-two, is married, with one child in college and another soon to be. Noting that she is in the early stages of the transition, she said she finds it difficult to balance her yearnings with her body's stalled physical response. "Just the fact that you may have the desire mentally but physically your body is not cooperating as much as you'd like. You have to—it may require more foreplay, it may require lubrication, things that you didn't need when you were young and you can't—I tell my husband I'd love to be able to be turned on like this, but physically your hormones aren't letting you. It doesn't go that way anymore. And it's frustrating."

Miriam, age sixty-one, a mother with older kids, remarried in her fifties. She felt disappointed about her diminished desire when menopause began.

> I wanted to have more interest 'cause it was fun and it was nurturing and it was a connecting. And yet I was sort of "take it or leave it." And then all the physical things, too. . . . In my twenties I would just be dripping with hormone goop. And then you see these ads for people who need lubricants and stuff like that. That was me, so that was sort of not so much fun. I'm not interested in feeling sexual, I don't think . . . It used to be that I would be very attention getting, and I realized as I got older that that was a big part of how I assumed things would always be, okay? And . . . there was a time when I realized, "Gee, that's not happening anymore."

Dawn, age fifty-four, pointed out that having to plan and be prepared for sex makes it a different experience. "Things change. You have to use lubricant and you're drier, and it's like a pain. You just feel kind of like, like it's a—not a chore, I was going to say, 'Chore,' and then I would feel bad. It becomes more tedious. It's not as natural. It's not as easy because you have to actually think about it." Spontaneity is something many women liked about sex in their experimental years; and Dawn, Miriam, and Faith all told me that they wished they were now more easily or naturally aroused. Although motherhood constrained impulsive sex for many women, their bodies still responded physically when aroused. When sex was not natural or required effort and forethought, that necessary attention almost ruined the mood.

When Menopause Enhances Sexual Subjectivity

For some women menopause inspired self-acceptance. As Heather Dillaway (2012) found, reproductive histories affected perception of menopause and allowed some women who never had children freedom from anxiety or guilt about not being mothers. Georgia, a fifty-two-year-old woman who remained emotionally disconnected from her sexuality because she had been molested by her former stepfather, had grappled with many issues associated with her body and sexuality throughout her life. Reproduction was a major one, and "I think that in a way [menopause] gets me off the fence. . . . I did this whole dance, I think, through a lot of my adult life about children, not children, and it's like okay, that is removed now. It's like okay, whatever it is I feel about it."

Throughout her adolescence Georgia had felt helpless and lacked control over her body. She did not decide when to become sexually active: her first experience was molestation. As I discussed in chapter 3, Georgia did not know her stepfather had impregnated her until she was taken on a surprise trip to an abortion clinic. Consequently, it was difficult for her to make decisions about her body or her sexuality because she had never developed a sense of subjectivity. Her body always felt more like an object that others acted on or controlled. The experience of menopause as a natural transition gave one of her very first feelings of control. Although other women lamented their inability to become aroused naturally, menopause and aging liberated Georgia from making a major decision and led her to accept herself as a child-free woman. With fewer consequential decisions, she began to feel empowered.

I think that what you can get as you get older is more in touch with who you are and what makes you happy, what pleases you. I think that earlier it's easy to get caught up in what pleases the other person, that it becomes wanting to be pleasing as opposed to actually being aware of pleasing yourself in some way.

So I think that as we get older you maybe have a chance to be more in touch with how you're feeling about all of this, which is a kind of cool thing. . . . So then it becomes more of a choice. And maybe that takes pressure off of it: I can either choose to do this or I can choose [not] to do this. . . . As you get older I think that the choice becomes more like you really do make a choice here.

Georgia developed greater sexual subjectivity when she no longer felt burdened by expectations for a sex life or sexual desire. After she passed through menopause and could no longer become pregnant, she did not have to think about doing something that had never felt right for her.

A few other women, notably those past the stage of daily hot flashes and night sweats, described menopause as freeing. Shannon, age sixty-four, declared that menopause was "underrated," explaining that it had allowed her to feel more rational and less influenced by hormones. She commented, "I think it's wonderful. . . . I think women in menopause can really enjoy their sexuality more." Shannon said that she no longer felt lustful, which gave her a greater sense of control over her sexuality and sexual decision making. She could have less sex or choose to have sex because she felt like it. She also felt less dependent on her husband, which she saw as a positive change. Married for forty years, her sex life had had ups and downs, most recently with the discovery of her husband's infidelity. Angry with him and uncomfortable about masturbation, she had felt both emotionally and sexually frustrated during the aftermath of his affair. So she welcomed menopause because she believed it allowed her to respond to her husband rationally and it reduced her sexual desire.

Alice, age fifty-five, also appreciated menopause because it provided "freedom from like raging hormones [*laughs*] which really is sort of hard!" Alice started menopause after her divorce. Once she was out of that relationship and involved in a new, highly sexual one, she spent some time feeling "out of control" and hypersexual. Menopause, she believed, helped her to scale back her sexual urges and, in her mind, act more sensibly. Women are socialized to rein in their sexual desires, and they learn that expressing lust or showing their sexuality is a bad thing (Tanenbaum 2000; Tolman 2002). In this context, both Alice and Shannon appreciated their decreased desire and liked controlling their bodies rather than being controlled by them. Thus, menopause enhanced their sexual subjectivity because they felt greater power over their libidos.

A number of women in their fifties and sixties noted that dating after menopause allowed them to feel more sexual. Although their bodies did not always respond and they sometimes needed lubricant, the fact that they never had to think about pregnancy or menstruation made them feel more spontaneous. Debra, age fifty-nine, who recently ended a long-term relationship, made this point: "It's a little bit freeing, actually, because you don't deal with the mess and bother of having a period. You know, what if you're going on a date and you're gonna have sex and you have your period and is this guy gonna be thinking about that and you're gonna have to say no." Leslie, age sixty, white, and divorced, also noted benefits of being menopausal and dating. "When I was fifty I was dating a guy who was twelve years younger and let me tell you, there were some advantages to that. . . . Even though I was just at the end of my periods, [now] there was always . . . 'oh, my God, I don't have to worry about getting pregnant.' . . . So there's always that sort of 'wow, we don't have to think about that all the time,' especially if you're in a committed and monogamous relationship when both people are not having extra activity, that you feel comfortable with that."

Women who were dating or single were least likely to communicate a sense of decreased desire during or following menopause. Perhaps the excitement of new sexual partners or spontaneous sex facilitated arousal. For example, Iris, age fifty-eight and single, "was going through menopause in [her] last relationship, and it was kind of nice because while friends, girlfriends had told me, 'Oh, you get so dry and all this stuff and sex is difficult,' I never had that happen to me. I was physiologically just the same as I ever was, and excited about sex . . . at the beginning of that relationship. And it was nice because there was no problem with birth control, so that was like not an issue, . . . so menopause has been good to me."

New sexual relationships are exciting and characterized by lust and fascination with one's partner (Kingsberg 2002). Thus, relationship status can influence women's perception of the impact of menopause (Dillaway 2012). Women in my study who were divorced, dating, or in new relationships were more likely to view menopause positively because it enabled them to enjoy sex and not worry about pregnancy prevention (Gott and Hinchliff 2003). Paige, age sixty-four, remarried in her fifties. She said that although her physiological response is not the same as it was, being in a newer relationship minimizes the emotional consequences of this transition. "Menopause kicks in and even though you want to be sexual and there's something that says, 'Okay, physically it's not going to work the way it used to work.' So then you have to start using enhancements like lubricants and things like that to feel sexual that way, physically sexy. But I still felt.... I was still in my honeymoon—[my friend] always says, I'm still on my honeymoon, kind of thing. So for us, I felt really good. Also, I had a partner who made me feel really good." Although sex was not as impulsive as it once was, Paige used tools to make it work, which gave her control over her body in a new way. Motivated by a new partner and a desire to maintain their sexual connection, she learned more about her body and her desire. Menopause did not impede her sexual subjectivity but inspired her to think about and cultivate her sexuality in a new way.

In contrast, a number of women who had been married for longer periods of time mentioned that their relationships were already far from "hot and heavy." For them, menopause did not have much of an impact on their sexuality. Celeste, age fifty-eight, commented that when she went through menopause, she was in a long-term relationship in which the lust had waned. "I didn't have that desire the way I did in prior years. And like I think you just—when you're with someone, when you're with the same partner for years, at that point it was twenty-five or so years, then you don't have that steady passion." Other research corroborates decline in passion, activity, and desire over time (Das, Waite, and Laumann 2012; Edwards and Booth 1994; Waite et al. 2009). Like Celeste, most of the women in my study expected to feel less interested in sex as they aged and experienced menopause. Given our lack of sexual scripts for women older than forty, most of them had normalized the waning of desire.

AGING

More women described the physical aging process as one of transformation and self-discovery (Kingsberg 2002). Erika, age sixty-two, told me,

> I think that ... in your twenties and thirties you have this puzzle called sexuality, and it's got different pieces to it—the way you were brought up, the influence of your parents, and other things. But there's this big piece of the puzzle that's sexual activity. I think that the pieces of the puzzle are all still there as you go through life—it's just that they take on different shapes and sizes, so

in the fifties and sixties all the pieces are there. If you throw in nurturing to a female's sexuality, maybe the nurturing piece of the puzzle gets bigger in the fifties and sixties, and the sexual activity or the desire for sexual activity is— the piece is still there but it's not this huge hulking piece that was there earlier.

As Erika so eloquently said, women assemble the puzzle of their sexuality throughout their lives, influenced by socialization, experience, and consequent personal growth. Laura Carpenter and John DeLamater (2012) have suggested that these pieces can yield advantages or disadvantages in subsequent experiences. Cultural scenarios from certain generations or a national culture influence intrapsychic scripts, which affect interpersonal scripts and interactions (Plummer 2010; Schalet 2011; Simon and Gagnon 1984; Waite et al. 2009). Women learn that the older they get, the further they are from societal ideals of conventional desirability. They must process and accept this transformation and develop a broader, more complex sexuality than the one encouraged in their youth, one that is *not* wholly focused on physical appearance. Among the women I interviewed, the aging process sometimes enhanced sexual subjectivity when they learned to accept their bodies or when years of experience made them feel as if they had mastered sexual pleasure. In other cases, aging diminished sexual agency when women felt insecure about their desirability, given the correlation between youth and sexual appeal (Furman 1997; Gullete 1997; Montemurro and Gillen 2013b; Twigg 2007).

Although women in their twenties and thirties acknowledged the expectation that desire and desirability decrease with age, only a few expressed concern about aging and their sexuality. Women in their thirties were more focused on motherhood and marriage or dating and were still in a process of sexual beginnings. A number of women in their forties, however, reflected on feeling older and noticing changed bodies, beyond those associated with perimenopause. Kristen, age forty-one, a remarried, stay-at-home mother of teenagers, observed, "Women really are very much more interested in the . . . physicality of sex during their thirties. . . . I was so happy through my fortieth year that . . . nothing changed. And now, it's the end of forty-one and I'm going, 'Hmm, yeah, now I know it's important.' So I don't know, it doesn't feel—it's more mental now—like I have to think about it and I have to remember not to let too much time go by. Where in my thirties it was the physical taking over and you didn't let too much time go by." Although she hadn't yet experienced any signs of menopause, Kristen attributed her lack of passion to both hormones and habituation. In her thirties, physical desire had spurred sex. In her forties, she makes an effort to do it, not because she necessarily feels aroused but because she recognizes its importance in her marriage.

Celeste, age fifty-eight, who went through menopause as her marriage was ending, now recently separated and dating, felt perplexed about her sexuality, given her perception that older women are not supposed to be sexual. At times, she said, she needs to talk herself into feeling sexual because cultural scenarios influence her intrapsychic scripts about sexuality and age. "I think sometimes you think, 'Well, that's—I can't do that anymore. I can't have these kinds of feelings because I am past my prime.' Like you kind of talk yourself into it." Although age made Celeste question her sexual expression, it also allowed her to realize that arousal is partly mental and under her control. "I think that sex, a lot of sex is in your mind, in your head. And you're gonna, like if you talk yourself into the fact that you're gonna be feeling turned on, then you're more likely to be turned on than the opposite. If your mind is wandering and you're not concentrating on things and you just don't feel connected in a sexual nature or relationship, then I think that has its effect."

When I spoke to her, Celeste had already gone through self-discovery and new sexual experiences after her divorce. This made her less likely than other women to be deterred by lack of arousal. Instead, she recognized that her mental state can change this when the conditions are right. Like Kristen, she may not feel desire, but she knows how to induce it. It is likely that hormonal shifts are also partly responsible for Celeste's slower sexual response. As Sheryl Kingsberg (2002) has suggested, once aroused, older women experience desire, but they may need more stimulus, seduction, or, like Celeste and Kristen, mindful decision making to reach that state. In other words, for many postmenopausal women "desire *follows* arousal" (434).

Several women in their sixties or late fifties experienced little change in their penchant for sex, which surprised them, most likely because of the ways in which cultural scenarios influence intrapsychic scripts. Regina, age sixty-two and divorced, told me about having recently been turned on. "Well, you do get shocked when you, especially if you don't use something, it's like 'Oh, okay.' So I knew that in the old shower it was like 'Ohhh, okay.' [*laughs*] . . . So it's still there." Sandra, age fifty-eight and married, said she had expected that she would be "over" sex by this point in her life. "It's surprising to me that I am so interested because . . . I would have thought that fifty, which I thought would have been menopause, would have been the end of it. I did not expect—I heard people say, women say, that after menopause you get another surge and then you have that freedom because you're not worrying about periods. . . . So I would not have expected myself to be worried about sex at this point." Because sexual activity decreases for most women as they age, and there is little public recognition of older women's sexuality, Sandra and Regina believed they would follow the same pattern. But both still had strong physical urges and sought sexual gratification either through masturbation or partnered sex. Recent publications about sexual activity for women over age sixty-five suggest that, though they may be in the minority, these two women are far from alone in their desire and probably have many years of sex ahead of them (Fisher 2010; Gott and Hinchliff 2003; Kingsberg 2002; Loe 2004b; Meadows 1997; Schwartz 2007; Waite 2010; Waite et al. 2009).

Defined by Desirability

By and large, my interviewees were well aware of older women's desexualization. Several raised questions about the appropriateness of sexual expression among older women and whether they could, should, or would feel sexual after the age of fifty (or forty, for some) (Montemurro and Gillen 2013a, 2013b). Because youth and desirability are culturally linked, women felt desire decrease when they felt less physically attractive and wondered what that meant as far as their own sexuality. Joyce, age fifty-seven, said,

> I'd have to say later in my forties my sexuality started to wane. . . . [I have] a relationship that's sort of comfortable, we do the same things, we know each other and we don't have to—I don't have to feel needed or I don't need somebody. I don't need to have sex every night to feel desirable, I assume my husband loves me and whatever. . . . And so I think that starting in my late forties my sexual drive started going down and I'm getting older so I feel less, well, I wouldn't say less desirable, I feel less attractive. And I guess all of us to a certain extent, whether we're happily married or not, would like to seem attractive to other people . . . and when you begin to feel that no matter what you do you can't be attractive, I think that deadens some things.

Joyce's assessment of aging and allure illuminates the role that physical appearance plays in women's sexuality. Their sexual body image influences their sexual desire and their perception of their desirability (Montemurro and Gillen 2013b). Joyce spoke at length about self-acceptance and the comfort of her marriage, both of which certainly enhanced her sexual subjectivity. Yet she also acknowledged the critical role of feeling visually appealing. Like most of the other women with whom I spoke, she did not feel desire when she did not feel attractive.

In Charles Horton Cooley's (1964) concept of the looking-glass self, individuals imagine themselves through the eyes of others. The image they see in the mirror is not simply a reflection; rather, they see themselves as they perceive others see them. Women such as Joyce, who know how older women are viewed in American society, thus have a hard time feeling attractive when their appearance deviates from convention. As Margaret Gullette (1997) has noted, culture ages us as much as biology does—perhaps even more so. How women are viewed in a culture has great influence on how they view themselves. Because North American culture has very few images of sexually appealing older women, Joyce and her peers have difficulty seeing themselves that way.

Gail, age sixty-five, white, and married, made a similar observation. "When you get into your sixties there is the component of 'I'm not an attractive woman anymore. I am aging.' And there's an awkwardness in it because you don't know whether someone is responding to you because you're attractive or you're not. . . . You don't have that security of who you are physically anymore 'cause it's changed." Several women in their sixties and even a few in their fifties spoke of this awkwardness in interactions that used to be sexually charged. A number used the word *invisible* when describing encounters in public—a feeling that no one reacts to them as *women* anymore—and other studies of aging women reveal similar sentiments (Furman 1997; Twigg 2004). Because women are socialized to tie identity to looks, older women need to discern who they are internally and externally in a new way. Feeling less attractive may inhibit sexual confidence; but when women feel less appealing to others they may ponder their identity as women. As Gail told me, they must figure out who they are beyond appearance and accept biological changes. Thus, aging may inspire self-discovery beyond the physical.

Older women in my study were likely to believe that a partner's lack of sexual interest was either a response to aging and declining attractiveness or a sign of infidelity. Sandra, age fifty-eight, had maintained a strong and active sexual relationship throughout her marriage, with peaks and valleys following the birth of her children. However, once her children became teenagers, she worried that her husband was not interested in seizing their long-awaited opportunity for intimacy.

> Our sexual relationship has just died, and I can't figure out why. So I talked to his doctor and his doctor said physically there's nothing wrong with him, and if there is, we can fix it. . . . And so I'm thinking—I told him just this morning that I was not satisfied with our lack of sexual relationship. . . . It was always very vigorous, it was very frequent. And then I'm like "What happened to you? I was afraid it was gonna happen to me, but what happened to you?" And he does not like to talk about it. . . . So what do I see? Right now I see a very boring future. I see me on my way to some device store, which I may really do. . . . I feel like I'm not gonna live as long as I want to because I also feel that sex is part of a healthy life. I feel that I'm definitely not gonna be as happy as I would be.

Sexually frustrated, Sandra felt rejected by her husband and questioned her appeal. She wanted to have sex and did not know how to change things in her relationship.

The usual stereotypes portray women rebuffing their husbands' sexual advances, but many women suggested it was the other way around. Although they maintained sexual desire, despite the distractions of parenthood or career, their husbands did not. But Sandra seemed to lack sexual agency. She told me she imagined she would eventually use a "device" for sexual gratification, yet she had not brought herself to take that step. Taboos about the use of vibrators and masturbation, particularly for women in relationships, inhibit many from seeking sexual pleasure independently (Rutter and Schwartz 2012; Waskul, Vannini, and Wiesen 2007). In my study, unpartnered women in their late fifties or sixties tended to speak most often and frankly about masturbation, in stark contrast to married women in their sixties, who rarely mentioned it, even when they were in celibate relationships. Given their age, generation, and taboos about sex generally, I believe that few of these married women have ever engaged in self-gratification or considered sources of sexual satisfaction beyond intercourse.

Physical Changes: Hers and His

Bodies age, and sex is complicated by bad knees, aching joints, impotence, and fatigue, among other conditions. Connie, age sixty-four and in a long-term relationship, explained, "You develop arthritis, you get a little less flexible. There are things that definitely impact on it. . . . Just the sheer physicality of the sexual act and partaking of it, yeah, you go, 'Wait a second, that hurts,' you know, 'Can't do that.' The neck doesn't want to bend that way anymore." Some women were deterred by these changes and gave up on sex, but others, including Connie, simply readjusted their expectations and practices.

And although many women in their sixties complained of vaginal dry-ness or hormonal changes associated with menopause, very few mentioned other physical problems of their own that interfered with sex. Far more often, partners' issues derailed sexual adventures, as other studies have noted (Ellison 2000; Waite et al. 2009; Waite 2010). When talking about sex in her sixties, Angela, age sixty-two, said, "[My friends and I] sit around and joke about it. . . . 'Oh, yeah, well, it's there but we don't use it anymore.' . . . The ability and the desire [are] there, but sometimes Mr. Happy doesn't work." Carol Rinkleib Ellison (2000) reported a similar situation in her research on women's sexuality, noting that some women desired more sex than their partners did and that a group of women between the ages of forty and sixty complained of sexual dissatisfaction due to partners' performance issues and disinterest in sex. Linda Waite and her colleagues (2009) found that approximately 63 percent of women between the ages of fifty-seven and seventy-four cited a partner's health problems as explanation for sexual inactivity, compared with only about 25 percent of men.

Several women in my study mentioned that a husband's chronic illness or heart trouble had led them to accept celibacy. When Wanda, age sixty-four and married, called in response to the flier I had posted at a senior citizens' center, she wanted to make certain that I was open to speaking with sexu-ally inactive women. After I assured her that I was, we soon met at her cozy home in a rural riverfront town. I noticed that she had difficulty walking, which she said was due to injuries from a car accident in her fifties. When I asked about the current importance of sex in her life, she replied, "I guess I do have a sense of my sexuality, but it's like I'm sixty-four, what is there to be sexual about? There's like no conquests, no one to impress, no one to—I think in that equation, too, is both my husband and I are disabled, so that goes into part of the equation. We've had our children, yeah, so it's sort of a—you think about it and you hear about people having sex at our age so it's like—there's a curiosity but then it's 'Oh, what the hell.'"

Wanda's lack of interest in sex was both biological and cultural. Certainly she and her husband had physical limitations that made intercourse difficult, but cultural barriers also impeded her sexual interest. In the question "What is there to be sexual about?" we can hear the influence of cultural scenarios about asexuality and old age on her intrapsychic sexual scripts. Although most interviewees in their sixties told me they were both sexually active and interested, Wanda could not imagine or understand their motivation.

Wanda told me that she had lived a full life and had enjoyed her "femininity" in her youth. Before committing to marriage, she made the decision to date one hundred men. Though "dating" implied dancing or flirting rather than sex, she wanted to have a lot of experience and interactions before settling down. Yet she did not believe in premarital sex and held fast to that rule as a way of reining in her sexual feelings. "I was restrained. I always thought when I went out with a guy and I thought about having sex, I'd say, 'Do I want to spend the rest of my life with this guy?' Because that's the way my feelings were." Like many others in my study, Wanda was disappointed by her early sexual experiences; and after she married, her main focus was having and caring for her children. In her thirties and forties, she was "exhausted raising those two. So by that time sex was really slowing down. And the husband is tired and the wife is tired, so, yeah, it changes then. For me, it changed." By her fifties, "I was sick of sex . . . It was sort of disgusting [*laughs*], for me. I had friends having affairs. I wondered, 'How the hell do they do it?'" Although Wanda set limits and felt in control of sexual decision making, sex was never a priority for her; so as she aged and other issues interfered, she accepted celibacy. In fact, however, her husband, who needed assistance to walk and took medication for several ailments, would not have been able to have sex even if Wanda had wanted to.

Some women in my study would have liked to remain sexually active but found emotional relationships more important than physical ones. Harriet, age sixty-eight, married her second husband when she was in her early fifties. Several years into their marriage, he developed prostate cancer, which ultimately rendered him impotent. Timidly, she confided, "The operation didn't go well. So I love him dearly, we love each other, but there's not the sex part. But I wouldn't trade him for the world. So that's where sexuality gets to be so different in your—it all depends on what happened to you in life. And I wouldn't cheat on him, nothing, we're very compatible." Harriet had had a long journey to reach this relationship. She was young when she first married, after she unexpectedly became pregnant, and was unhappy throughout most of that twenty-three-year relationship. Her husband was emotionally unavailable, so she focused on her children. After a while, she became dissatisfied with her husband's distance and their lack of compatibility and began a fifteen-year affair with a man who was also married. That relationship was very sexual. Harriet said it was like going "from one extreme to another." Although she divorced during the affair, she and her paramour also eventually broke up. However, when she met her current husband, she knew she had finally found a partner who respected her and was committed to her. Even after they could no longer have intercourse, she readily traded physical intimacy for companionship. While most of my interviewees in their twenties and thirties could not conceive of staying in a relationship in which they could not have intercourse, most long-married women could not conceive of leaving one for that reason. As Merryn Gott and Sharron Hinchliff (2003) have also found, long-term relationships provide a foundation for emotional support that makes declines in sexual frequency less problematic.

Changes in men's bodies affect heterosexual women's sexuality because these women largely define it through relationships (Holland and Eisenhart 1990; Kingsberg 2002). Although sex may remain important to women such as Harriet, they accept its absence because they value partnership more than sex. The joke that older married women are not interested in sex may be a myth constructed in part to disguise the fact that men's sexual problems seem to contribute so greatly to a couple's decrease in sexual activity and desire. In other words, older women's lack of desire or sexual activity may be a reaction to men's reduced libido or sexual functioning rather than a sign of frigidity or aging (Deeks and McCabe 2001; Gott and Hinchliff 2003; Kingsberg 2002).

Masculinity is defined clearly and specifically by both sexual performance and tacit support of sexual scripts that link men's power to sexual virility (Bordo 2000; Loe 2004a). Interestingly, however, men's sexual problems may lead women to learn more about their own desire, acknowledge the existence of desire whether or not they are pursued, or experience satisfaction using other means of intimacy. Nonetheless, some of the women in my study were frustrated. Joan, age sixty-six, single, and dating, lamented both older men's performance problems and their delicate sexual egos.

"When men have sexual dysfunction, it's always your fault and that's still the way they feel or at least say. And who wants to be put in that predicament?"

I asked, "What might a man say? Like, that the woman wasn't turning him on enough or something like that?"

She responded, "Yes. [He might say,] 'This never happens to me, it must be you.' I mean they say that!"

Rose, also single in her sixties, told me that she has trouble relating to men of her own age because they seem so much older. Though she said she does not have the energy of her youth, she finds that men have more stamina problems than women do. "There's a quote that says the spirit is willing but the flesh is weak. I don't think there would be many men my age that could go all night—two or three times a night. I doubt that."

Most women spoke of the limitations associated with the physical aspects of aging. Yet a couple of them strongly felt that the ways in which their bodies had changed, in concert with emotional changes and experience, had allowed them to reach unprecedented heights of physical pleasure. Joan, for instance, was finding sexual satisfaction in her sixties. Although she noted that partnered sex is hard to come by, she was amazed by the power of her body. After many years of confusing and disappointing sexual experiences, she said, she now accepts herself and finds self-gratification as satisfying as partnered sex.

> I think it took probably until my fifties to figure out how to get to a really good orgasm. Can we talk? [leans toward me] . . . I'll tell you how it happened. My friend and I were in a yoga class and it was a fabulous yoga class and at the end, you know, you do the meditation part and, um, the chakras opened up—have you had this experience? Oh, my God, you must try it. All the chakras opened up and I thought, 'Oh, my God!' I've talked about this with other women and it wasn't just me. And so it has to do with this thing rather than a male penis and oh, my God, but believe me, oh my God! So, and my friend, so I looked at her and . . . I had tears running down my face, I said, as soon as we got out of there, "We have to talk! What was that?" Then when you're intimate you can see—the combination of the two that the chakras opening up and that mind-blowing kind of orgasm. Oh, my God! Yes. . . . And so then in the past, like it was, like never enough and that was because it wasn't right that it was never enough. If it had been, it would have been, once would be good! Once would be fine! But always the need to try to get to that place that you never got

to and then once you figured it out for yourself, and this is what I want to tell like other women—and then I do tell women all the time, and tell eventually my granddaughter and stuff, don't go to any stupid parties and blow off some guy—yuck—no. Because that is—there's nothing for you in that and that feeling of well-being that you get from an orgasm that oxytocin kind of glow and stuff is just—it's worth it if you can get there and there's ways of doing that without debasing yourself.

Joan exemplifies the power of self-discovery. As she explored the physical abilities of her body through yoga and meditation, she began to feel more in touch with it, more centered, and more aware of herself. This enabled her to relax and climax in a way that had never been possible during partnered sex, when her focus had always been on pleasing someone else. Joan's experience changed not only her understanding of her body but also her outlook on sex as a woman in her sixties. Rather than believing that her sex life was over or hopeless without a partner, these physical experiences led her to discover a new dimension of both her sexuality and herself and made her feel powerful and in control.

Less Sex, More Satisfaction

As I have already discussed, for many women, relationships provide comfort and assurance. When they feel loved and validated, they are usually more at ease with their sexuality, their desire, and their desirability. Although habituation is related to decline in sexual frequency (Edwards and Booth 1994; Rutter and Schwartz 2012), it does not necessarily indicate sexual dissatisfaction. Women told me that being in long-term relationships led them to reprioritize sexual intimacy or the frequency of sex. Having a reliable, supportive partner was what long-married women said that they valued most. Most suggested that, over time, sex became less important because the pair had developed many ways to show their love for one another. Even as women in these partnerships aged and lost sexual stamina or desire, they remained generally content because they did not rely on sex to demonstrate commitment or affection.

Dawn, age fifty-four and married for thirty-two years, noted the naturalness of this transition and her acceptance of it.

> I think . . . aging has changed [sex]. We used to be a lot more sexually active than we are now. But I don't see that as a bad thing necessarily. It's just we're older, it's

like you get tired at eight o'clock. It's just, that's just life. And I think that he and I both feel comfortable with that. . . . Because we've been married so long, . . . it's not just about sex. It's about closeness more, I think. And I think the older you get, that becomes, for me it becomes, a realization that it's not just sex, it's living in the same space and sharing, and it's a lot more than sex.

Aging has given Dawn perspective. She still enjoys sex and feels attracted and attractive to her husband, yet simply being together is satisfying enough.

Faith, also in her fifties and married for almost thirty years, expressed a similar attitude.

I think when you're younger it's much more important, you feel like it's more at the forefront of the relationship. Whereas as you get older, you value the other parts of your relationship more. You value the quality of your friendship, being able to rely on somebody else, [knowing that] somebody else will provide you [with] emotional support. I think there are so many more difficult situations that happen when you're older—the illnesses or operations or people dying or the problems with your kids are so much bigger, and you value that connection you have with somebody else who's willing to go through all that crap with you. And I think that's what being in a long-term loving relationship is: the willingness to go through all that.

Both Dawn and Faith had developed sexual subjectivity within satisfying long-term relationships, thanks in part to the sexual experience, affirmation, and encouragement of their partners. They and many long-married women in their fifties and sixties told me that they felt confident about their sexuality because they rarely had occasion to question it. They knew their husbands loved and appreciated them, which mattered more to them than lust or having sex less often than some of their divorced or remarried peers were.

The Wisdom of Maturity

Some women made explicit connections among aging, long-term relationships, and self-confidence. Heather, a forty-six-year-old married woman, noted,

I've grown as a person. I think sexual satisfaction when you're young, it's thought of more in a very physical sense. You know, the ultimate physical experience will give you this great satisfaction, and that has to do with a stage, if it's a relationship that's moving forward. When you're young, you don't have all those other depths of a relationship. When you have time with someone or history, . . . we have so much to talk about and I think that adds a dimension [to] things. When you're young, your life experiences are less, you don't have as much to talk about or as much to draw from. And when you're older, even if you haven't had those tumultuous experiences with the same person, you've gone through financial struggles, health struggles, you know, different things, jobs, all that kind of thing. And those things are sort of a big part of your level of satisfaction in the relationship, how you've weathered those things.

Several other women in their forties agreed that aging could inspire reflection and sexual self-discovery. The process enhanced their sexual subjectivity because, as with menopause, they were reevaluating the priority of physical intimacy or were reminded of the importance of sex in their lives. Although Robin, age forty-eight and married, does not see herself as a sexual person, she told me that how she thinks about sex and its role in her marriage have changed as she has matured. When I asked if she thought sex was more meaningful to women in their twenties or thirties than to those in their fifties or sixties, she (like most women over forty) said no.

I think it means more to them in their fifties and sixties. As far as like I'm concerned, I'm learning more about my own self because you can—you can concentrate. Back then I just think it's like, . . . I don't even think they really know what they're doing. But when you're at this age, you're learning more about your body and stuff. . . . I just think it's more—it's the importance of it, I think, that changes. . . . You realize it's not gonna be here forever, and I think you dwell on it being very important and you make special time because you can be here today and gone tomorrow. . . . I just think it's getting better, it just gets better. You grow with each other more, you know what the other one wants, you know what he likes, and I just think it gets better after the kids are grown.

Because most of her children were now out of the house, Robin and her husband had more opportunities to have sex with fewer distractions or interruptions. Moreover, she prioritized reconnecting with her husband, focusing on their relationship as husband and wife, not mother and father, in a way that allowed her to learn more about her body and sexual pleasure.

Sex also became more important to Robin because she recognized her mortality and the limitations of her body. At some point, in a future she can imagine, she will not be able to be sexually active, so her late forties are a time for action.

CUMULATIVE ADVANTAGES AND DISADVANTAGES ASSOCIATED WITH AGING AND MENOPAUSE

Aging stifled sexual subjectivity when women felt less desire and less desirable than they had at any other point in their lives. Such women had often grown up with negative stances on sex or had had few or bad sexual experiences, and many lacked validation of their desirability or affirmation of their desire. For other women, however (mostly those with more positive early stances on sex or who had learned self-acceptance through motherhood or relationship transitions), aging increased sexual subjectivity. These women better understand their bodies' functioning and thus felt more comfortable with their sexuality.

This is the one of the last stages I chart in the development of sexual subjectivity. Because the oldest woman I interviewed was sixty-eight, I do not know how positive experiences with menopause or self-acceptance might benefit women in their seventies and beyond. While studies find that interest in sex decreases with age, researchers are curious about a cohort effect among the baby-boom generation that may lead current generations of seniors to continue the adventurous and expansive sexual practices of their youth (Waite et al. 2009; Waite 2010). In other words, given our more liberal sexual climate and our greater attention to health- and age-related sexual problems, we may discover additional advantages beyond self-acceptance.

9 ❻ SELF-ACCEPTANCE
Staying Sexual Subjects

In the forties I was claiming it. In the fifties I owned it. . . . I never had a better time in my life than I had in my fifties—except I'm hoping that I'll be able to say it about my sixties. . . . I worked to avoid committed relationships in my fifties, which was different for me. But it's like I don't want an everyday person, I just don't want that. I want to be my own person. It was totally liberating. I was fifty years old, I cut off all my hair, I dyed it blond, and I said I'm just gonna start the next half of my life in a completely different way than I had lived the first half. That's what I did. I started to date younger men. I started to date men of different races. I just had a whole attitude shift at fifty that had a lot to do with "who cares?" I don't care what anybody else thinks, and if they care about what I'm doing, that's their problem. I'm really good with all of this.

—Delia, age sixty

Delia, a writer, welcomed me into her cozy home, which was located in a busy suburban area. Now sixty years old, she has been married twice, and several other relationships have also contributed to her understanding of her sexuality and her peace with it. In chapter 4, I described how her relationship with her first husband inspired self-confidence when he genuinely expressed interest in her sexual satisfaction and encouraged her to strive for it. Through that exploration, she became more self-assured and aware of what she wanted, liked, and could do without.

During her childhood, Delia's open parents influenced her "sex is natural" stance. Coming of age during the sexual revolution also liberated her and helped her feel sexually secure.

I read *The Feminine Mystique* and I read *Fear of Flying*—and this [was] like hot off the presses, this was brand-new stuff back then. . . . I was very much in the mix of all of this, and quite aware of it. And so, yeah, it was a part of my life. . . . I remember being—I was a newlywed, and sitting down with a girlfriend flipping through the very first *Our Bodies, Ourselves,* and that was something I could not imagine my mother doing with her best girlfriend when she was in college. . . . Beyond the sexual freedom that birth control pills gave women, the ability to actually have this conversation about your body and to talk with another woman about it and to feel not embarrassed or like it was weird or shameful in some way was good.

Among Delia's peers in the countercultural movement, sexual self-discovery had become acceptable, and Delia had many beneficial experiences in her twenties and as she moved through midlife that helped her, in her words, "claim" the right to be sexual, to have desire. In those years she was still in the process of declaring her sexual entitlements, but in her fifties she embraced that desire and accepted herself accordingly.

Delia does not feel a steady partner is necessary for her to feel good about her sexuality. Unlike most of the women with whom I spoke, her sexuality is about *her,* not a relationship. She appreciates herself, has high self-worth, and no longer needs someone else to validate her desire. She has dated many men—younger men, white men, foreign men. She has stopped caring about how other people might judge her behavior and started acting decisively.

When I asked what changed for her during her fifties that allowed her to accept herself without prejudice, she said that she thinks that women in general, by virtue of the aging and maturity process and fewer caregiving responsibilities, can be more self-centered, which cultivates greater self-awareness.

I think that [women in their fifties] are at a place that allows them to focus more on themselves. And once they start to do that, if you really start to listen to your body and your head and what it's really saying and you respond to what you're listening to, you will find that you will get—I don't know, answers to questions you didn't even know you had. I just think that that's the time, in the late forties, mid-fifties, when women really are confident and comfortable and relaxed. And I also think they're less concerned about their bodies. . . . You stop obsessing about the fact that you don't have the hips and thighs of a supermodel. It's like "Okay, I never had 'em. I'm not gonna have them now. Get on with it." And I think that [when] you're less concerned about those sorts of things, it frees you up to feel what you're actually feeling as opposed to worrying about what you don't have. You start to appreciate what you do have. You may not have supermodel hips but you don't need hip replacement surgery, either. You have to shift the way you see things.

Having been in relationships with partners whose sex drives were incompatible with her own, Delia has also learned that sex is critical for her. "It is important to me and . . . it is a priority in my life and in any kind of relationship that I would have. It's not something that could go on the back burner. It's not something that it would be okay if it didn't happen. That was not acceptable for me. And I learned that and I accepted that that was just a part of who I was, that it was just in me, it had nothing to do with some kind of outside force, this is just the way that I felt about it."

Delia's experiences epitomize the final stage in the development of sexual subjectivity: *self-acceptance.* When women "shift the way [they] see things," start to appreciate rather than criticize their bodies, and recognize their capacity for sexual pleasure, they free themselves from constraints that limit desire. Desire no longer only precedes conventional desirability. Women cultivate it and feel alluring when they accept and take pride in their accomplishments, relationships, and selves. When women accept themselves, they, like Delia, confidently act in their own interest rather than focus on pleasing others.

Women have many pathways to self-acceptance. As in other stages, they can want or not want to have sex; the key is recognizing and being in touch with sexual needs and preferences and having the self-assurance to hold them fast. Although most of the women in my study who had reached this stage were in their fifties and sixties, a few younger women had also fully embraced their sexuality and desire. Thus, I look at the role of aging and accomplishments as key influences in inspiring sexual subjectivity.

As women age, they must deal with changing perceptions of what sexuality means and how it should be communicated. Many of my interviewees noted a shift from a need to display their sexuality to the creation of a sexuality that is more about themselves and their own satisfaction. When I asked women when in their lives they felt most comfortable with their sexuality, most said, "Right now." (The exception was mothers with young children.)

In the present, one has the benefit of hindsight, the wisdom gained from past experiences, and the advantage of having learned what does and does not work. Yet women in their fifties and sixties said, "Right now," with the most conviction. Older women had more years of experience and more familiarity with their bodies.

AGING, EXPERIENCE, AND SELF-ACCEPTANCE

Aging often yields emotional maturity, and with that maturity many women learn to accept their bodies as they never have before (Montemurro and Gillen 2013b). This self-acceptance inspires a kind of sexual confidence that most women reported they lacked in their early years. As Tiina Vares and colleagues (2007) also found in their study of "mid-later life" women in New Zealand, many of my interviewees said that sexual activity improves with age because they have begun to challenge the male sex-drive discourse (Fine 1998; Gavey, McPhillips, and Dougherty 2001). Women came to realize that they, too, deserved sexual pleasure. They also learned to stop focusing on how others viewed them and trying to live up to unrealistic media-driven standards. Finally, they were able to appreciate what their bodies had allowed them to do throughout their lives.

A few women under the age of forty were in the beginning stages of self-acceptance. Lila, a thirty-five-year-old Middle Eastern woman, explained that her attitudes had started to change over the past few years.

> I can't still figure out exactly what I like, but I know what I don't like and that kind of leads me to what I like sometimes. And that kind of creates more of a balance for me. So thirties, forties, you kind of know what you like a little better and then you know how to express exactly the sexuality you are look-ing for. . . . I think it's kind of when I got over my inhibitions that I had maybe when I was younger. . . . I'm more experienced, I know what I want. I kind of know what the other person might want and that makes it a better experience for me.

Lila was generally self-confident and did not worry about her sexual body image in the way that most other interviewees did or had. But as a bisexual woman, she knew that other people judged her. So when she got older and moved to the United States, which was considerably more liberal than her homeland had been, she became more comfortable with her personal sexuality. After a long hiatus, she was now in a serious relationship in which she had the opportunity and comfort of expressing herself and discovering and defining her desires.

Serena, age thirty-one and white, is in a committed relationship; and like Lila, she is moving toward self-acceptance. As a child, she was embarrassed by her early physical development and endured both sexual molestation and the weight of religious proscriptions about sex. But validation from her current partner and life in a large, liberal, northeastern city have helped her to feel good about her sexual proclivities and entitled to her own pleasure. "I care less and less each day about what other people think. I used to care a lot about what other people thought, and now I don't care as much." Her move from a conservative southwestern state was a key trigger for this changing attitude. In her hometown she had concealed her desires because she feared her parents would reject her and she would stand out as deviant. In her new home, exposure to many different kinds of people and cultural acceptance of variations in sexual expression have helped Serena make peace with her desires.

Both Serena and Lila found validation in committed relationships and liberal environments that helped them to accept themselves. Clearly, positive experiences during other phases in the development of sexual subjectivity—particularly *validation, affirmation, and encouragement; learning through doing;* and *self-discovery through relationship changes*—can bolster self-acceptance, which is the ultimate step in this process. For other women born after 1960, self-acceptance was tied more closely to physical appearance. As women age and their bodies change in ways that make them less and less able to look like mediated ideals of sexual desirability, some feel liberated because they no longer need to do the body work that once seemed compulsory. Heather, age forty-six, white, and married, spoke about this change.

I think, unfortunately, teenagers and extremely young adults are very affected by the media in terms of body image, and I think the more comfortable you are with your body—that occurs over time. I think my attitudes about myself over time, I mean I'm certainly not, physically speaking, the standard that the world would think is, you know, a beautiful person or a sexual person or someone that should be comfortable with themselves, but I am. And that comes over time and that has to do with a lot more facets of yourself than just your sexuality. . . . When I turned forty, I just didn't care what anybody thought. I care about what I think, and I don't let anybody's influence, anybody's opinion of me, change who I am. I'm very, very comfortable with who I am, and I'm not afraid to tell anybody that, and I don't take any crap from anybody about anything.

For Heather, loving herself and her body became easier over time. When she recognized that her value extends far beyond her looks or sexual worth, she stopped worrying about how others viewed her and decided her self-satisfaction was more important. As with other older women in my study, Heather's self-acceptance was not just *sexual* self-acceptance. Once she began to disregard others' views of her choices and focus on her own wishes, she grew more comfortable with who she is, and that includes her sexuality.

Lila, Serena, and Heather were unusual. Most of the women in their twenties, thirties, and forties had not yet reached self-acceptance. As I have discussed throughout this book, different life-course experiences can suppress sexual subjectivity; and as the GSLC model asserts, negative early experiences can produce cumulative disadvantages that make it difficult for women to feel sexually self-confident (Carpenter and DeLamater 2012). The self-assurance these three women displayed was far more common among women in their fifties and sixties. Such women talked about what they had been through and how aging had facilitated this transition. Regina, age sixty-two and single, laughed and declared, "Sixties is spicy! Sixty is 'I don't-give-a-damn-I-can-do-what-I-want,' you know? I've lived a life and whatever I feel I wanna do at this point, I can. . . . So there's a better sense of tranquility . . . that only comes with time."

Joyce, age fifty-seven and married, told me, "When I was younger, . . . sex was all about power, . . . a man's power over you. And part of my awakening in my thirties was that that's not true. And I don't know whether that's from my time or whether that's still now, that maybe when you're younger that you feel sort of that it's the man instigating, it's the man that has the power. And there's something about when you find out that you have power over yourself, . . . power over the relationship that is liberating." Sexual scripts and double standards reinforce men's dominance in sexual relationships and emphasize their sexual pleasure and satisfaction (see, for example, Gavey et al. 2001; Kiefer and Sanchez 2007; Martin 1996; Simon and Gagnon 2003). Thus, it was pivotal for Joyce to learn that this is not necessarily the way it has to be or even the way it actually is in relationships. Once she recognized her entitlement to desire and pleasure, she became more confident.

As Joyce aged, she learned to define her sexuality on her own terms, without pressure from media or other societal messages. When I asked her to discuss why women are more self-possessed as they age, she noted that they do not fear rejection as much because they learn they have value beyond their sexuality and that someone will appreciate this.

> I think once you get into your thirties today, and even in my time, that you begin to have, you begin to be in a place to say, "I don't need to have that guy look at me, I'm fine, and if I want to have a relationship with that guy I'll go over and ask him." And then forties, more so. I think forties, ... you can begin to get your life in a place where you're doing—you're again more in charge of the things you want to do. That you're gonna take a night class, that you're gonna do yoga, that you're not just like changing diapers and cooking dinner. Married or not married, you're again a little more maybe in charge of your desires and [can] say, "I don't want to do that," or "I do want to do that." [You can say,] "I can walk away from this relationship if I don't like how it's going," as opposed to saying, "Well, I can't walk away from this relationship unless I have somebody else." So I perceive women getting more powerful and more in charge of themselves as they get older, but I guess that would be in lots of things, not just sexuality

For Joyce, feeling confident comes from feeling authoritative, and authority is very much a part of sexual subjectivity. A subject acts on desire or holds back when lacking desire. As she pointed out, confidence in one's self-worth can come from many sources, not just from sexual experiences. When women are able to make space to cultivate their own interests and engage in activities beyond caring for others, they are more likely to feel self-assured in general and less obliged to always put the needs of others first. Self-possession yields self-acceptance. Women who recognize their value no longer feel the need to change for someone else or to remain preoccupied about others' views. The looking glass now reflects the actual woman, not the woman through the eyes of society (Cooley 1964). She develops her own lens, and this frees her to pursue her own happiness, sexually and beyond. In Joyce's words:

I can say, "I want to dress up as a, you know, as a nun before we go to bed because, darn it, that's what I feel like doing." And when you're younger, you say, "Oh, no, . . . he'll never call me back." So, yeah, I think that self-assuredness allows you to say basically, "This is how I want to be and this is what I want and, you know what, if you don't want to go down this path, I'm good with that. I'll wait until I find somebody that does." . . . I felt more powerful and self-assured in my thirties, that I began to come into my own and feel like—you know what?—I am a person who people like and who people would think was attractive.

Women in their fifties and sixties, both in and out of relationships, repeated this theme of self-acceptance, of recognizing a value that extends far beyond what a woman can do for someone else or how attractive or sexually appealing she is. Leigh, age sixty-five, commented, "Women in their sixties can be, depending on where they are in their heads, they can feel free, they can feel accomplished, they can feel it's time for me. I can now do whatever I want to do. I can exercise and I can bike-ride and I can hike and I can do whatever I want to do. So I think the sexuality is based on an accomplishment of a long time." For Leigh, her decade signifies freedom. As Joyce remarked, younger women are more tied down by family, work, expectations, and responsibility. In their sixties, women can take time for themselves and feel good about what they have done and what they are free to do. It's important to note, however, that socioeconomic status may impede a women's sense of freedom in her sixties. Because most of my interviewees were middle or upper middle class, they had the ability to pursue other passions. Working-class or poor women may not have the same feeling of liberty at this stage in life.

More in Touch

I asked interviewees if they thought women over the age of fifty were less in touch with their sexuality than women in their twenties and thirties were. Most women over forty-five emphatically said no, remarking that because older women know themselves better, they are much more self-aware and more likely to act on their own desire rather than put on a show for a partner or men in general. Dawn, age fifty-four, stated,

I think [older women] might be more in touch. They've had lot more experience and also . . . when you're older, you've gone through menopause and your desire has either gotten more or less. Or you've gone through enough changes that I think you find the spot that's comfortable for you or at least you should. . . . I think that the longer you live and deal with things, you become more comfortable in your own skin. I think you tend to be more balanced and not care as much what society or people think. And again, I'm sure there's people that's not true for, but I think for me, definitely more comfortable in my own skin.

Alyssa, age fifty-one, had similar perceptions.

I think you get more confident about—I mean, personally I have more confidence in myself as I've gotten older and feel more comfortable about my body, whether anyone else is comfortable with it or not, kind of like "oh, well, here I am." . . . And I think also you're just comfortable inside your own skin, you know? And I think that that just comes with age. . . . I think you have time to think about yourself and you think about what is good for you and, you know, you've experienced someone. I think you're probably more in touch with your body at that point in your life.

All of the women I've quoted in this chapter recognized the importance of self-realization as they age. They no longer felt obliged to emulate unattainable socially driven standards and sexual scripts. James J. Dowd (2012), influenced by Jochen Brandtstädter (2006), has noted the significance of self-acceptance in cultivating desire and a sense of personal security as people age. They enhance their well-being when they accept their limitations and scale their desire to their capabilities. Among the women with whom I spoke, those who had stopped trying to live up to others' expectations of their physical appearance or sexual interest felt more secure about their sexuality than did those (mostly younger women) who were still chasing or feeling pressured to follow inaccessible conventions or uncomfortable, other-driven sexual scripts.

Certainly, older women still had insecurities about their desirability, but more communicated self-acceptance overall. Some unpartnered women lacked validation and affirmation from long-term relationships and thus had more motivation for personal self-discovery and self-acceptance. Several noted that although they hoped to find companionship and a sexual partner in the future, they would do so only on their terms and would be content with themselves if no one came along. Leslie, age sixty and single, said,

It's just—it's harder, you're more self-conscious because you just know that you're not the way that you used to be. But it's still . . . a pretty exciting time, I think. It's more of a freeing situation than anything else, where you just accept yourself for the way you are and say, "Okay, you know, this is me. I spent fifty-some years fashioning it and here it is and I'm happy with it." . . . Finding something, the likelihood of that happening, is pretty, pretty tiny at this point, I think. I'm sixty years old. I know it happens to people, and that would be so curious and interesting, but if not, not. And I think that acceptance allows you to know that you can still be sexual because it doesn't mean you're not interested in meeting somebody. Or if someone looks at you, you know whether you look good or you don't. Or when you think about being in bed with somebody, you don't think, "Oh, my God, you know, he's gonna see my stomach," or something like that. You're comfortable with who you are and you know what you have to offer and if something happens, that's great, and if it doesn't, you know, I think you get to the point where you realize being grateful for what you do have is really what's important. . . . I think my sexuality is pretty good. I'm pleased with my physical self, I'm pleased with my inner self and I know I can still respond as a woman, which is pretty exciting at age sixty. . . . I'm not hesitant about a whole lot anymore [*laughs*]. That's part of the great things about getting older, you know? Don't hold back.

Leslie's self-acceptance is inspiring. Although she is aware of how others might view her and at times feels self-conscious, she focuses on how she feels and what she has accomplished. She likes that she feels desire and appreciates her body and the pleasure it has afforded her through the years. She knows that she is getting older, and this is both freeing and motivation for living life to its fullest.

Beyond Sex: The Significance of Other Accomplishments

Women described how accomplishments in work, family, or other areas of life gave them more self-confidence in general, which helped build sexual self-confidence. As Dowd (2012) has asserted, people remain connected to society when they feel desire, whether that longing is sexual or the need to be engaged in a community or activity. Desire is as socially motivated and constructed as it is personally inspired, yet American cultural images repeatedly paint older women as uninterested in sex, asexual, and unappealing (Gullette 1997). Thus, maintaining personal desire and engagement in society is a way of rallying against societal expectations. For some of the women in my study, a feeling of social worth and value was crucial to their social and sexual identity.

Gail, age sixty-five, said that she was most comfortable with her sexuality in her forties and that much of her comfort was related to her professional accomplishments. "I think in [your] forties, you are simply much more confident in all ways. Much more confident with your skill set, you had a chance to look back on your life and say, 'I've done x, y, and z, gee, I did that okay.' . . . I went out into the workplace and that was part of that confidence builder. And it was like, you had children, you had a family, that was working. You went out into the workplace, found yourself there, so you're just more confident."

Brenda, a fifty-one-year-old professional woman with a graduate degree, pointed out that her work achievements made her feel like an equal partner in her marriage and consequently as focused on her own needs as those of her husband. "Career success. Education, pursuing education. Success with how we've raised my son. Things that my husband has accomplished in his life that aren't necessarily directly related to our sex life but certainly make me respect him more and have caused both of us to grow in different areas and maybe being more interested in one another than had we not gone out and done some of the things that we did as individuals." For Brenda and Gail, confidence came from triumphs in multiple realms. They expressed pride in their achievements, which made them feel interesting and worthy and thus able to accept themselves and recognize the depth of their value. Among many of the professional women with whom I spoke, physical sexuality was not the most consequential element in their definitions of identity. This made it easier for them to enjoy sex, feel comfortable, and accept their sexual feelings.

Penny, age fifty-one, concretely described the relationship between sexual subjectivity and work. Having worked for many years in a masculine occupation, where she is often a minority, she has learned the importance of assertiveness. "I think all of the experiences you have in business, all my experiences I've had when I was single—and I tell my daughter this all the time—it's like 'stick up for yourself.' If you're in a situation where you're out with a guy or whatever, and you know that he just wants to take you back and go to bed but you don't really feel like it, you know, don't be submissive. I mean, we are in a generation now that, you're as tough as he is, so it's like 'say no.'" Penny's career has required decisive action and confidence, the ability to turn down persistent offers, and sometimes the need to stand up against sexual harassment. Early on, she recognized the importance of not being submissive to men; and once she developed the skill and confidence to do so, she became more self-assured in general.

Bonnie, age forty-seven, also suggested that her career has helped her accept and appreciate herself because it has pushed her to focus more on her internal rather than her external value.

> I think once you're . . . in the workforce and developing your expertise and becoming knowledgeable and just growing as a person, the need to express yourself that way goes—well, it doesn't go away completely because everyone wants to be attractive, . . . but I think it becomes less important as a way to define ourselves as you become older. And I'm just thinking about me personally—when I was first out of college and I was working with men and women, I was very, very unsure of myself and kind of held back a little bit, especially in mixed company. . . . But somewhere in my forties it was like, okay, I—I like what I do, I'm comfortable in my life. I've got a marriage that's been going on for a while. I really don't feel the need to go out and make everybody love me anymore. And this is good. And I'm not sure necessarily that it has to do with age as much as where you are in life, that you've accomplished goals. . . . Women in the forties, I think we want to be more than just the female in the room. We want to hold our own in terms of accomplishments, in terms of what we know. . . . . I think that's all kind of woven into what we've been talking about in terms of . . . every major accomplishment or major goal that's met, major promotions, getting a job with a company that maybe I wanted to work for, changing a career path, getting the master's degree, that kind of stuff. Each of those just made me a stronger person and I keep going back to this but I'm more comfortable and happy with myself as a person, which does have a positive impact on sexuality.

Bonnie's work accomplishments improved her self-esteem. When she was younger and less experienced, she sometimes deferred to men and felt that her gender was a limitation in the eyes of others. But as she matured and gained experience and confidence, she began to recognize her value, power, and abilities and felt pride in her achievements, which increased her confidence in all areas, including sexuality.

STAYING SEXUAL SUBJECTS

Throughout my interviewees' lives, many experiences and encounters affected their development of sexual subjectivity. Once girls discovered the existence of sex, they took a stance on it that influenced their future experiences. Different generations more or less understood, discussed, or tacitly condoned the actual process of sex. Women born before 1960 rarely spoke openly about it in their youth or received direct information. Those born in or after 1960 more often discussed sex with peers, learned about it (insufficiently) in schools, and grew up with scripts for sexual interaction and mediated models of girls' and young women's sexual expression. Women who had been raised as conservative Christians, particularly those who were raised as Catholics, were more likely to feel fearful about sex and were generally slower to develop sexual subjectivity. And some never had an opportunity to develop a stance on sex because their first experiences were nonconsensual.

Part of becoming a sexual subject is constructing and revealing a public sexual self. When girls are younger and learning about or imagining sex, their sexuality is hidden and private. As they get older and begin to experiment with others, they present a public sexuality in how they talk, display their bodies, and express desire, pleasure, and satisfaction. Girls and women who mirror hegemonic images of hypersexuality may lack authenticity in their public sexual self, but they still put forth an image and allow others, even if only their partners, to see them as sexual.

When early encounters were positive and when my interviewees felt supported by others, their subjectivity was enhanced. However, women raised in proscriptive religions, those from conservative ethnic backgrounds, and those who were immigrants or first-generation Americans tended to lack sexual confidence in early sexual experiences because they felt guilt or shame about violating cultural or religious norms. For a number of women reared with conservative religious values, generation mediated the impact of religion. Given the many available models of hypersexuality, women born after 1960 were far more comfortable about premarital sexual experimentation and their sexuality.

Overall, for the women I interviewed, desirability preceded desire. When partners in early sexual relationships affirmed or validated their physical appeal, women felt more confident and interested in sex. Partners who encouraged self-gratification, were eager to please, or supported women's interest in sex and sexual satisfaction helped them recognize their entitlement to sexual pleasure. In contrast, men who showed little concern for or recognition of women's sexual pleasure and desire did not bolster sexual subjectivity and sometimes suppressed it. This situation was common among married women born before 1960. Women from all generations noted that the transition to marriage enhanced their feelings of sexual allure because it was a public statement of desirability. Among younger married women, marriage often increased sexual confidence because it gave them a sense of trust and respect or allowed them to reconstruct their sexual identity in a culturally legitimate way. Compared with women in relationships, unpartnered women under the age of fifty felt decidedly less sexual or sexually appealing.

Common midlife experiences, such as motherhood, divorce, and menopause, inspired self-discovery. In motherhood, women felt transformations in their body. Though most expressed diminished interest in sex and did not feel desirable in the early years of motherhood, over time many recognized and appreciated the power of their bodies. They noted the strength it takes to carry and bear a child and were proud to realize that they possessed such fortitude.

Divorce, though rarely welcomed, often gave women an opportunity to reinvent a sexual self. They reflected on failed marriages, considered their personal desires, and often sought them out in new relationships or sexual encounters. Many ultimately found breakups liberating because they helped the women become more independent and self-aware. Those who divorced in their twenties, thirties, and early forties fared better in the development of sexual subjectivity than did women who divorced later in life. Younger women had physical desirability, fecundity, and a larger pool of available men on their side, all of which were advantageous in a culture in which men tend to marry younger partners and women tend to marry older ones (England and McClintock 2009). The women I interviewed were well aware of these advantages in the dating market. Mothers who divorced had difficulty balancing their roles and identities as mothers with those of sexual women, which complicated their post-divorce sexual agency. Most of the single mothers told me that they compartmentalized their identities and hid their sexual sides for fear of sending inappropriate messages to their children.

As women aged and experienced menopause, they came to terms with declining fertility and changed physical appearance. For some, particularly those who were dating or in newer relationships, these experiences were freeing as they no longer worried about pregnancy or menstruation. More often women complained about the lack of sexual spontaneity and felt saddened by their increasing inability to keep up with conventional standards of attractiveness. Many women's decreased sexual activity or desire was spurred by their partners' health issues and difficulties with intercourse. These women still desired sex but were with partners who could not have it. Such women generally prioritized emotional connection over physical gratification and accepted celibate futures.

Among most of the women in their fifties and sixties, aging stimulated self-acceptance. Over time, they learned to care less about others' expectations and defined and refined their own sexual interests and needs. Accomplishments in work, family, and lived experience inspired strength and self-confidence, which facilitated sexual subjectivity. Middle- and upper-middle-class women, those with bachelor's and graduate degrees, expressed greater self-acceptance, given that they had resources for self-discovery and tangible accomplishments to reflect on with pride.

I found that generation mattered most in the development of sexual subjectivity. Women born after 1960 were quicker to become confident and shed negative stances about sex because they came of age in an era in which premarital sex was normative, hypersexuality was embraced, and information about sex was readily available. Religion, particularly Catholicism, had a strong influence on women of all generations. Those from conservative religious backgrounds recalled early proscriptive messages about sex and said that sexually active girls were tagged as immoral. Ethnic background also influenced women. All of the first-generation American and immigrant women noted the liberality of American culture and said that their cultural backgrounds made talking about sex uncomfortable, particularly with parents. Many of these girls, except for a few born in the 1980s, identified themselves as late bloomers and had less sexual confidence than did their peers born in the United States or to American parents.

Among American-born women, race mattered less than I might have expected. However, because approximately three-quarters of the women identified themselves as middle or upper middle class, socioeconomic status may have obscured any racial differences. A couple of African American women did mention that they appreciated being black because it allowed them to be more sexually expressive, which was their perceived expectation of black women. Likewise, a couple of Asian women noted playing into stereotypes of the eroticized Asian woman. But when asked about how their race had influenced their sexuality or others' expectations of it, the vast majority had little or nothing to say. Nor did I find many class- or raced-based differences in my analyses of the development of sexual subjectivity.

Given a wealth of information and the diversity of women's sexual experiences, I was not able to address all of the experiences that shaped my interviewees' sexual development. Although I have detailed the major influences on women's development of sexual subjectivity, episodes such as a health crisis, the loss of a child, or a period of depression also played significant roles in suppressing interest in sex. While I do not overlook or minimize these experiences, my purpose here has been to chart and explain the commonalities of heterosexual women's journey to sexual subjectivity through the life course.

THE SIGNIFICANCE OF SEXUAL SCRIPTS AND DOUBLE STANDARDS

Throughout my interviewees' lives, sexual scripts influenced sexual decision making and self-image. The women with whom I spoke communicated strong awareness of sexual double standards; and though some suggested that these standards are changing, the vast majority believed in the dominance of gendered norms that differentiate women's and men's sexual desire and behavior. Showing keen interest in sex or sexual pleasure outside (and sometimes inside) of committed relationships was generally perceived as deviant. According to sexual script theory, the internalization of cultural scenarios influences intrapsychic scripts—that is, how women think about their personal expression of sexuality and sexual desire (Simon and Gagnon 1984, 1986, 2003). Even when women rejected sexual double standards personally and felt confident in their desire, they had to negotiate such noncompliant behavior within a gendered world (Hamilton and Armstrong 2009; Tolman 2002). As the personal is political, the sexual is social. Women do not simply act on or have physiological desires. Desire is influenced by cultural constructions (Elliott and Umberson 2008), and heterosexual American women navigate among mixed, age-variant messages about sexual expression.

Developing sexual subjectivity and a sense of entitlement to sexual desire and pleasure may be easier as women get older because sexuality becomes more private. As women age, marry, or become mothers, they are culturally desexualized. Thus, they deal with fewer expectations about expressing or displaying their sexuality. They must construct their sexuality in a personal way because the roles that most take on as they move through life define them as nonsexual. In other words, aging can be liberating. Although women of all ages wanted to feel attractive and appealing, the audience with whom they hoped to curry favor narrowed as they grew older. Married women wanted their husbands to continue to find them desirable but cared much less about men in general. Older single women wanted to look and feel good for themselves as a way of staying youthful and connected with the world (Dowd 2012; Furman 1997).

Women also defined their value more broadly as they aged. In adolescence and young adulthood, many girls and women put much more effort into their physical appearance and sought validation of their allure by attracting men's attention. Relationships brought status. But as women grew older, motherhood, friendships, work, and physical health or strength helped them cultivate pride and self-esteem. Validation of self-worth and desirability on multiple levels also bolstered sexual subjectivity. For some women, most of whom were middle or upper middle class, success in education or career reinforced the value of intellect, creativity, leadership, or other tangible skills, which in turn deemphasized the value of appearance and physical allure. Women with less education, who had never been taught about the women's movement or feminism, or who had been encouraged to see marriage and motherhood as their calling and jobs as economic necessity seemed to put more weight on their sexual desirability and romantic relationships, as studies of working-class adolescent girls have also noted (Bettie 2003; Martin 1996).

Women with greater sexual subjectivity are women with greater power. Sexual experiences, relationships, and role transitions can enhance sexual subjectivity when women feel in control of decisions about sexual activity and the use of their body. In contrast, nonconsensual sexual interaction, the sense of being at the mercy of sexual pressures or expectations, and a belief in gendered sexual scripts based on a male sex-drive discourse all stifle sexual subjectivity. Among my interviewees, women who lacked information as girls or young adults were more likely to feel alienated from their bodies and objectified during sexual activity. Knowledge functioned as power for girls whose families were open about sex.

Sexual subjects have self-confidence; they act judiciously. They know their bodies and generally feel mentally and physically in control of their sexuality and sexual decision making. Possessing sexual agency and self-confidence gives women the power to write and tell their own sexual stories. And "the power to tell a story, or indeed not to tell a story, under the conditions of one's own choosing, is part of the political process" (Plummer 1995, 26). Women's sexual power is compromised by sexual double standards and scripts that make their expression of sexuality deviant. Nonetheless, most of the women with whom I spoke developed sexual subjectivity during their lives. Though the plots and characters in their stories varied, the stories were their own. Their decision to share them with me and with you has been powerful.

APPENDIX A: DEMOGRAPHIC CHARACTERISTICS OF RESEARCH PARTICIPANTS

WOMEN IN THEIR TWENTIES

Name	Age at Time of Interview	Race	Education	Self-Reported Socioeconomic Status	Relationship Status	Mother	Current Religious Identification
Blair	20	White	Some college	Upper class	Dating	No	Christian, unspecified denomination
Bridget	25	White	B.A.	Working class	Single	No	None
Brittany	21	White	High school diploma	Working class	Married	Yes	Catholic
Caitlin	27	White	B.A.	Middle class	Separated	No	Catholic
Chloe	24	White	Some college	Middle class	Married	No	Christian, unspecified denomination
Erin	22	White	B.S.	Working class	Dating	No	None
Hailey	20	Biracial	B.A.	Upper middle class	Dating	No	Spiritual
Holly	21	White	Some college	Upper middle class	Single	No	Unitarian
Hope	21	Asian	Some college	Middle class	Single	No	Catholic
Jia	22	Asian	B.S.	Middle class	Single	No	Buddhist

(continued)

WOMEN IN THEIR TWENTIES (continued)

Name	Age at Time of Interview	Race	Education	Self-Reported Socioeconomic Status	Relationship Status	Mother	Current Religious Identification
June	20	Asian	Some college	Middle class	Single	No	Christian
Kara	26	White	M.Ed.	Upper middle class	Engaged	No	Jewish
Kendra	21	Black	Some college	Working class	Single	No	None
Leann	29	White	Some college	Middle class	Married	No	Christian, unspecified denomination
Marcia	22	Asian	B.S.	Working class	Dating	No	Christian, unspecified denomination
Melissa	23	White	Some college	Working class	Dating	Yes	Agnostic
Olivia	24	White	Some college	Middle class	Single	No	Unitarian
Nia	29	Black	Some college	Working class	Married	Yes	Christian
Vanessa	26	Hispanic	Some college	Middle class	Single	No	Catholic
Vanida	22	Asian	Some college	Middle class	Married	No	Spiritual

WOMEN IN THEIR THIRTIES

Name	Age at Time of Interview	Race	Education	Self-Reported Socioeconomic Status	Relationship Status	Mother	Current Religious Identification
Adena	30	Middle Eastern	Some college	Middle class	Separated, dating	No	Spiritual
Adrianna	38	White	B.A.	Working class	Single	No	Atheist
Amanda	39	White	B.A.	Upper middle class	Divorced, dating	Yes	Russian Orthodox
Amber	36	White	M.Ed.	Middle class	Single	No	None
Amy	34	White	Some college	Working class	Divorced, dating	No	Christian, unspecified denomination
Charlotte	36	White	M.A.	Middle class	Married	Yes	None
Courtney	31	Black	B.A.	Upper middle class	Dating	No	Jewish
Danielle	35	White	M.S.	Middle class	Married	Yes	Christian, unspecified denomination
Emily	33	White	B.A.	Middle class	Engaged	No	None
Jane	38	White	M.A.	Middle class	Married	Yes	None
Jessica	38	White	B.A.	Middle class	Married	Yes	None
Kelly	35	White	M.F.A.	Middle class	Married	Yes	None
Lila	35	Middle Eastern	M.B.A.	Middle class	Dating	No	Agnostic
Marisa	30	White	B.A.	Upper middle class	Dating	No	Christian, unspecified denomination

(continued)

WOMEN IN THEIR THIRTIES (continued)

Name	Age at Time of Inter- view	Race	Education	Self- Reported Socioeco- nomic Status	Relation- ship Status	Mother	Current Religious Identification
Misty	31	White	M.A.	Middle class	Divorced, dating	Yes	Christian, unspecified denomination
Monica	35	Black	B.S.	Middle class	Married	Yes	Christian, unspecified denomination
Naomi	39	White	M.S.N.	Upper middle class	Married	Yes	Christian, unspecified denomination
Serena	31	White	B.A.	Middle class	Dating	No	None
Stephanie	32	White	B.A.	Working class	Wid- owed, dating	No	Agnostic
Tara	31	Asian	B.A.	Middle class	Single	No	Agnostic

WOMEN IN THEIR FORTIES

Name	Age at Time of Interview	Race	Education	Self-Reported Socioeconomic Status	Relationship Status	Mother	Current Religious Identification
Autumn	41	White	B.A.	Upper middle class	Married	Yes	Spiritual
Bonnie	47	White	M.B.A	Middle class	Married	Step-children	None
Camille	47	White	Associate's degree	Middle class	Divorced, dating	Yes	Catholic
Eve	48	White	M.A.	Upper middle class	Married	Yes	Jewish
Gretchen	42	White	M.A.	Upper middle class	Single	No	None
Heather	46	White	Associate's degree	Middle class	Married, previously divorced	Yes	Christian, unspecified denomination
Irina	46	White	M.A.	Middle class	Married, previously divorced	Yes	None
Jacqueline	44	Black	Some college	Middle class	Separated	Yes	Catholic
Jamie	40	Asian	B.A.	Middle class	Married	Yes	None
Jennifer	40	White	B.A.	Working class	Married	Yes	Catholic
Kiko	47	Asian	M.B.A.	Working class	Married	Yes	Christian, unspecified denomination
Kristen	41	White	Some college	Middle class	Married, previously divorced	Yes	None

(continued)

WOMEN IN THEIR FORTIES (continued)

Name	Age at Time of Interview	Race	Education	Self-Reported Socioeconomic Status	Relationship Status	Mother	Current Religious Identification
Nadia	40	Hispanic	Some college	Upper middle class	Married	Yes	Catholic
Robin	49	White	High school diploma	Upper middle class	Married	Yes	Catholic
Sara	49	White	B.S.	Middle class	Married	Yes	Catholic
Sherry	47	White	M.F.A.	Middle class	Divorced	No	Christian, unspecified denomination
Tamara	48	Black	B.A.	Working class	Divorced	Yes	Baptist
Tammy	45	White	Some college	Middle class	Married, previously divorced	Yes	Christian, unspecified denomination

WOMEN IN THEIR FIFTIES

Name	Age at Time of Interview	Race	Education	Self-Reported Socioeconomic Status	Relationship Status	Mother	Current Religious Identification
Alice	55	White	Associate's degree	Working class	Divorced	Yes	None
Alyssa	51	White	Associate's degree	Upper middle class	Married	Yes	Catholic
Brenda	51	White	M.B.A.	Upper middle class	Married	Yes	Catholic
Celeste	58	White	B.A.	Middle class	Separated, dating	Yes	Catholic
Cora	51	Black	Some college	Working class	Married	Yes	Methodist
Dawn	54	White	B.A.	Upper middle class	Married	Yes	Agnostic
Debra	59	White	M.Ed.	Upper middle class	Divorced	Yes	Jewish
Faith	52	White	B.A.	Middle class	Married	Yes	Christian, unspecified denomination
Georgia	52	Black	B.A.	Middle class	Married	No	None
Iris	58	White	B.A.	Middle class	Divorced	Yes	None
Joyce	57	White	Some college	Middle class	Married, previously divorced	Yes	None
Pamela	55	White	M.A.	Middle class	Married	Yes	Spiritual
Paula	53	White	M.B.A.	Upper middle class	Married	Stepchildren	Christian, unspecified denomination

(continued)

WOMEN IN THEIR FIFTIES (continued)

Name	Age at Time of Interview	Race	Education	Self-Reported Socioeconomic Status	Relationship Status	Mother	Current Religious Identification
Sandra	58	Black	M.A.	Upper middle class	Married	Yes	Christian, unspecified denomination
Shirley	56	White	B.A.	Middle class	Married, previously divorced	Yes	None
Thelma	50	Black	B.A.	Working class	Married	No	Methodist
Wendy	59	White	High school diploma	Middle class	Married	Yes	Catholic

WOMEN IN THEIR SIXTIES

Name	Age at Time of Inter- view	Race	Education	Self- Reported Socioeco- nomic Status	Relation- ship Status	Mother	Current Religious Identification
Angela	62	White	Some college	Middle class	Married	Yes	Jewish
Connie	64	White	M.A.	Middle class	Divorced, dating	Yes	None
Delia	60	Black	M.A.	Middle class	Divorced	No	Christian, unspecified denomination
Erika	62	White	B.A.	Middle class	Divorced	Yes	Christian, unspecified denomination
Gail	65	White	B.A.	Middle class	Married	Yes	Spiritual
Hannah	66	Asian	Some college	Upper middle class	Married	Yes	Jewish
Harriet	68	White	High school diploma	Working class	Married, previously divorced	Yes	Catholic
Helen	62	Black	Some high school	Working class	Widowed	Yes	Baptist
Jeanne	66	White	M.A.	Upper middle class	Married	Yes	Jewish
Joan	66	White	M.A.	Working class	Divorced	Yes	Spiritual
Leigh	65	White	M.A.	Upper middle class	Widowed, previously divorced	Yes	Catholic
Leslie	60	White	M.A., M.Ed.	Middle class	Divorced	No	Jewish

(continued)

WOMEN IN THEIR SIXTIES (continued)

Name	Age at Time of Interview	Race	Education	Self-Reported Socioeconomic Status	Relationship Status	Mother	Current Religious Identification
Paige	64	White	B.A.	Upper middle class	Married, previously divorced	Yes	Spiritual
Regina	62	Black	M.A.	Upper middle class	Divorced	Yes	Christian Scientist
Rose	65	White	High school diploma	Middle class	Divorced	Yes	Christian, unspecified denomination
Shannon	64	White	M.A.	Upper middle class	Married	Yes	Catholic
Wanda	64	White	Some college	Working class	Married	Yes	Christian, unspecified denomination

APPENDIX B: METHODOLOGY

This research is based on in-depth interviews with twenty women in their twenties, twenty in their thirties, nineteen in their forties, eighteen in their fifties, and eighteen in their sixties. I sought participants by asking women I knew to refer me to women in the relevant age groups and then asking those women for referrals. Additionally, I posted recruitment fliers at colleges, health clubs, local markets, and senior centers.

Initially, I intended to interview bisexual and lesbian women as well as heterosexual women, but the diversity of sexual development experiences among these subgroups as well as existing studies on sexual orientation and sexual development (for example, Diamond 2008) led me to focus on heterosexual women only. Furthermore, because heterosexual women appear to be "normal," they have become an invisible and neglected group in sex research (Meadows 1997; Waskul and Plante 2010). Before deciding to focus on heterosexual women, however, I did interview two bisexual women. In addition, two married women who had identified as heterosexual during recruitment later described their sexual identity as more fluid, noting that they had had sexual relationships or encounters with women in the past. Thus, of the women I interviewed, ninety-one identified themselves as heterosexual, four as either bisexual or undefined.

Because I was particularly interested in diversity of age and relationship status, I selected a stratified snowball sample. I aimed to interview relatively balanced numbers of women in each age bracket: a minimum of fifteen and a maximum of twenty. I also wanted a sample of women whose marital and parental statuses mirrored the larger population of women. Thus, I looked at the 2008 U.S. Census to determine whether the majority of women in each bracket were married or unmarried, mothers or not. As a result, most of my interviewees over the age of thirty were married (or had been married) and mothers.

I conducted ninety-one interviews. Allison Cooper, a research assistant who helped during the first year of data collection, conducted the remaining four, all with women in their twenties. Interviews took place at locations that were convenient for participants, such as their homes, my home, public parks, quiet coffee shops, restaurants with tall booths, or my office. The average length of each interview was about an hour and forty-five minutes, and questions focused on women's attitudes about sexuality and on how their sexuality had developed and changed during their lives.

The women I interviewed were diverse in terms of demographics, experiences, and feelings about sexuality. All but three lived in Pennsylvania (seventy-one), New Jersey (thirteen), or New York (eight). Seven were born and raised outside of the United States: two in Asia, four in Europe, and one in the Caribbean. About two-thirds of the women lived in suburban areas, and a quarter lived in urban areas. Only four lived in rural areas. Sixty-one percent were mothers, and most of those who did not have children (seventeen) were in their twenties. Half of the women were currently married, 25 percent had never been married (though three were engaged and ten were in relationships), 17 percent were divorced, 5 percent were separated, and 2 percent were widows.

Fifty-two percent of the women self-identified as middle class, 22 percent as working class, and 24 percent as upper middle class. One person self-identified as upper class. Overall, these women had more education than the general population does, with one-third of the women holding bachelor's degrees and slightly less than one-third holding graduate degrees. Five women had associate's degrees, and twenty-three noted that they had "some college" (fifteen of whom were current students). Only six women had a high school education or less.

Seventy-two percent of the women were white, 14 percent were African American, and 10 percent were Asian. Two women were Hispanic, two were Middle Eastern, and one was biracial. Sixty-one women were Christian (including Catholics), ten were Jewish, and three were Buddhist. Eight stated that they were agnostic, and thirteen did not presently identify with a religion, though many noted they were "spiritual" and most had been raised in a Christian denomination.

Interviews were audio-recorded and either professionally transcribed or transcribed by the interviewer. Using Nvivo qualitative software, my assistants and I analyzed transcripts for themes and patterns following a grounded theory approach (Glaser and Strauss 1967). In other words, I built a theory from data rather than imposing data on a theory. In addition to coding data by themes and subthemes, I also constructed summaries of women's sexual development and the development of sexual subjectivity. This allowed me to chart significant episodes and transitions in women's lives. Because this was not a random sample, I cannot generalize from the experiences of my interviewees to all or most women.

REFERENCES

Acker, M. 2009. Breast is best . . . but not everywhere: Ambivalent sexism and attitudes toward private and public breastfeeding. *Sex Roles* 61 (7/8): 476–490.

Ahlborg, T., L. Dahlof, and L. R. Hallberg. 2005. Quality of the intimate and sexual relationship in first-time parents six months after delivery. *Journal of Sex Research* 42: 167–174.

Allen, L. 2003. Girls want sex, boys want love: Resisting dominant discourses of (hetero)sexuality. *Sexualities* 6 (2): 215–236.

Amato, P. R. 2000. The consequences of divorce for adults and children. *Journal of Marriage and the Family* 62: 1269–1288.

Apt, C., and D. F. Hurlbert. 1992. Motherhood and female sexuality beyond one year postpartum: A study of military wives. *Journal of Sex Education and Therapy* 18: 104–114.

Bartky, S. L. 2010. Foucault, femininity, and the modernization of patriarchal power. In *The politics of women's bodies: Sexuality, appearance, and behavior,* edited by R. Weitz, 76–97. New York: Oxford University Press.

Bettie, J. 2003. *Women without class: Girls, race, and identity.* Berkeley: University of California Press.

Blumstein, P., and P. Schwartz. 1983. *American couples: Money, work, and sex.* New York: William Morrow.

Bogle, K. 2008. *Hooking up: Sex, dating, and relationships on campus.* New York: New York University Press.

Bordo, S. 2000. *The male body: A new look at men in public and private.* New York: Farrar, Straus, and Giroux.

Braly, J. 2012. Breastfeeding and sex: Is latching on a turn-off? *New York Times,* July 15. http://parenting.blogs.nytimes.com/2012/07/15/breastfeeding-and-sex-is-latching-on-a-turn-off/.

Brandtstädter, J. 2006. Adaptive resources in later life: Tenacious goal pursuit and flexible goal adjustment. In *A life worth living: Contributions to positive psychology,* edited by M. Csikszentmihalyi and I. S. Csikszentmihalyi, 143–164. New York: Oxford University Press.

Browning, C. R., and E. O. Laumann. 1997. Sexual contact between children and adults: A life course perspective. *American Sociological Review* 62: 540–560.

Call, V., S. Sprecher, and P. Schwartz. 1995. The incidence and frequency of marital sex in a national sample. *Journal of Sex Research* 36: 180–190.

Carbone-Lopez, K. 2012. The life course consequences of childhood sexual assault: Effects on relationship formation and intimate violence across relationships. In *Sex*

for life: From virginity to Viagra, how sexuality changes throughout our lives, edited by
L. M. Carpenter and J. DeLamater, 88–106. New York: New York University Press.

Carpenter, L. M. 2005. *Virginity lost: An intimate portrait of first sexual experiences.* New
York: New York University Press.

Carpenter, L. M., and J. DeLamater. 2012. Studying gendered sexualities over the life
course: A conceptual framework. In *Sex for life: From virginity to Viagra, how sexuality changes throughout our lives,* edited by L. M. Carpenter and J. DeLamater, 23–41.
New York: New York University Press.

Carpenter, L. M., C. A. Nathanson, and Y. J. Kim. 2005. Sex after 40? Gender, ageism,
and sexual partnering in midlife. *Journal of Aging Studies* 20: 93–106.

Centers for Disease Control and Prevention. 2012. *Breastfeeding report card—United
States.* Atlanta: Centers for Disease Control and Prevention. http://www.cdc.gov/
breastfeeding/pdf/2012BreastfeedingReportCard.pdf.

———. 2013. *Key statistics from the National Survey of Family Growth.* Atlanta: Centers
for Disease Control and Prevention. http://www.cdc.gov/nchs/fastats/fertile.htm.

Chandra, A., G. M. Martinez, W. D. Mosher, J. C. Abma, and J. Jones. 2005. Fertility, family planning, and reproductive health of U.S. women: Data from the 2002
national survey of family growth. *National Center for Health Statistics. Vital Health
Stat* 23 (25): 1–160.

Chodorow, N. 1978. *The reproduction of mothering: Psychoanalysis and the sociology of
gender.* Berkeley: University of California Press.

Christina, G. 1992. Are we having sex now or what? In *The erotic impulse: Honoring the
sexual self,* edited by D. Steinberg, 24–29. New York: Tarcher.

Cooley, C. H. 1964. *Human nature and the social order.* New York: Schocken.

Crawford, M., and D. Popp. 2003. Sexual double standards: A review and methodological critique of two decades of research. *Journal of Sex Research* 40: 13–26.

Daniluk, J. C. 1998. *Women's sexuality across the life span: Challenging myths, creating
meanings.* New York: Guilford.

Das, A., L. J. Waite, and E. O. Laumann. 2012. Sexual expression over the life course:
Results from three landmark surveys. In *Sex for life: From virginity to Viagra, how
sexuality changes throughout our lives,* edited by L. M. Carpenter and J. DeLamater,
236–259. New York: New York University Press.

Deeks, A., and M. McCabe. 2001. Sexual functioning and the menopausal woman:
The importance of age and partner's sexual functioning. *Journal of Sex Research* 38:
219–225.

De Judicibus, M. A., and M. P. McCabe. 2002. Psychological factors and the sexuality
of pregnant and postpartum women. *Journal of Sex Research* 39: 94–103.

Dempsey, J. M., and T. Reichert. 2000. Portrayal of married sex in the movies. *Sexuality
and Culture* 4: 21–36.

Diamond, L. 2008. *Sexual fluidity: Understanding women's love and desire.* Cambridge,
Mass.: Harvard University Press.

Dillaway, H. E. 2012. Reproductive history as social context: Exploring how women
talk about menopause and sexuality at midlife. In *Sex for life: From virginity to*

Viagra, how sexuality changes throughout our lives, edited by L. M. Carpenter and J. DeLamater, 217–235. New York: New York University Press.

Douglas, S. 1995. *Where the girls are: Growing up female with mass media.* New York: Random House.

Dowd, J. J. 2012. Aging and the course of desire. *Journal of Aging Studies* 26: 285–295.

Dunn, J. 1998. Defining women: Notes toward an understanding of structure and agency in the negotiation of sex. *Journal of Contemporary Ethnography* 26: 479–510.

Edwards, J. N., and A. Booth. 1994. Sexuality, marriage, and well-being: The middle years. In *Sexuality across the life course,* edited by A. S. Rossi, 233–259. Chicago: University of Chicago Press.

Elliott, S., and D. Umberson. 2008. The performance of desire: Gender and sexual negotiation in long-term marriages. *Journal of Marriage and Family* 70: 391–406.

Ellison, C. R. 2000. *Women's sexualities: Generations of women share intimate secrets of sexual self-acceptance.* Oakland, Calif.: New Harbinger.

England, P., and E. A. McClintock. 2009. The gendered double standard of aging in U.S. marriage markets. *Population and Development Review* 35 (4): 797–816.

Fasula, A. M., K. S. Miller, and J. Wiener. 2007. The sexual double standard in African American adolescent women's sexual risk reduction socialization. *Women and Health* 46: 3–21.

Fine, M. 1988. Sexuality, schooling, and adolescent families: The missing discourse of desire. *Harvard Educational Review* 58: 29–53.

Fisher, L. L. 2010. *Sex, romance, and relationships: AARP study of midlife and older adults.* Washington, D.C.: AARP.

Friedman, A., H. Weinberg, and A. M. Pines. 1998. Sexuality and motherhood: Mutually exclusive in perception of women. *Sex Roles* 38 (9/10): 781–800.

Fullilove, M. T., R. E. Fullilove, K. Haynes, and S. Gross. 1990. Black women and AIDS prevention: A view towards understanding the gender rules. *Journal of Sex Research* 27: 47–64.

Furman, F. K. 1997. *Facing the mirror: Older women and beauty shop culture.* New York: Routledge.

Gavey, N., K. McPhillips, and M. Dougherty. 2001. If it's not on, it's not on: Or is it? Discursive constraints on women's condom use. *Gender and Society* 15: 917–934.

Geller, J. 2001. *Here comes the bride: Women, weddings, and the marriage mystique.* New York: Four Walls Eight Windows.

Gilligan, C. 1982. *In a different voice: Psychological theory and women's development.* Cambridge, Mass.: Harvard University Press.

Glaser, B., and A. Strauss. 1967. *The discovery of grounded theory.* New York: Aldine.

Goffman, E. 1959. *The presentation of self in everyday life.* New York: Doubleday.

Gott, M., and S. Hinchliff. 2003. How important is sex in later life? The views of older people. *Social Science and Medicine* 56: 1617–1628.

Guendouzi, J. 2005. 'I feel quite organized this morning': How mothering is achieved through talk. *Sexualities, Evolution, and Gender* 7 (1): 17–35.

Gullette, M. M. 1997. *Declining to decline: Cultural combat and the politics of the midlife.* Charlottesville: University Press of Virginia.

Hamilton, L., and E. A. Armstrong. 2009. Gendered sexuality in young adulthood: Double binds and flawed options. *Gender and Society* 23: 589–616.

Heath, H. 1999. *Sexuality in old age.* Nursing Times Clinical Monograph, no. 40. London: Nursing Times Books.

Hesse-Biber, S. 1996. *Am I thin enough yet? The cult of thinness and the commercialization of identity.* New York: Oxford University Press.

Hinchliff, S., and M. Gott. 2004. Intimacy, commitment, and adaptation: Sexual relationships within long-term marriages. *Journal of Personal and Social Relationships* 21: 595–609.

———. 2008. Challenging social myths and stereotypes of women and aging: Heterosexual women talk about sex. *Journal of Women and Aging* 20: 65–81.

Holland, D., and M. A. Eisenhart. 1990. *Educated in romance: Women, achievement, and the college culture.* Chicago: University of Chicago Press.

Holland, J., C. Ramazanoglu, S. Sharpe, and R. Thomson. 2004. *The male in the head: Young people, heterosexuality, and power.* London: Tuffnell.

Howard, H. 2011. Vibrators carry the conversation. *New York Times,* April 30. http://www.nytimes.com/2011/04/21/fashion/21VIBRATORS.html?pagewanted=all.

Hyde, J. S., J. D. DeLamater, E. A. Plant, and J. M. Byrd. 1996. Sexuality during pregnancy and the year postpartum. *Journal of Sex Research* 33 (2): 143–151.

Ingraham, C. 2008. *White weddings: Romancing heterosexuality in popular culture.* New York: Routledge.

Jhally, S. (producer and director). 2007. *Dreamworlds III: Desire, sex, and power in music video.* Northampton, Mass.: Media Education Foundation. DVD.

Kiefer, A. K., and D. T. Sanchez. 2007. Scripting sexual passivity: A gender role perspective. *Personal Relationships* 14: 269–290.

Kingsberg, S. A. 2002. The impact of aging on sexual function in women and their partners. *Archives of Sexual Behavior* 31 (5): 431–437.

Kitzinger, S. 1983. *Women's experience of sex.* New York: Penguin.

Langer, M. 2000. *Motherhood and sexuality.* New York: Other Press.

Laumann, E. O., J. H. Gagnon, R. T. Michael, and S. Michaels. 1994. *The social organization of sexuality: Sexual practices in the United States.* Chicago: University of Chicago Press.

Leiblum, S. 1997. Love, sex and infertility: The impact of infertility on couples. In *Infertility: Psychological issues and counseling strategies,* edited by S. R. Leiblum, 149–166. New York: Wiley.

Levy, J. A. 1994. Sex and sexuality in later life stages. In *Sexuality across the life course,* edited by A. Rossi, 287–309. Chicago: University of Chicago Press.

Lichtenstein, B. 2012. Starting over: Dating risks and sexual health among midlife women after relationship dissolution. In *Sex for life: From virginity to Viagra, how sexuality changes throughout our lives,* edited by L. M. Carpenter and J. DeLamater, 180–197. New York: New York University Press.

Loe, M. 2004a. *The rise of Viagra: How the little blue pill changed sex in America.* New York: New York University Press.

———. 2004b. Sex and the senior woman: Pleasure and danger in the Viagra era. *Sexualities* 7: 303–326.

Lowder, J. B. 2012. Has Rush Limbaugh finally gone too far in slut-shaming Sandra Fluke? *Slate,* March 2. http://www.slate.com/blogs/xx_factor/2012/03/02/has _rush_limbaugh_finally_gone_too_far_in_slut_shaming_sandra_fluke_.html

MacNeil, S., and S. Byers. 2005. Dyadic assessment of sexual self-disclosure and sexual satisfaction in heterosexual dating couples. *Journal of Personal and Social Relationships* 22: 169–181.

Martin, K. A. 1996. *Puberty, sexuality, and the self: Girls and boys at adolescence.* New York: Routledge.

Masters, W. H., and V. E. Johnson. 1966. *Human sexual response.* New York: Bantam.

Mead, G. H. 1937. *Mind, self, and society.* Chicago: University of Chicago Press.

Meadows, M. 1997. Exploring the invisible: Listening to mid-life women about heterosexual sex. *Women's Studies International Forum* 20: 145–152.

Montemurro, B. 2005. Add men, don't stir: Reproducing traditional gender roles in modern wedding showers. *Journal of Contemporary Ethnography* 34: 6–35.

———. 2006. *Something old, something bold: Bridal showers and bachelorette parties.* New Brunswick, N.J.: Rutgers University Press.

Montemurro, B., and M. M. Gillen. 2013a. How clothes make the woman immoral: Impressions given off by sexualized clothing. *Clothing and Textiles Research Journal* 31 (3): 167–181.

———. 2013b. Wrinkles and sagging flesh: Exploring transformations in sexual body image. *Journal of Women and Aging* 25 (1): 3–33.

Montemurro, B., and J. M. Siefken. 2012. MILFs and matrons: Images and realities of mothers' sexuality. *Sexuality and Culture* 16 (4): 366–388.

———. 2014. Cougars on the prowl: New perceptions of older women's sexuality. *Journal of Aging Studies* 28: 35–43.

Nack, A. 2008. *Damaged goods: Women living with incurable sexually transmitted diseases.* Philadelphia: Temple University Press.

Nicolson, P. 1986. Developing a feminist approach to depression following childbirth. In *Feminist social psychology,* edited by S. Wilkinson, 142–158. Milton Keynes, U.K.: Open University Press.

Ogletree, S. M., and H. J. Ginsburg. 2000. Kept under the hood: Neglect of the clitoris in common vernacular. *Sex Roles* 43: 917–926.

Oliver, K. 2010. Motherhood, sexuality, and pregnant embodiment: Twenty-five years of gestation. *Hypatia* 25 (4): 760–777

Otnes, C. C., and E. H. Pleck. 2003. *Cinderella dreams: The allure of the lavish wedding.* Berkeley: University of California Press.

Plummer, K. 1995. *Telling sexual stories: Power, change, and social worlds.* New York: Routledge.

———. 2010. Generational sexualities, subterranean traditions, and haunting of the sexual world. *Symbolic Interaction* 33 (2): 163–190.

Renaud, C. E., S. Byers, and S. Pan. 1997. Sexual and relationship satisfaction in mainland China. *Journal of Sex Research* 34: 399–410.

Rich, A. 1976. *Of woman born: Motherhood as experience and institution.* New York: Basic Books.

Rose, T. 2003. *Longing to tell: Black women talk about sexuality.* New York: Picador.

Rosenthal, S. 1987. *Sex over 40.* Los Angeles: Tarcher.

Rossi, A. S. 1973. Maternalism, sexuality, and the new feminism. In *Contemporary sexual behavior: Critical issues in the 1970s,* edited by J. Zubin and J. Money, 145–173. Baltimore: Johns Hopkins University Press.

Rubin, L. 1983. *Intimate strangers: Men and women together.* New York: Harper Perennial.

Rutter, V., and P. Schwartz. 2012. *The gender of sexuality: Exploring sexual possibilities.* 2nd ed. Lanham, Md.: Rowman and Littlefield.

Sarracino, C., and K. M. Scott. 2008. *The porning of America: The rise of porn culture, what it means, and where we go from here.* Boston: Beacon.

Sassler, S. 2010. Partnering across the life course: Sex, relationships, and mate selection. *Journal of Marriage and Family* 72: 557–575.

Schalet, A. 2009. Subjectivity, intimacy, and the empowerment paradigm of adolescent sexuality: The unexplored room. *Feminist Studies* 35: 133–160.

———. 2010. Sexual subjectivity revisited: The significance of relationships in Dutch and American girls' experiences of sexuality. *Gender and Society* 24: 304–329.

———. 2011. *Not under my roof: Parents, teens, and the culture of sex.* Chicago: University of Chicago Press.

Schwartz, P. 2007. *Prime: Adventures and advice on sex, love, and the sensual years.* New York: HarperCollins.

Siebel, J. (producer and director). 2011. *Miss Representation.* Ross, Calif.: Girls' Club Entertainment. DVD.

Simon, W., and J. H. Gagnon. 1984. Sexual scripts. *Society* (November/December): 53–60.

———. 1986. Sexual scripts: Permanence and change. *Archives of Sexual Behavior* 15: 97–120.

———. 2003. Sexual scripts: Origins, influences, and change. *Qualitative Sociology* 26 (4): 491–497.

Steinberg, B. 2010. Now safe for TV: Female desire; Trojan "vibrating massager" ads suggest topic no longer so taboo—but it might depend on who's talking. *Ad Age,* December 8. http://adage.com/article/mediaworks/tv-advertising-trojan -vibrating-massager-ads-safe-tv/147517/.

Sternheimer, K. 2003. *It's not the media: The truth about pop culture's influence on children.* Boulder, Colo.: Westview.

Tally, M. 2006. "She doesn't let age define her": Sexuality and motherhood in recent "middle-age chick flicks." *Sexuality and Culture* 10 (2): 33–55.

Tanenbaum, L. 2000. *Slut! Growing up female with a bad reputation.* New York: Harper Perennial.

Thompson, S. 1995. *Going all the way: Teenage girls' values of sex, romance, and pregnancy.* New York: Hill and Wang.

Tolman, D. 2002. *Dilemmas of desire: Teenage girls talk about sexuality.* Cambridge, Mass.: Harvard University Press.

Traina, C.L.H. 2000. Maternal experience and the boundaries of Christian sexual ethics. *Signs* 25 (2): 369–405.

Trice-Black, S. 2010. Perceptions of women's sexuality within the context of motherhood. *Family Journal* 18 (2): 154–162.

Trice-Black, S., and V. A. Foster. 2011. Sexuality of women with young children: A feminist model of mental health counseling. *Journal of Mental Health Counseling* 33 (2): 95–111.

Twigg, J. 2004. The body, gender, and age: Feminist insights in social gerontology. *Journal of Aging Studies* 18: 59–73.

———. 2007. Clothing, age, and the body: A critical review. *Ageing and Society* 27: 285–305.

Urban, A. 2012. "Reclaim your wife": Advertising leaps back 50 years. *Care 2,* July 23. http://www.care2.com/causes/reclaim-your-wife-advertising-leaps-back-50-years.html.

Vares, T., A. Potts, N. Gavey, and V. Grace. 2007. Reconceptualizing cultural narratives of mature women's sexuality in the Viagra era. *Journal of Aging Studies* 21: 153–164.

Vaughan, D. 1990. *Uncoupling: Turning points in intimate relationships.* New York: Vintage.

Wade, L. D., and J. D. DeLamater. 2002. Relationship dissolution as a life stage transition: Effects on sexual attitudes and behaviors. *Journal of Marriage and Family* 64: 898–914.

Wade, L. D., and C. Heldman. 2012. Hooking up and opting out: Negotiating sex in the first year of college. In *Sex for life: From virginity to Viagra, how sexuality changes throughout our lives,* edited by L. M. Carpenter and J. DeLamater, 128–145. New York: New York University Press.

Waite, L. J. 2010. Sexuality has no expiration date. *Contexts* 9 (3): 80.

Waite, L. J., E. O. Laumann, A. Das, and L. P. Schumm. 2009. Sexuality: Measures of partnerships, practices, attitudes, and problems in the National Social Life, Health, and Aging Study. *Journal of Gerontology* 64B (supp. 1, November): i56–i66.

Ward, L. M., A. Merriwether, and A. Caruthers. 2006. Breasts are for men: Median, masculinity ideologies, and men's beliefs about women's bodies. *Sex Roles* 55 (9/10): 703–714.

Waskul, D. D., and R. F. Plante. 2010. Sex(ualities) and symbolic interaction. *Symbolic Interaction* 33(2): 148–162.

Waskul, D. D., P. Vannini, and D. Wiesen. 2007. Women and their clitoris: Personal discovery, significance, and use. *Symbolic Interaction* 30: 151–174.

Watson, W. K., and C. Stelle. 2011. Dating for older women: Experiences and meanings of dating in later life. *Journal of Women and Aging* 23: 263–275.

Weeks, J. 2006. *Sexuality.* 2nd ed. New York: Routledge.

Weisskopf, S. C. 1980. Maternal sexuality and asexual motherhood. *Signs* 5 (4): 766–782.

Yeh, H., F. O. Lorenz, K.A.S. Wickrama, D. Conger, and G. H. Elder. 2006. Relationships among sexual satisfaction, marital quality, and marital instability at midlife. *Journal of Family Psychology* 20: 339–343.

INDEX

abortion, 65, 145–147, 148–149
abstinence, seen by young girls as best
  policy, 32
abuse: childhood, 41, 186; cumulative
  disadvantage from, 103; difficulty in
  sustaining relationships as result of, 64;
  domestic, 64; by family members, 64;
  and first-time sex, 39, 58; lessons on
  compliance in, 61–62; lifelong costs
  of, 63–67; mind-body split during,
  66; sexual, 63–67, 87, 102, 103; sexual
  agency and, 15; verbal, 114
advantages, disadvantages associated with:
  aging and menopause, 181; embodied
  changes of motherhood, 157–158; learning through doing, 74–75; motherhood
  role, 133–134; relationship dissolution,
  120–121; taking a stance, 45–46; validation, affirmation, and encouragement,
  101
agency, sexual, 2; abuse and, 15, 87; confidence in expressing, 78; development
  of, 2, 76–101; differing levels of strength
  of during motherhood, 135–158; early
  experiences and, 9, 57; ethnicity and,
  15; family norms and, 15; immigrant
  women and, 15; inhibited by early abuse,
  87; religion and, 15; role of validation,
  affirmation, and encouragement in,
  76–101
aging: changes associated with, 14; decline
  in frequency of sexual activity and, 159,
  160; doubts about sex appeal and, 99;
  importance of relationships in, 178–179;
  inspiring reflection and enhancing sexual
  subjectivity, 179–181; lifestyle changes
  and, 160; loss of interest in sex and, 159,
  160; partners' differing levels of interest
  in sex in, 173–178; physical changes and,

173–178; problems faced by men in,
  173–178; remaining sexual subjects in,
  194–197; self-acceptance and, 182–199;
  self-discovery and, 168–181; significance of accomplishments in, 191–193;
  transformative nature of, 168; validation,
  affirmation, and encouragement and,
  99–100; wisdom of maturity in, 179–
  181, 185–193; and women's ability to be
  self-centered, 183
Armstrong, E., 5, 6, 10, 13, 22, 79, 197
assault, sexual, 39–41, 58, 61–62, 63–67, 87

Blume, J., 51
body: alienation from, 53; discovery of, 13;
  feeling alienated from after miscarriage,
  144, 145; learning about, 50; motherhood and, 135–158
Bogle, K., 10, 13, 79, 85, 93
breasts, 40, 129, 136–137, 150–153, 156
breastfeeding, 150–153; barriers to, 150;
  body changes due to, 153; Oedipal competition and, 137; perceptions of sexuality and, 14; public, 137; sensual nature
  of, 150–153; sexual neglect of fathers
  and, 136; stigmatization of, 136–137

Carbone-Lopez, K., 41, 63, 87, 103
Carpenter, L., 8, 9, 16, 44, 57, 59, 70, 85, 88,
  109, 161, 169, 187
celibacy, 174–175
childbirth: perceptions of sexuality and,
  14, 135–137; postpartum changes and,
  149–153; understanding capacity of
  body and, 14. See also motherhood;
  pregnancy
children: changes in sexuality and, 2; effect
  on mother's development of sexual subjectivity, 123–128; prioritized over

ABOUT THE AUTHOR

BETH MONTEMURRO is an associate professor of sociology at Penn State University Abington. Her research focuses on social constructions of gender and sexuality. She is also the author of *Something Old, Something Bold: Bridal Showers and Bachelorette Parties* (Rutgers University Press, 2006).

www.ingramcontent.com/pod-product-compliance
Lightning Source LLC
Chambersburg PA
CBHW031128270326
41929CB00011B/1541